LIFE AFTER DEATH

LIFE AFTER DEATH

◆

Tom

Harpur

M&S

Canadian Cataloguing in Publication data

Harpur, Tom
  Life after death

1st ed.
Includes bibliographical references and index.
ISBN 0–7710–3939–5

1. Immortality   I. Title

BL530.H37 1991   291.2'3   C90–095863–4

Printed and bound in Canada.
The paper used in this book is acid free.

McClelland & Stewart Inc.
The Canadian Publishers
481 University Avenue
Toronto, Ontario
M5G 2E9

To all those whom we have
"loved long since, and lost a while."

"For now we see through a glass, darkly; but then face to face: now I know in part; but then shall I know even as also I am known."

The Bible
I Cor. 13:12

"What happens after death is so unspeakably glorious that our imaginations and our feelings do not suffice to form even an approximate conception of it."

Carl Jung

CONTENTS

ACKNOWLEDGEMENTS

This is a book that "wanted to be written" from the very start. Much, however, is owed to many who assisted me along the way. I am particularly grateful to the readers of my syndicated columns. Their personal experiences helped enormously during my original research and their continuing letters of encouragement served to spur me on. Thank you to Sidney Katz for allowing me access to his notes on Leslie Sharpe. My thanks also to the Canada Council for a grant at the outset of this project. Finally, my appreciation to Dinah Forbes at McClelland & Stewart for her editorial skill and insight in the final shaping of the manuscript for publication.

T.W.H.

INTRODUCTION

"Eternal Life, here?" a recent headline in a major newspaper trumpeted. The lengthy feature article bore the subtitle "Scientists are making some amazing finds." The story dealt with humanity's age-old, universal dream of discovering the fountain of youth, or some other elixir, to stave off the hour of our death. While carefully documenting the latest research into the ageing process, however, in the end the account had very little to say about the headline. The best it could offer was the hope that future scientific progress in this field will increasingly ensure that people "die 'young' as late as possible."

Media stories on this and allied themes – not just in the mass-market, sensationalist tabloids but in mainline outlets as well – continue to underline our perennial preoccupation with the problem of death and the quest for eternal life. Hollywood, too, has a renewed interest in this subject. To the utter surprise of everyone in the movie industry, the top-grossing film as I write is not the highly hyped *Dick Tracy*, Bruce Willis's *Die Hard 2*, Tom Cruise's *Days of Thunder*, or even Arnold Schwarzenegger's *Total Recall*, but a modest-budget supernatural film, *Ghost*. The film is basically a tender love story about the protective, ghostly caring of a murdered young man for his surviving partner, who is at risk herself of a violent end. Another film, *Flatliners*, released a few weeks after *Ghost*, is also drawing capacity crowds. It deals with the story of a group of young medical students who become obsessed with discovering what lies beyond death's door. They decide to explore "the one frontier the Yuppies haven't cracked yet" by experimenting with "clinical death" and what is known as the near-death experience.

Not long after the newspaper article quoted above appeared, the same paper ran a story billed "Advocates of Cryonics Defy Death."[1] It told of the American Cryonic Society's ventures in freezing recently dead bodies and brains as a logical step "toward immortality." At the rather sparsely furnished Trans-Time warehouse in West Oakland, California, two human bodies, two heads, one brain, and a dog and cat are "on ice" in cryonic suspension inside shiny, stainless-steel containers, which resemble giant silver thermos bottles. They have been frozen, with instructions that they be thawed some time in the next couple of centuries and, with luck and presumed scientific advances, brought back to life. Altogether, about seventy members of this society have made similar arrangements to be frozen when they die. One of them, Art Quaife, has reportedly arranged for his freezing to be paid for through life insurance. "Fifty cents a day for immortality," he is quoted as saying. "I like the deal."

All of this gives further emphasis to the ancient truth that there is indeed nothing new under the sun. It's just that today, at least in the West, we tend more and more to rely on technology in what was once the exclusive territory of God and religion. We now know that the graves of Neanderthal man, dating to some fifty thousand years ago, contained spherical stones and other ritual objects, including food and weapons, which strongly suggest their belief in a life after death. On October 21, 1987, newspapers everywhere carried the story of how American and Egyptian scientists, using space-age technology, discovered a five-thousand-year-old pharoah's funeral boat at the Cheops pyramid near Cairo. The team, co-ordinated by the National Geographic Society, lowered cameras through a hole some four inches in diameter into a pit sealed by the Egyptians in or about 2,600 B.C. They took a picture of this "solar boat" and found it to be similar to one found nearby in 1954. Under the ancient Egyptian custom of the solar cult, a cedar boat was left in the tomb to transport the soul of the dead king to the afterworld.[2]

In the Egyptian Book of the Dead, dating from about 1500 to 1400 B.C., the chief features of the myth of Osiris are elaborated. Osiris was the "king of eternity," and the Egyptian doctrine of eternal life was based upon the story of his resurrection in a transformed body after an unjust and cruel death. Since Osiris was the mythical way of speaking of the fate or destiny of every person, the way to eternal life was described in terms of identification with him, just as Christians speak of their identification with a crucified and resurrected Lord. Just as happened to Osiris (or to Jesus Christ, according to St. Paul) at death, the body of every individual germinates or is transformed into a spiritual, glorified body. The Egyptian Book of the Dead says that when a person enters heaven, he becomes "God" or the "Son of God." He or she receives a crown, feeds upon the Word of God as "bread," is clothed in white raiment, and eats of the tree of life.[3]

In this book, I am more interested in current phenomena and thought than I am with those of the far distant past. But, unless we can see the matter in its proper context, unless we sense the longevity and the universality of the question, Is there life after death? we are destined to go badly astray.

There is today a major paradox in the fact that, while more people than ever are concerned about dying and what may lie beyond, fewer and fewer turn to traditional religion to find the answers they seek. Little of what the churches teach today about life after death – and my research suggests that many of them avoid the topic completely – makes much sense to many people. To the increasing number of those outside the church, life after death often seems like a childish mish-mash, a boring prospect, and the product of mere wishful thinking. Yet there has seldom been a time in history when more men and women held some form of belief in survival beyond the grave. Indeed, in many ways the present spiritual searching in our culture is a rebuke to organized religion and suggests that its essential message is failing to communicate reasonable answers to life's most basic and most urgent concerns.

Surely the most momentous personal question of our day – or indeed any other – is, having once died, is that the end or do we somehow live again? Moreover, if the answer is in the affirmative, what kind of life can we expect? While for obvious reasons this is not an area where categorical finality of thought or utterance will ever be possible, nevertheless there is an extraordinary need for some clear thinking and analysis just now. This book is an attempt to provide that. What is the evidence, if any, for life after death? What are we to make of the contemporary surge of interest in near-death experiences? Is there any truth the New Age insistence upon reincarnation, with all the tales of past lives that now appear so frequently in the popular press and other media? Have we really lived before and have we already died a thousand times? What is the teaching of Christianity and of other major world religions about life after death? Is there a flaming hell for sinners and a heaven above the stars for all the redeemed? Has modern science anything to say to all of this? Then, having reviewed and sifted this material, what is left for an intelligent, modern man or woman to believe? It is to these issues that we now must turn.

Before we do so, however, it is important that we make a few basic distinctions at the outset. Evidence for the belief in a life after death has to be sharply distinguished from evidence for life after death itself. Humans have always and nearly everywhere held some form of belief that life does not end with the grave or funeral pyre. Anthropology, sociology, and the history of world religions all provide ample evidence of the extent to which our species has expressed its solid, near-universal faith that death is not the last word. But evidence of such a faith, however abundant or moving, is not the same thing as evidence for the reality of a life beyond.

This doesn't mean we must simply discount faith or ignore it altogether. That would be highly unscientific to say the least. The fact that something is obviously very widely believed must itself be accounted for. If there is an inherent conviction in the human psyche that there is some kind of eternal life or survival after death, this has to be explained. It may be a form of indirect evidence of the truth of what is believed. In other words, such an effect could testify to such a cause. But, in and by itself, it doesn't necessarily do so. When I speak of evidence for life after death itself, on the other hand, I have in mind material – whether historical documents or recent experiences – that bears directly upon the subject. Yet, it must be said, even this evidence, however solid and weighty, or even at times sensational, does not establish absolute certainty.

This brings us to the second important clarification. Evidence and proof are by no means one and the same thing. For example, I am fully convinced that there is considerable evidence to be taken into account when trying to answer the question, Is there a God or not? But, because of the very nature of the inquiry, there can be no proof of God's existence in the normal, scientific use of the word "proof." This should not, however, discourage us or make us think that any discussion of what we call metaphysical (beyond the physical or material) concepts is a matter of "Your guess is as good as mine." In science, as in courts of law, those areas where absolute empirical proof is possible are far more limited than many of us imagine. With regard to many important and far-reaching scientific theories or legal cases, the best one can do is to gather all the available evidence, weigh it judiciously, and then make a decision based on a reasonable conclusion about where the evidence leads. I propose to follow the same principle here.

One final brief observation – a personal one. Most married couples have a very vivid memory of their first date. I certainly do. It was the spring of 1979, and Susan and I went for a picnic lunch beside Lake Ontario, not far from *The Toronto Star* offices where we both worked at the time. When we had eaten, we decided not just to talk but to have a discussion. I asked Susan: "What would you most like to talk about?" She replied very calmly, "Let's talk about death. What do you really believe about death?" Considering it was our first time alone together and that it was a simply glorious day, I could tell this was no ordinary woman! Now, roughly ten years later, I have written this book as my answer to her question.

◆

PART ONE

THE
SECULAR
WITNESS

1

◆

Strange
Encounters

RECENT POLLS IN NORTH AMERICA REVEAL A REMARKABLE upsurge in the number of people reporting that they have had one or more paranormal experiences. For example, priest-sociologist Father Andrew Greeley has done several major surveys showing that millions of Americans undergo psychic and mystical experiences, from extra-sensory perception (67 per cent of all adults) to being in some form of contact with the dead (42 per cent). In all, Greeley and his associates discovered that 74 per cent of Americans believe in a life after death where they will be reunited with their loved ones.[1] In a special survey of Canadian beliefs about life after death, published in 1983 as *Death and Beyond: A Canadian Profile*, a University of Lethbridge sociologist, Reginald Bibby, found that 40 per cent of the population believed it might be possible to communicate with the dead. Only one in three ruled it out as a total impossibility. Some 70 per cent said they believe in "something after death." A 1990 Gallup poll of Canadians had almost identical findings. Slightly over 70 per cent of those interviewed stated they "believe in heaven."[2]

Greeley, whom I got to know in Rome during the "year of the three Popes" in 1978, says he first became interested in what are generally referred to as "paranormal" experiences in the early 1970s when he began to be aware of just how many people have them "even if they don't tell anyone." He found that in the case of those North American adults who now believe they have had experiences of contact with someone who has died, the dead person is usually a spouse or sibling. His latest sociological study was done at the University of Chicago's National Opinion Research Council, and his data show that there has been a marked increase in the number of people claiming to have had contact with the dead – up from 27 per cent in 1973 to 42 per cent in 1986. Among widows alone, the figures are 51 per cent in 1973 and 67 per cent in 1986. What is perhaps most striking is that there seems to be a split between scientific belief and personal realities. Greeley states, "For example, 30 per cent of Americans who do *not* believe in life after death still say they've been in personal contact with the dead."

Greeley quotes a theologian friend, Father John Shea, who says these encounters may well be real and the cause, not the result, of man's tenacious belief in life after death. One argument in support of this thesis is that Greeley and his colleagues found that many of the widows who reported contact with a dead spouse said they had not believed in life after death before their experience. Another important finding in this study was that the people making such reports were "anything but religious nuts or psychiatric cases." In fact, Greeley maintains, "They are . . . ordinary Americans, somewhat above the norm in education and intelligence and somewhat less than average in religious involvement."

Other researchers confirm the vividness of these experiences. At the University of North Carolina, a team led by an associate professor of family medicine, P. Richard Olson, found that nearly two-thirds (64 per cent) of widows at two Asheville nursing homes had felt they were in touch with a dead person at least once or twice. Of those reporting such contact, 78 per cent said they saw the deceased. Some 50 per cent said they heard, 21 per cent touched, 32 per cent felt the presence, 18 per cent talked with the departed one, and 46 per cent had some combination of these experiences.[3] Most found the contact "helpful," and not one had mentioned it to her doctor! Greeley himself did another survey in 1984, which, among widows and widowers in the general population, just about replicated Olson's findings in North Carolina.

In England, the Oxford biologist David Hay, director of the Alister Hardy Research Centre, conducts scientific research in religion. In one large survey of English nurses, he discovered that two-thirds of them reported mystical events, "brought on mainly by close involvement with people in dire and dying moments."[4] In the spring issue (1990) of the Oxford University magazine *Oxford Today*, Peter Snow reports that the Alister Hardy Centre has recorded thousands of mystical experiences by ordinary Britons as well. Visions, out-of-body "trips," and transcendental dreams have been coded for computerization by the centre. One "staggering" statistic emerges, he says: Nearly 40 per cent of the British population will have a profound religious or spiritual experience at some time in their lives. "Clearly there is something in us struggling to get out," Snow concludes.

Colin Wilson cites similar results obtained by Dr. Karlis Osis of the New York Parapsychology Foundation. In 1960, Osis sent out ten thousand questionnaires to nurses asking about their patients' deathbed visions, and found that in a large number of cases, at the moment of death, the dying believed they saw a dead relative. The same discovery was made, Wilson relates, when Sir William Barrett, founder of the Society for Psychical Research, was gathering materials for his own book, *Death-bed Visions*.

Before we go on, I want to make one thing clear. Although I

was raised in an intensely religious home and have not just studied but have experienced the spiritual dimension of reality all my life, I have never had what I would label a paranormal experience of any kind. One doesn't go around looking for such experiences. They either happen or they don't, and in my case, it seems they don't. In other words, there is no hidden agenda here.

At the same time, however, as a parish priest I have had firsthand encounters with some seemingly extraordinary phenomena. Several times, when attending the deathbed of a parishioner, something was either said or observed to lead me to the conclusion that the dying person had had a vision or foretaste of a glory to come. One such incident stands out in my memory and illustrates what I mean.

One day in June, many years ago, I was leaving the hospital closest to my church, St. Margaret's-in-the-Pines, in West Hill, Ontario, when a young couple stopped me in the entrance. They had spotted my Roman collar, and, not knowing a minister themselves, suddenly asked me for help. They said the woman's mother was in a coma suffering from a terminal illness. They asked me whether I would mind paying her a brief visit. We went up to a private room, one of those reserved for the dying, and I saw the patient, a woman in her mid-sixties, lying unconscious under an oxygen tent. I said a brief prayer at her bedside, and, because I had learned that even when in a coma our sense of hearing can often still be operative, I read a brief passage to her from the New Testament. It is the one which speaks eloquently of the fact that nothing can ever separate us from the love of God, not even death itself. Then I put my hand through the opening of the tent and placed it on her forehead as I said a final blessing.

Two days later, the daughter called me to say that, to their complete surprise, her mother had regained consciousness for a brief time the following day and had told her in great detail about my visit. "She said she heard the prayer and the reading and that suddenly her whole being had been flooded with an incredible sense of light," the daughter said. "It seemed to envelop her and give her an assurance of wholeness and peace she had never known before. She had a kind of radiance about her face that was quite wonderful to see." The dying woman relapsed into the coma shortly afterwards and died peacefully later that evening.

Since I had been only too aware of my own limitations on that occasion – it had been a very hot day, I was tired and looking forward to getting home, and there seemed to be nothing anyone could do for her at that point – I am certain that whatever happened had absolutely nothing to do with me. Yet I know that something strange and spiritually healing did occur.

Because of my university background in the Classics, particularly in Ancient History (ten years in all, including four years of undergraduate and then graduate study at Oxford), coupled with my training in journalism, I have always been reluctant to accept things on the basis of secondhand evidence. Shortly after the latest Greeley results came out, I decided to test them with the readers of my syndicated Sunday column. In a brief footnote to a July 1987 column, I said simply: "I am doing some research and would like to hear from you on the following: Do you believe in life beyond death? Have you ever experienced anything that amounts to solid evidence for this *as far as you yourself are concerned?* Please write briefly. . . ."[5] I was quite aware it was not a scientific poll. It wasn't intended to be; there was little point in duplicating the many that had already been done by qualified researchers. What I wanted was a live sample, as it were, to get the flavour or feel of this phenomenon for myself.

In all, I received nearly two hundred letters in answer to my request. While some were brief, most ran to several pages. They came from people of all ages, all walks of life, and from various regions of the country. Roughly 3 per cent of the respondents said they did not believe in a life after death. Typical of these was the man from a small Ontario town who concluded his articulate rebuttal with the words, "What is after your life is what was before your life – nothing. Sorry, but at times the truth hurts."

Another sceptic wrote as follows: "I find it sad that so many people's grip on their life is so precarious that rather than face the bleak truth of their mortality they will embrace any preposterous delusion promising them immortality." To cover all his bases, though, he added, "In any case, from what I have read and heard of heaven I am sure I would find it incredibly boring and unpleasant existing under the critical eye of a humorless dictator whose compassion is all too capricious and fleeting."

The overwhelming majority, however, obviously wrote because they now feel positively about a future life. Several themes or characteristics stood out sharply as I read and reread what they had to say. Most of those who described one or more mystical experiences involving some form of "contact" with a deceased person said that this was the first time they had ever told anyone else about it. They expressed a sincere relief not just at the opportunity to share this with somebody else, but at learning that they were not going to be looked upon as eccentric or even deranged for talking about such intimate and unusual psychic happenings. I was also greatly impressed by the number of respondents who prefaced their story with the observation that they had not previously held strong convictions about an afterlife. In other words, it seems that it was an unusual experience that awakened belief in them rather than the other way around. Greeley's researches have uncovered the same phenomenon. Closely related to this was the way in which the psychic event, in most instances, came unexpectedly, both as to place and time, as well as content. There were certain similarities, on the one hand, but there was a striking range of variables on the other. To tell the truth, I was surprised by the originality or creativity involved in whatever it is that is going on at such times.

One final word about the methodology. The letters went through several stages once I began to read them. The process was admittedly a subjective one. While nearly every letter was interesting, some were obviously more interesting than others. All I can say is that, using whatever critical powers I have, I gradually sifted them down to a final score or so. The overriding criterion was believability: Does this account have about it the ring of authenticity and of truth-telling? This is what Colin Wilson refers to as the "boggle threshold" – how far can we trust the person concerned? The credibility of any witness, whether in a court of law or elsewhere, has much to do with how sane and balanced they seem in other ways. None of this, of course, makes any pre-judgement about the status of such reports as hard "evidence" of a life to come. We'll come back to that issue later on.

◆ M. B. is a widow whose husband died in 1984. They were "always very happy together" and his death has left a great void. She writes: "I have had the feeling many times that my husband was there in the room with me, but it is the experience I had on September 30, 1987, I wish to tell you about. I had stretched out on the chesterfield for a nap before watching a program due to come on TV in an hour. I fell sound asleep but soon the presence of someone standing beside me caused me to wake up. I knew it was Jack, my husband. There he was. He bent over and offered me a bottle of beer. I remember thinking 'Oh yes, he's taken the cap off and he wants to pour it into two glasses for us' (we had always done this and really consumed very little; in fact, I haven't bought any since I've been alone). I reached out to touch him but, in a flash, he was gone! But I actually saw him. And I had a warm feeling for days after. I know it must have been an apparition – but it was the most realistic one I have ever known. I speak to him and feel he guides me in many things."

◆ On December 22, 1986, at 4.15 a.m., F. P.'s father died. He was ninety-six years old and remained completely lucid and alert to the very end. She had visited him the day before, a Sunday, and they had talked about Christmas plans and the new house his son had bought. He wanted to see it "when the weather gets better." Out of the blue, the old man asked her: "What do you know about double vision?" When she asked if he had some problem with his eyes, he said: "Not really, but this morning when I came into my room there was a woman sitting on my bed." She asked him whether he knew the woman (there were no women in the wing of the seniors' home where he lived) and he answered that she had had her back to the doorway. He turned to leave the room and, glancing back as he did so, noticed the woman "was gone." F. P. felt intuitively that it had been the spirit-form "of my mother who died long ago."

When she went home, she told her husband she had a strange feeling her father's death was not too far away. The old man himself had a normal day for the balance of December 21, but after he went to bed that night his heart began to fail and he was rushed to the hospital for oxygen. A few hours later, he died.

His daughter comments: "While his death came as a surprise, since he was normal when I left him, it wasn't the shock it might have been because of what he told me he had seen. I can't explain it, but I accept what happened as a real event."

◆ M. H. begins her letter with the terse statement: "I doubt a lot. I'm not superstitious; I'm fairly intelligent." She then relates how on Mother's Day 1978 she was with her grandmother, holding her hand as the old lady was dying. She says she told her over and over, even though she seemed unconscious, that she would help her with dying and that she would soon see her mother and sister, to be with them as she had longed to be. "She died at about 4 p.m. After about ten minutes, while I was looking at her, not touching, I felt a sudden and very powerful aura in the room. It felt as though my grandmother was all around me, in the air of the room, and as though she was most intensely projecting her personality toward me. I have never felt anyone, ever, as strongly as then. It was one of the happiest moments of my life. I have tried to analyze it, tried to be objective, but those few minutes were so incredible, so very happy, and the world all around was brilliant, jubilant, everything in super-technicolor. I can't begin to explain how powerful it was."

◆ A. G. lost his wife five years ago. The day after her sudden death, he was alone in the house thinking how glad he was that her will, which they had often discussed, had been finally drawn up only a couple of days before she died. "I spoke her name and said I had fulfilled all her wishes. The room was suddenly filled with her perfume and looking up I saw a form all in white which gradually faded away. I knew then that she knew what I had said. I firmly believe that my wife's spirit remained in the house for some time afterwards. This has been on my mind a lot and I am very glad to write to you about it because when I mentioned the above to anyone I got funny looks. But, I'm certain I did not just imagine it."

◆ R. B., an Anglican priest, who says he feels somewhat "ridiculous and exposed" in recounting several paranormal experiences of his own and of his immediate family, tells the following: "My maternal grandfather died in 1965. My mother often thought of him and wondered 'how he was.' About 1968–69, she answered the telephone one day only to hear his voice faintly at the other end, as through static. She was deeply traumatized and asked: 'Dad, where are you?' He replied: 'You know where I am. I'm O.K.' Then the phone went dead. It was years before I heard that story because, of course, my mother thought everyone would think she was crazy. My eldest sister was greatly relieved, however, because, as she explained to us, she 'knew' she had seen my grandfather about 1971 but had been afraid to speak of it to anyone else."

◆ H. B. describes a "vision" she had the night after her mother died: "My mother stood before me, smiling, and told me not to grieve for her, that we would eventually be together again. Even before I woke from it, I was surprised that I had had no difficulty recognizing her. She appeared to be about seventeen or eighteen . . . She was wearing a long garment of a beautiful mulberry shade, and she had a radiance as if, as I thought later, she had seen God. My mother was forty-one when I was born so

I never knew her except as a middle-aged and then elderly woman. Her favorite color was a shade of mulberry but I had never seen her wear it. Then, as now, it is a most difficult dye to achieve. I told my husband about the experience and, while he was very kind and sympathetic, he thought I had become unstrung by grief and was raving. Until now, I have never told anyone else about it but remain convinced that it was what it seemed to be: a genuine message from my mother who had gone on to a higher life. The memory has not faded but remains as vivid as when I experienced it some thirty years ago."

◆ D. W. lived in Owen Sound, Ontario, and his mother was quite ill in hospital in London, over 150 kilometres away. He was driving down to visit her and stopped overnight at his aunt's home in Goderich. In the middle of the night he was awakened to see his mother as a younger woman standing at the foot of the bed. She told him she had come to say goodbye. In the morning, when he got up, his aunt informed him that his mother had died during the night. He knew that "it hadn't been a dream; it had really been her."

◆ A baptist minister, T. B., was away at college in Evanston, Illinois, when he got word that his father had died. He came back to Canada for the funeral feeling very badly that he had been away and had not seen his father in over a year. "We had always been close in a quiet, empathetic way." Life went on, and that summer he and his wife were vacationing at a small lake in Wisconsin. T. B. got up at six o'clock one morning and wandered down to the deserted shore. "As I stood gazing across the water, I suddenly became aware of my father's presence. I simply cannot describe the sensation. There was nothing visual or auditory – just a 'spirit' awareness that he was there. I never moved a muscle. It lasted for maybe five minutes and left as quickly as it came. I believe God allowed Dad's spirit to return to communicate with me since I had been away at the time of his death . . . I have never had a similar experience nor sought one.

Whatever the explanation, I know beyond all doubt that my father was there with me."

◆ W. K. had what could be described as an "auditory" experience some three and a half years after the death of her mother. She describes herself as having been "fairly neutral" on the subject of life after death prior to this. The death of her mother came after she had been living with W. K. for four years, and the two were "very close." At the time of the "event," W. K. had been having a series of medical tests and had an appointment to go into hospital for more. Her mother was the furthest thing from her thoughts as she wrestled with her growing reluctance to go to the hospital. "Much to my surprise, since I wasn't even thinking of her, my mother's voice came into my head and all she said was: 'Go on, you can do it!' It was definitely her voice and not a thought – she had an English accent which I could never imitate. I want to stress I know the difference between a voice and a thought! At the same time it wasn't coming in my ear but inside my head." She concludes her letter, "I am not a religious person and would love to hear an explanation as I'm sure nobody believes me."

◆ S. B. describes a time she was on a bus with some friends in London, England: "A woman opened a car door on the wrong side and a man on a bicycle swerved violently to avoid a collision. So did the bus-driver. The bus hit the cyclist and dragged him some distance before coming to a stop on the sidewalk. We were all pretty shaken and everybody was staring, not doing anything. I got off the bus and tried to help the young man. Someone ran to call an ambulance and I covered him with my coat. He was fully conscious so I sat on the curb amid all the glass and the blood and tried to console him. Later that night I was in bed reading – at about 2 a.m. – when this man appeared. I was scared at first but all he did was to mouth 'thank you.' There was no sound. I was still shaking the next day when the papers reported the accident and said he had died at 2 a.m."

◆ A. G. wrote to tell of an unexplained happening just after his wife died on July 15, 1986. Attached to his letter is a sworn affidavit signed by the nurse who was in attendance at the time of his wife's death. A. G.'s wife fell ill with cancer in January 1986. During her illness he took care of her and, although they had been childhood sweethearts, marrying soon after leaving school, they became even closer as they discussed every aspect of dying. "My wife helped me plan the life I would lead after she died and I asked her to try to find a way of letting me know if there was indeed a life after death and if there was, was she happy."

Sometime between one and three hours after his wife ceased breathing and had been pronounced dead by the coroner, "she closed her mouth and smiled with unmistakable bliss. Her face that was so drawn and haggard due to the stress leading to her death, became once again full and happy in appearance. Her color returned and her countenance took on a look that I can only describe as the appearance I remember when she was about fifteen to twenty years younger. I felt I was witnessing a miracle." The nurse confirms the "miracle" in her statement, noting that the woman was indeed smiling and that she "looked twenty years younger." A. G. discussed the case with the undertaker and two attending phsyicians. "They know that it actually happened but they stated that it is impossible. For the body's mouth to close and for a smile to appear, the brain would have to be alive. This, of course, is not possible after hours of not breathing." As far as A. G. is concerned, what happened was his wife's way of assuring him she was still alive, although in a new mode, and that she was happy. He concludes: "I have written to you because I feel that not to record this event in some form is wrong. It did happen."

◆ M. M. says that her husband, who was a "total disbeliever in God," died in 1982 after being ill for some time. She says they both knew he was leaving her but that they never spoke of this. When she reached her doorstep, still stunned and in shock after coming from the hospital and seeing his dead body, M. M. felt a sudden sense of desolation. "Where is this Comforter Jesus spoke of?" she asked herself. Immediately she felt a powerful presence at her left shoulder. "It was so strong that I even turned to see who it was; and my heart was touched by something which seemed to say 'You will be all right!'" She was able to carry through all the arrangements for the funeral and to care for the needs of her family "almost as though someone were guiding me."

About a week later, she accidentally locked herself out of the house. (She could see her keys inside on the kitchen table.) It took her about forty-five minutes to open a basement window which her husband had previously nailed shut. "And I would take an oath he was there watching me and laughing, his presence was so strong." M. M. goes on to say that the whole experience has taught her there is a "centre where we can 'radio' for help when we get beyond our depth in this life." She admits her friends wouldn't understand her if she related any of this to them, "but I felt compelled to pass this along to you."

◆ A. M. writes that fifteen years ago she was very ill at home. One day she awoke to find a tall, well-dressed man standing just outside her bedroom door. When she looked at him, he asked, "Are you ready?" "I quickly said 'No,'" she relates. For many years, she supposed she had dreamed this odd incident. Seven years ago, her husband was diagnosed as having terminal cancer. Near the end, she brought him home from hospital as he had expressed a deep wish to die at home. "As our two sons helped the ambulance men to carry my husband to the bedroom, my husband pointed to the same spot where I had seen the stranger and asked me, 'Who is he?' When I asked him later who was who, he described the same well-dressed man I had seen years before. I have never told anyone about this, but felt I had to write. No, I do not know who this man was, and as we bought the house new thirty years ago no one else had lived here. I still wonder who this stranger was." (This theme of a friendly stranger, sometimes male, sometimes female, who comes at the hour of approaching death and in some way helps the surviving relative or spouse, appeared in several of the responses I received.)

◆ B. Y., who says he was raised in the United Church of Canada but always felt very sceptical about such beliefs as those concerning life after death, had been very close to his grandmother as a boy. He was in his early twenties and recently married when he learned that she was quite ill in hospital in a northern town many miles away. One morning, he awoke very early and saw his grandmother standing at the entrance to his bedroom. "She was wearing the mauve suit that I always recognized as one of her favorites. Her face was very taut and sunken and would have looked terrible had it not been for the fact that she looked joyful at the same time. She just stood there silently. I closed my eyes before taking another look. She was gone but the phone began to ring. It woke my wife – it was on her side of the bed – and as she reached for it, I told her 'Grandma is dead.' She picked the phone up and my aunt told her what I already knew." (I received several other letters corroborating this kind of telepathic awareness, sometimes with apparitions, sometimes not, communicating the fact of a loved one's demise.)

◆ R. H. of Toronto had never given much thought to what happens at or after death. Her mother, to whom she was devoted, had once told her, "When we die, that's the end," and she had mentally agreed. Mother and daughter had been through great times of crisis and difficulty together, first as refugees in Europe and then as immigrants in Canada. Her mother died during the night of June 25, 1977, and was buried on Monday, June 27.

A few weeks later, in obedience to something her mother had said a few days before she died – "When this is all over, you must take a holiday" – R. H. and her husband were travelling by train down the beautiful Agawa Canyon in northwestern Ontario.

She was thinking how sad it was that her mother wouldn't be able to see "all this" any more when, "Suddenly, she spoke to me, but not with a voice one hears with one's ears. It came right through my heart some way and Mother had reverted to her native tongue, German. Translated, what she said went like this: You can't do anything for me any more. Don't grieve so. We will be together again. Please look after yourself!" All the words, she says, seemed underlined as though to emphasize their importance. As the train moved on, "It was not as though we were moving from her, but as if she was moving away from me as she seemed to float away, unable to stay. This experience gave me strength. My plucky, courageous mother . . . had to let me know that we will be together again one day." She concludes that while sceptics may not see this as "solid evidence" of anything, it was "proof enough" for her.

◆ The final example in this mini-review of phenomena is perhaps the strangest of all. E. M. of Oakville, Ontario, had lost her son some years before she wrote me her story. "We were a young family that had just moved into our new home in Oakville. Our street was the (then) last one bordering farmland between Oakville and Bronte. We drove past these old farms on our way to church each Sunday. In one field we passed, an old grey horse spent the days of his retirement watching the traffic go past. Our son, Bobby, almost seven, was delighted by that horse. We had Sunday conversations about it over many months. Bobby would say, 'That horse is lonely. I could be his friend. Can we take him home?' I would have to answer, 'No, dear. You can't just take somebody else's horse.' He once replied, 'I have four dollars saved up. I could buy him from the farmer.' But, of course, even if he had had more money we didn't have a stable, etc. Bobby insisted he could build a small house, cut grass, and feed him: 'He really is my horse,' he argued. Ten weeks later, Bobby was dead. He drowned while playing with some friends. My spirit silently screamed, 'Where are you my little one? I know where your body is, but where are you?' Now, our street is a crescent-shape with about fifty homes on it. We live near the middle of the crescent. The horse's field was almost a mile from us with orchards, lanes, and old farms between us. The Sunday following Bobby's burial, when we were getting ready to drive to church, we looked out and there on our front lawn, peacefully cropping the grass, was the old grey horse. Only the spirit that never dies, the spirit of Bobby, could have known the perfect assurance this meant for us that there is, without doubt, a life of the spirit after bodily death. Thank you for letting me tell this reality. It is true."

◆

There are a number of responses we can make to such testimonials. The determined sceptic will naturally scoff at all of this and dismiss it out of hand. The true believer will tend to take it all as some kind of proof positive that humans survive death in some mysterious way. Both responses, I believe, are inadequate. In spite of every attempt to be as scientific as possible in methodology and outlook, none of the results of the surveys – either my own or those of the experts – can claim to be scientific proof. About that, we must be very clear. These experiences cannot be repeated in a laboratory under scientific conditions; they cannot be verified by any normal, empirical methods. They are, by their very nature, highly subjective.

Having said that, however, it should once more be pointed out that simply to dismiss them as nonsense on those grounds would in itself be highly unscientific. Something major, something highly significant is clearly going on here, and it would be irresponsible to try to ignore it or brush it away. The fact that intelligent, non-religious people, as well as those with faith in life after death, have had such experiences, together with the vividness and unexpectedness of the happenings themselves, combine to suggest there is much more to all of this than wishful thinking or projection. Whatever else we may say, these experiences are intensely real to the millions who have them. The possibility, even the probability that they witness to an objective reality "out there" has to be taken with full seriousness. I was personally enormously intrigued by what my readers had to say, and this was what led me to look further into the topic for the next chapter, the near-death experience.

One final comment, though, before we move on. When the bishop gave me my first parish, out in the "wilds" of Scarborough, Ontario, he sent me a young priest from the Church of South India, who was studying at Wycliffe College, to be my Sunday assistant. His name was T. K. George, a small, gentle man of deep faith and intelligence. Just as I was writing this chapter a letter came from a former parishioner of mine saying that she had just heard from T. K.'s wife. She wrote that my former associate had died very peacefully at his home in India after a long illness. What she particularly wanted to share with those who had known him was that, just before the moment of his last breath, he told his wife he could see "my spiritual body coming to meet me."[6]

2

◆

The
Near-Death
Experience

THERE ARE MILLIONS OF PEOPLE TODAY – EIGHT MILLION IN the United States alone – who claim to know what death is like. They have "died" in the sense that they have suffered a cardiac arrest or have been otherwise declared clinically dead and then have regained consciousness. Others, under the influence of various anaesthetics, in the throes of giving birth, at moments of extreme crisis and danger, or simply in a "natural" out-of-body event, report curiously similar perceptions of a transitional state of being between this world and another. All have come back from this experience remarkably changed and with an amazing story to tell.

For many people, ever since Dr. Raymond Moody described this phenomenon in his trend-setting, pivotal book *Life After Life*, published in 1975, the near-death experience (NDE) is the final proof they have been waiting for that life goes on beyond the grave.[1] The sceptics and serious critics disagree. So much more has been written on this subject in the period since that first book by Moody, and so much invaluable research has been done by doctors and scientists, among others, that we must now attempt to come to terms with the possibilities and problems raised. What light does the NDE throw upon the belief in life after death? The fact that the experience does occur on an extraordinarily vast scale in all cultures and climes is not in doubt. Researchers who are officers of the International Association for Near-Death Studies (IANDS), of which I am a member, report that as many as 35 to 40 per cent of all those who have almost died can recall a near-death experience.[2]

Moody must be given credit for having given a name to the phenomenon and for having brought it dramatically to the forefront of public consciousness, but he certainly did not invent the NDE. Plato wrote about it, and current research shows that it has appeared in various forms since the dawn of literature.[3] But does the NDE really constitute evidence that there is some kind of afterlife, a state of blissful existence beyond "the valley of the shadow of death?" It is to this question that we now must turn.

Since all of the basic data about the NDE phenomenon is of necessity highly personal and anecdotal – flowing as it does from firsthand accounts of the experiences of ordinary people – it is essential to make this chapter as personal as possible. Let me begin, then, by saying that, while the statistical evidence for the prevalence of the NDE is quite arresting and should not be underplayed (some NDE researchers have used a figure as high as 60 per cent of all those who experience clinical "death"), it is by no means true that everyone who comes close to death, has a narrow escape, endures cardiac arrest, or is declared clinically dead and then survives has some kind of mystical revelation of a life beyond. I haven't. But, I have, however, had several uncomfortably close brushes with death.

In the summer of 1949, I was teaching school on a Cree reserve in the remotest corner of northwestern Ontario, about a thousand miles from Toronto. I was struck down with a violent fever and dysentry and had to be flown out on an emergency basis in a single-engine float-plane to Sioux Lookout, a tiny frontier town. For about two weeks I hovered in and out of consciousness while the two doctors at the rudimentary hospital debated over whether to perform surgery on my seriously ulcerated intestines. In all, I was in hospital for six weeks and finally emerged a pale, skinny vestige of my former self. I was told I had had a severe case of amoebic dysentry and that neither nurses nor doctors had expected I would leave the place alive. All I remember of the crisis part of the illness was that, while I might have been able to utter a few, brief mental prayers at moments of lucidity, my chief awareness was of not having the strength to care whether I lived or not. I just wanted to be left alone. There were no mystical overtones whatever, although, naturally, once it was all over I felt extremely grateful to be alive and on the road to recovery.

During my research, I found many people who have had a cardiac arrest while in intensive care or during surgery, or who have had close encounters with death such as I have described, who yet have had nothing dramatic to report. My own father-in-law is a case in point. He recently suffered a severe heart attack while undergoing kidney surgery. A few weeks later, he had to have open-heart surgery to remove the scarring caused by the attack and was in a coronary intensive care unit for several days. While he had some mild hallucinations as a result of the medications, there was nothing he could identify as truly mystical, nothing approaching an NDE.

Leading figures in NDE research admit they don't know why some have the experience and others do not. In an interview, Dr. Bruce Greyson, a psychiatrist at the University of Connecticut's Medical Center and one of the best-known researchers in this field, told me he considers it quite possible that all those who "die" and come back have an NDE, but that for unknown reasons some of them repress it. Greyson said, "It could be either that they didn't actually come close enough to really dying or that some other factor, say the medication, interfered in some way. In situations like this people are under extreme stress, so it's hard to calculate all the variables."

Intrigued, I followed this up by interviewing three anaesthetists, including Dr. Richard Cooper, assistant professor in the Department of Anaesthesia at the University of Toronto Medical School. They told me that there are usually three components in any general anaesthetic: analgesics to prevent pain, muscle relaxants to prevent bodily movement during the surgery or other procedure, and amnesics to ensure the experience is forgotten. As Cooper explained, the amnesics are to erase or prevent the formation of memories of the operation. "People don't want to be aware of what has gone on," he said. Those rare few who do manage some recall generally are plagued by a sense that "something has gone wrong." They can even have recurring nightmares in which they sense danger or risk of death but are unable to move to avoid it. The amount of amnesic given (usually one of the benzodiazepines) varies with each patient, and the effects vary as well, depending on other drugs being administered at the same time. Some surgery, the doctors said, is done without the use of amnesics if it is thought they might interfere with, for example, the heartbeat of cardiac patients. However, given the wide use of memory suppressants in most serious operations, I find it noteworthy, not that many who experience clinical death during surgery don't have an NDE, but that so many appear to remember so clearly that they did.

In his first book on near-death experiences, *Life After Life*, Moody analysed the "otherworld journeys" of those who have been to the brink of death and have reported "miraculous" glimpses of a world beyond. They found a plane of existence glowing with love and understanding, a place of bliss and light that can apparently be reached only "by an exciting trip through a tunnel or passageway." In his later book, *The Light Beyond*, he summarizes the characteristics of these "near-death visions" in this way: "NDErs experience some or all of the following events – a sense of being dead, peace and painlessness even during a 'painful' experience, bodily separation, entering a dark region or tunnel, rising rapidly into the heavens, meeting deceased friends and relatives who are bathed in light, encountering a Supreme Being, reviewing one's life, and feeling reluctance to return to the world of the living."[4]

By chance, a few days after I had read *Life After Life*, back in 1975, I noticed a story in *The Toronto Star* about a man who had been critically wounded in the abdomen by a shotgun blast at close range. He was a night watchman at a Canadian Tire store outlet in the west end of Mississauga, Ontario, and had surprised two thieves in the act. What caught my eye was the statement in the story that this security guard had "died" twice during the many hours of surgery required to save him. I kept the clipping for three months and then tracked him down by phone. He was by then well on the road to a near-miraculous recovery and was willing to give me an interview. I told him nothing in advance of my area of interest. I spent several hours with him and discovered that, although he was reluctant to talk about it at first, he had had an experience that he described as "a kind of religious conversion." It turned out that during the moments or minutes when his vital signs had totally flattened out on the monitor and the doctors were certain they had lost him, he had in fact had an NDE.

It was my first direct encounter with anything of the sort, and it gave me a strange feeling to hear him describe roughly the same phenomenon outlined in *Life After Life*. Incidentally, at that time he had not read the book and had been afraid to speak to anyone else about his experience for fear of being thought strange. Not every detail matched the complete profile of an NDE just given above, but there were enough of the major traits – the tunnel, the sense of shining light, and the reluctance to "go back" – to make me realize he was talking about essentially the same thing. I wrote the story and it gained a considerable response from readers and other media.

I was not the first *Toronto Star* journalist, however, to have reported such a case. In May 1971, well before Moody set off the NDE floodtide with *Life After Life*, a colleague of mine at the newspaper, Sidney Katz, wrote the strange story of Leslie Sharpe. Sharpe, who at that time headed a successful Toronto-based printing firm, had never concerned himself with the ultimate mystery of life after death. But, as Katz told it, ". . . late one spring afternoon a year ago, Sharpe, sixty-eight, had an experience that changed all that. He died." Katz, basing his account on an article by Sharpe that had just been published in the Canadian Medical Association *Journal*, told how the man had gone to the Toronto General Hospital complaining of sharp pains in his chest and left arm.[5] Once in bed, his symptoms vanished and blood pressure, heart sounds, everything seemed completely normal. Later that same day, however, at two minutes to four in the afternoon, he looked at his watch. A few seconds afterwards, he gave a very deep sigh and his head flopped over to the right.

He reported: "I remember wondering why my head flopped over because I hadn't moved it. I figured I must be going to sleep. That was my last conscious thought." Immediately, Sharpe was looking down at his own body from the waist up. "Almost at once, I saw myself leave my body, coming out through my head and shoulders. The body was somewhat transparent, although not exactly in vapor form. Watching, I thought, 'So this is what happens when you die.'" Next, the businessman found himself sitting on a small object, tilted at a forty-five-degree angle, and travelling through a blue-grey sky at great speed. He had the feeling he didn't know where he was or where he was going but that this was "one journey I must take alone." He felt safe and that everything was "being taken care of." Then he began to feel a "delightful" floating sensation as he was bathed in a bright yellow light.

He wrote: "I have a scar on my right leg, the result of an old injury. Although at the time I was not conscious of having any lower limbs, I felt the scar being torn away and I thought, 'They have always said your body is made whole out here. I wonder if my scars are gone?'" Continuing to float, he tried unsuccessfully to locate his legs. The sensation of tranquillity and joy engulfed him so fully that he could only describe it afterwards as "something beyond words to tell." Just then, a series of hard blows to his left side brought him back to consciousness. His heart had been restarted by means of shocks from an electric paddle. Looking up, he could see the doctors and nurses. He heard someone say that he'd taken "a bad turn." In the article he wrote in the medical journal and in his interview with Katz, Sharpe said he then told the medical team not to resuscitate him if he suffered another relapse. He wanted the experience to "go on and on. If that was eternity, I wanted to stay there. I was annoyed at being brought back to earth."

Some facts given in Katz's article are important. Sharpe was not a member of any religious group and had not been to church for many years. In his own mind, he had "long ago reached the conclusion that death was the final end and that beyond that there was nothing." He had, according to the hospital staff, received only Demerol and was not on any hallucinogenic chemical. (Demerol, a strong narcotic, normally produces extreme drowsiness and some confusion of mind as it numbs pain. In rare cases it can contribute to hallucinatory experiences of a confused nature, quite unlike what Sharpe describes.) Having "returned from death," he had lost any fear of it he previously had. "I've had the rare privilege of seeing behind a closed door that's never opened. I'm no longer afraid to go." Finally, Sharpe wrote his story for the Canadian Medical Association's *Journal* at the urging of his physicians, Drs. Robert L. MacMillan and Kenneth W. G. Brown of the Toronto General's coronary care unit. It bore the very conservative title "Cardiac Arrest Remembered."

Those familiar with the writings of Dr. Carl Jung will be aware that the great psychoanalyst, at first a colleague and then a critic of Sigmund Freud, had a very similar experience to that of Sharpe, one which he later said ranked among the most meaningful of his eventful life. During a brief clinical "death" after a heart attack, he said, "It seemed to me I was high up in space. Far below I saw the globe of earth bathed in a glorious blue light.

Ahead of me I saw a shining temple and was drawn towards it. As I approached, a strange thing happened. I had the certainty I was about to enter an illuminated room and meet there all those people to whom I was beloved in reality. There I would understand at last the meaning of my life." Jung then realized he was being pulled back into his physical body. It happened at the same moment his doctor injected him with a strong heart stimulant.[6]

Of the roughly two hundred readers who responded to the request in my column to describe briefly any experience they had had which for them constituted evidence of an afterlife, about forty responded with a story of NDE. What was significant, in my view, is the fact that no two of them were exactly the same and none was a replica of the full, classical NDE which is regularly discussed in the media. That, plus the way in which most respondents stressed that this was the first time they had ever told anyone outside their own immediate family circle about the experience, gives considerable credibility, I believe, to the conviction that what they describe did actually happen.

◆ R. H. D., of Burlington, Ontario, wrote: "Prior to quadruple by-pass surgery in 1979, I experienced cardiac arrest while in the intensive care unit at Joseph Brant Hospital. The arrest occurred during sleep but I was brought 'back to life,' as it were, by a very alert and able nursing staff. I have retained a very vivid recollection of the few minutes that I was 'dead.' Whether it was a dream or a temporary entrance into eternity I will obviously never know. However, just prior to administration of electric shock by the staff, I travelled through a long and misty-white tunnel, the end of which I never reached and the surroundings of which were immensely peaceful. I can remember no other details but it was an experience which I can never forget. It was not just a matter of imagination."

◆ B. C. is the mother of three children. In 1960, when her children were very young, she was in hospital for major surgery.

"Following the surgery, I experienced 'death.' There was no tunnel, but I did sense I was floating in another realm. There were two ancients there who merely nodded when my mind said, 'I can't come now. My children still need me.' I floated away from these beings and awoke in my hospital bed with people thumping and rubbing my extremities." She goes on to say that "this is not a story I share with many people."

◆ P. W. L. is a physicist with one of the largest public utilities in Canada. He had an NDE in 1965, a decade before *Life After Life* appeared. P. W. L. only realized that other people had had a similar experience when he happened upon the condensation of Moody's book in *Reader's Digest* in 1976. He never spoke of it to others until 1989, when he took an introductory course on the New Testament at the Toronto School of Theology.

Early on a Saturday in January 1965, he was involved in a serious car accident on the Gardiner Expressway, the major arterial roadway running along the Toronto waterfront. The police closed the Gardiner immediately afterward and the story was carried in the final edition of *The Toronto Star* the same day. His memory of the actual crash was "wiped out," he says. He was not wearing a seatbelt and only learned later that he had been battered between the two doors and the steering wheel and then thrown clear. He does remember lying waiting for the ambulance and giving his girlfriend's phone number to some bystanders. He was rushed to St. Joseph's Hospital where, in emergency surgery, his ruptured liver was sutured and repairs done to a series of tears in his lower intestine.

While unconscious on the operating table, P. W. L. had "an amazing experience." He became aware of a bright, round, yellow light overhead. "Then, I was up there beside the yellow light, watching the operation from the vicinity of the ceiling. I could see myself in the yellow illumination, in sharp focus on the operating table below. There was medical equipment above my body but it didn't impede my view in any way. I had the feeling that I was in the arms of God. An overwhelming sense of unconditional love and concern and support completely saturated me, in direct mind-to-mind contact, and it persisted for an indefinite duration. There was no dialogue involved. And then I woke up in the recovery room. My immediate reaction was, "So *that* is what God is like!" Having graduated from university not all that long before in physics, he says he was a "nominal Christian" with considerable scepticism prior to his NDE. He is aware that what happened to him is not firm proof of anything, but it changed his religious outlook completely. "Before, I could only hope, but now I know what God is like and that God loves each of us, whether we deserve it or not."

One immediate result of the NDE, he says, is that he proposed to Jean, his girlfriend, while he was still in hospital, and they were married nine months later. I met with this man not long ago at the close of a lecture I had just given. We discussed his NDE briefly and I must say that I have seldom met anyone whom I would judge to be less given to hallucinations or flights of fancy than this particular scientist.

◆ J. A. C. served in a field artillery regiment in Italy during World War II, taking part in the seige and capture of Cassino. He wrote to say that in 1972 he had a "massive coronary" and was unconscious for three days in intensive care. "There were times when I knew that my family were around me and I was sorry to be leaving them. But, I was also able to see a warm, rosy, welcoming light and knew that there were friends waiting to greet me. I wanted to go and resented being called back. Each time that I roused enough to know that I was still alive I was sorry that I hadn't made it to the light. Then I realized that it was not yet time for me to go."

◆ Several women wrote about NDEs or out-of-body experiences they had had during the process of giving birth. Two of these were instances where the baby was either born dead or died during the delivery. P. R., for example, relates that on August 1, 1947, she had the following "unforgettable experience." She was in the delivery room of the local hospital. "Something had gone wrong with the way the baby was being born. Suddenly, I remember, I found myself walking up a path in a beautiful garden. The scent of the flowers was overpowering. I was walking towards a figure dressed in white, surrounded by a bright light. This person was holding a baby in his left arm and holding his right hand out to me. I heard someone calling me from what seemed a long distance away and suddenly I was out of the garden and back in the delivery room. One of the nurses, who happened to be a friend of mine, told me that the baby had died. I have not been able to talk about this very much but have told members of my prayer group."

◆ One of the replies I received came from the Reverend Ken Martin, pastor of Siloam United Church in London, Ontario. Martin wrote to me on August 22, 1989, to say he had recently had a remarkable out-of-body experience during a "silent heart attack." It was the first of two attacks, and Martin, who is forty-eight, had been feeling tired and overworked. He told me he had made notes in his diary the same night he had his NDE and offered to share them. I spoke with him on the phone, discovered that the NDE had had a profound effect upon him, and invited him to send me his account. Here it is, verbatim:

"I was sleeping earlier tonight with my wife, Beverley, when suddenly I awoke. There was an incredible pain in my chest and I was suddenly aware of being lifted up from the bed into the air. I took a fleeting, backward glance at the bed and saw Beverley sleeping, and then I was transported right out of the room into the sky. The sky was very dark in the background and yet there were swirls of very bright lights. I found myself caught up in one of these swirls. It was like being at the small end of a long funnel that was opening wider and wider. I was rushing through the funnel in a fast-moving swirl of light.

"It was incredibly bright. It was also warm and I felt very much at peace and extremely contented. It was as if there was a great strength lifting me and pulling me forward. I experienced the feeling that I was going home. There was no pain, no depression, and no worries about finishing my thesis, earning a living, or whether or not I would be able to return to work. It was as if these things were gone forever. I had a very definite feeling that I was coming home from someplace I had left a long time ago. Then I saw an extremely bright light ahead of me. All was so peaceful, warm, and well. I was rushing faster and faster into this ever-widening swirl of blazing light. It was as if someone was summoning me to come home but I heard no voice. The overwhelming feeling was one of incredible peace.

"Then, abruptly, I was yanked back and found myself in my bed again. I felt deeply disappointed and cried out: 'Oh no, not this again!' I guess that was a terrible thing to think and voice. Although there had been a few seconds as I first had felt myself being lifted into the dark sky when I felt disappointment at leaving my family, that feeling had quickly left me, overwhelmed by the sense of peace. Now I was back in bed with all the pain and depression and worry. I wept because I had come back. I now have a deep feeling that 'home' is somewhere else and would like to go back. When will I resume my journey? It was incredible!"

Martin has now lost forty pounds – he had been up to 195 – is swimming regularly on his doctor's orders, and is back at work in a busy parish. In his accompanying letter to me, he says he now knows firsthand that "there is nothing to be afraid of after death." He is also convinced that there is so much more to life than what we have known on earth. "Yet, I am also convinced that we Christians are in for a big surprise and that we have certainly made our God far too small." He added that, apart from his wife, he has told nobody else about his experience. He has not, at the time of my writing this, shared this experience with his congregation. "Why not?" he queries. "Likely because I'm afraid of being called eccentric, crazy, or worse."

◆

It is impossible to do more than skim the surface of my mail on this and related subjects, never mind describing in any adequate way all of what is now available on near-death experiences. Letters have come from the educated and the uneducated, from the religious and the non-religious, from believers in life after death and from those who previously were total sceptics. Many of those who wrote to me were not at death's door when their "glimpse of eternity" or their sense of being able to "look down on my body" from some other vantage point occurred. Nearly all of them spoke of the "light," of feelings of a peace beyond understanding, and of seeing loved ones or supernatural beings – God, Christ, Krishna, angels, or others – aware that they were using symbolic language to express what had happened to them. Most say their attitude to both life and death were changed in the process. One man wrote to say that he now feels as though he is living "with one foot in each of two different worlds." While there is generally some regret at not having passed on to the other side, there is, paradoxically, a greater commitment to this life, a desire to learn more, to love more. While those who have the experience do not necessarily become suddenly more religious, they invariably become more spiritual, more concerned with the depth dimension of living. All fear of death and dying, they say, is gone.[7]

"Hellish" Near-Death Experiences

It is tempting, given the overwhelmingly positive nature of the NDE portrayed in the bulk of both popular and scientific literature, to assume that, whatever is signified by this phenomenon, its main thrust is extremely good news about dying and death. However, there is another side to the story, one that has not yet been fully studied and assimilated by NDE researchers. That some people who come close to the gates of death experience a reality which is anything but reassuring was first fully discussed by Dr. Maurice Rawlings in his 1978 book, *Beyond Death's Door*.[8] Rawlings, an evangelical, fundamentalist Christian, argued from his medical experience that some people who have an NDE feel themselves to be in hell. *Beyond Death's Door* is not a particularly good book in my opinion, as Rawlings only manages to adduce a very tiny number of such stories, and one has the feeling throughout that he had already decided on his conclusions before he began his research. But Rawlings at least has raised the issue that possibly all is not light and bliss during the near-death experience.

When George Gallup, Jr. published his 1982 book, *Adventures in Immortality: A Look Beyond the Threshold of Death,* he too referred to respondents who said they had had a "hellish" experience while close to death. For the most recent and the most insightful look at this aspect of the NDE, though, one must look at Margot Grey's *Return From Death: An Exploration of the Near-Death Experience.*[9] Grey, a "humanistic psychologist," based her research on interviews with thirty-eight people claiming near-death experiences and many more patients she later worked with in her practice. Grey herself had an NDE when she had a close brush with death while travelling in India. She reports she too had an encounter with light accompanied by a "feeling of being very close to the source of light and love, which seemed to be one." Grey, who has no religious ties, states quite categorically that her studies have brought her to the conclusion that "conscious awareness survives physical death."[10]

Her chapter on negative experiences breaks some new ground. She bases her remarks here on five of her own cases and nine negative cases from the general literature, together with information gleaned from interviews with cardiologists who have been on the lookout for NDE reports from their patients. Like Rawlings, these doctors stressed that negative NDEs are only made known *very shortly after* the episodes happen. In other words, such experiences tend to be quickly repressed. Grey found that those who experience this type of NDE feel a sense of guilt or shame at hellish experiences and would rather not admit to them. She also concludes that they may indeed have had some terrible deed in their background that they felt accounted for their sense of being in or going to hell. In his review of her book, Karlis Osis says that in this finding Grey "has put her finger on the right spot. We might need to rethink our methods. Maybe we have relied too much on the self-reports of the patients and have failed to ascertain observations made through the cooler eyes of doctors and nurses who were around when the patients started to talk about the NDEs that were still fresh in their memories."[11]

Grey was able to come up with some quite significant similarities between the pattern of positive NDEs and that of the negative ones. In the negative NDE, instead of peace and a sense of well-being, there is a feeling of fear and panic. The sense of being out of the body is similar in both types. Instead of entering a tunnel, however, in the negative NDE one enters a black void. There is no light, but rather the sense of an evil force, and one enters what can only be described as a "hell-like" environment. In the negative cases, there are after-effects, too. "Like those respondents who had positive experiences, the people in this category returned from their encounters with an increased conviction that life continues after death. They also felt a strong urge radically to modify their former way of life."[12]

In all, about one-eighth of Grey's interviewees reported experiences that were hell-like. None of this, of course, means that such imagery has to be taken in a literal fashion or that there is such a "place" or state as a literal hell. But, it is clearly an area of research that needs much more careful examination. As Osis remarks, "If this pattern is replicated and sound, it would require nothing less than considering the positive and negative NDEs as one integrated whole – a sweeping reorganization of our views."

Problems with the Near-Death Experience

According to the International Association for Near-Death Studies, "An NDE may occur when a person is considered clinically dead, or even to one not close to death but who is under some biological and/or psychological stress. Somehow, the experience appears to be a biologically-based trigger for a spiritual event." For me, the most exhaustive and fascinating attempt to understand just what is going on in this "event" is a book by Carol Zaleski, *Otherworld Journeys: Accounts of Near-Death Experience in Medieval and Modern Times.* Ms. Zaleski, who wrote this work initially as her doctoral thesis in religious studies at Harvard, gives us a sparkling overview of the NDE and sets it in a more universal perspective by analysing examples from sources as diverse as the epic of Gilgamesh, Plato, St. Paul, and Dante's *Divine Comedy.* Her main focus, however, as the title says, is a comparison of medieval otherworld journeys with those described in the NDE literature of today. In addition, she reviews the modern scientific debate between the advocates of the NDE as a real glimpse of eternity and the hard-nosed sceptics who pour cascades of cold water over such "imaginative flights of fancy."

Zaleski finds amazing parallels between the experiences of medieval saints, mystics, and ordinary folk, and those relayed on talk shows or in the books of the NDE researchers of today. But she finds some remarkable differences too: "Gone are the bad deaths, harsh judgement scenes, purgatorial torments, and infernal terrors of medieval visions; by comparison, the modern other world is a congenial place, a democracy, a school for continuing education, and a garden of unearthly delights."[13] In other words, there is something very western about the terms in which the modern otherworld traveller conceptualizes his or her vision.

This brings us to one of the first observations I want to make about the NDE. The experience, though obviously universal in the sense that we can find examples of it at every period and in every culture, is nevertheless culture-specific. That is, it is expressed in forms of thought and language peculiar to its historical context. While those who have had the experience may all, or nearly all, "see" beings of light, these will be described variously as Jesus, Buddha, or Krishna depending on who is doing the "seeing" and where. Zaleski points out, for example, that Dante's heaven is much more hierarchical than any heaven in modern NDE experience. But the social order of Dante's time was itself a hierarchical one: "For medieval audiences, the ranking of the blessed in a series of concentric but ascending heavens ... derived its plausibility – or rather its imaginative power – from the fact that it reflected and affirmed the social order and provided an emblem for the structure of human intelligence." What this cultural component indicates is that, whatever is happening in the NDE, there is certainly a subjective element provided by the individual concerned. If they are indeed viewing a reality of some kind, it is a reality shaped by their own background, conditioning, and life situation. This, of course, does not automatically mean that the NDE itself can be dismissed as "totally subjective." Being human, it is impossible for us to apprehend any reality in this world or the next without bringing to it whatever we ourselves are, and shaping it accordingly. It is possible intellectually to conceive of a totally objective reality *in the abstract*, but in practice there is no such thing as the "unobserved observer." Even in science, allowance has to be made for the contribution we make in describing "the real world."

A second problem faced by Zaleski and admitted in varying degrees by even the most enthusiastic of the NDE proponents is that of defining death itself. No matter how moving some of the descriptions of journeying into this other realm may be, we have to keep reminding ourselves that the operative word in "near-death experience" is "near." All of these visionaries were near death; they were not actually dead, because, by definition, to be dead is to be at that point from which any kind of physical return is ruled out. Zaleski quotes from an article in the British medical journal, *The Lancet*: "Death is just beyond the point from which anyone can return to tell us anything." As she goes on to say, the "popular appeal of return-from-death stories rests partly on the assumption that temporary absence of vital signs is equivalent to death."[14]

The difficulty here is that it is now very hard, even for ethicists and medical experts, to agree on what constitutes death. What's more, as medical technology and skills advance and ever more amazing rescues of the dying are possible, even tentative definitions have to be constantly reexamined and updated. It should be remembered too, in this connection, that even NDE researchers themselves do not want to restrict the NDE too closely to death because they have documented so many cases where the same experience was encountered not near death but during meditation, in the face of extreme danger, while on a drug, or during childbirth. Even allowing for all of this, however, I agree with Moody that while those who experience NDEs are not really dead in the full sense of the word, they have come very much closer to this ultimate experience than the rest of us. Or, as Zaleski puts it, "Whether NDEs occur in the grip of death or only in the face of death, they may still constitute a revelatory encounter with death." These experiences are certainly not proof of a life after death, or of the other realities and entities reported. But, it is argued, they could supply at the minimum some evidence upon which a belief in life after death could reasonably take its stand.

The critics, as one would expect, have come up with a wide variety of natural explanations to account for what the proponents of the NDE claim is a vision of another world or plane of reality. Certainly, as both Zaleski and Moody admit – along with a host of other responsible researchers in this field – it is essential to look hard at the question of whether any sufficient, natural causes exist to explain the phenomenon before leaping to any transcendental conclusions. In *The Light Beyond*, Moody devotes his final chapter, "Explanations," to a detailed refutation of a range of natural possibilities. Zaleski, too, in an even more thorough manner, considers the critical literature and explanations ranging from the effects of stress on the body to drugs or sensory deprivation. Her chapter is called "Explanations and Counterexplanations." There is no need here to repeat everything that has been said pro and con. Instead, I propose to look at the most obvious alternative, the hallucination theory.

Since a large majority of those who have experienced near-death were on various medications at the time of their brush with death, and since altered states of consciousness can be produced by such physiological factors as an acute lack of oxygen (hypoxia or anoxia), or a sudden rush of endorphins, enkephalins, or other as yet unknown chemicals secreted by the brain when stress, pain, or fear occur, many scientists have argued that what we are dealing with here is some form of hallucination. As Zaleski says, as far as the debunkers are concerned, these "endogenous opiates are a neurochemical equivalent for and an answer to grace."[15]

I believe this theory deserves further consideration. There can be no doubt that the human mind is capable of quite extraordinary thoughts and visions under the right stimuli. Visionary experiences can be produced by extended fasting, by extremes of physical exhaustion, or by hallucinogenic substances. As I have already made clear, I am not personally subject to mystical visions or visitations of any kind. However, I do know what it is like to hallucinate on a chemical substance.

Let me explain. In the summer of 1962 I took a year's leave of absence from my parish in Scarborough, Ontario, to return to Oxford, England, for some postgraduate studies in Patristics, the writings of the early Fathers of the Church. In February 1963, Dr. Frank Lake, a British psychiatrist from Nottingham, came to the university for a series of lectures. Lake was one of the earliest pioneers in the use of lysergic acid, (LSD), in the treatment of the mentally ill. He had been a missionary doctor in India for a number of years, and had spent almost all of his time as a psychiatrist dealing with people heavily involved in organized religion. At his invitation, following one of his lectures, I joined a small group of other clergy who volunteered to assist in a research project. Lake had become discouraged by the difficulty and length of time required for traditional analysis and counselling and was experimenting with LSD as a psychiatric "shortcut." (I would remind the reader that this was well before LSD appeared in North America and became part of the drug scene in any way. At this point, none of us had even heard of it before.) I hitchhiked up to Nottingham one weekend that spring and joined Lake and the others at his centre, a place called Lingwood. An Anglican priest came, and along with four other priests, one of whom had been a distinguished Spitfire pilot in the Battle of Britain, I received Holy Communion and then was administered some LSD. Each of us had been assigned to a room of his own, and the doctor dropped by frequently to monitor what was going on.

Though it happened over twenty-five years ago, the experience remains perfectly vivid in all its details. I had known nothing like it before, and have never since. At first, it was like seeing technicolor movies run at a very high speed inside my head. The speeded-up images were mainly of various family members, often doing extremely funny things. A tremendous sense of exaltation flooded me and it seemed nothing would ever be impossible – writing a world best-selling novel, rivalling the greatest artists who had ever painted, or composing music as great as Mozart's or Beethoven's. There were sensations of glorious light, and then visions of great beauty, both of the human form and of natural landscapes.

Suddenly, the mood changed, and with a growing sense of dread I approached a tunnel, which was as arid and dry as dust. The sensation of drawing a fingernail over a slate blackboard is the closest I can get to describe the feeling on my skin as I was forced through. From that point on, the "trip" became much worse. Spider-like monsters threatened my very being. Even with my eyes open it seemed as though the room was filled with horrific presences with sinister intent. Quite frankly, it was terrifying until I felt myself growing increasingly angry and wanting to fight back. I imagined myself wielding a short, sharp sword and plunging it into the belly of the enemy creatures, much like Frodo did with Shelob in Tolkien's *The Lord of the Rings*. This was followed by a renewed sense of exaltation and awareness of a beauty I had never dreamed existed.

All of this went on for at least two hours, and even much later, when I was able to leave the centre and go for a walk in a nearby park, the "flashbacks" continued. One moment I was in the park watching the children playing and some adults busy with a cricket game, the next I was back in my own inner world with its exaggerated fears and glories. I remember looking across the park at some slumlike houses in the distance. Caught in the rays of the westering sun, they seemed to stand out with a glory that utterly transformed them.

I'm not sure what help any of us were to Dr. Lake in his research. The memory of the experience stands out much more sharply for me today than his conclusions with all of us afterwards. Though I gained no personal insights that could not have been acquired by other means, there was certainly a revelation of a kind. What was instructive was the glimpse into the incredible capacity of the brain to invent, to recall suppressed material, and to put it together in totally unexpected and original ways. There was, however – and this is in marked and important contrast with the NDE – no specifically religious content that I can remember, no visions of God or of Christ, no feeling of being in another realm of existence. Yet, while I would never care to repeat it, nor would I ever recommend it to anyone else, the experience was spiritual in that it further convinced me of dimensions of beauty only hinted at in ordinary life.

It is tempting to infer from this personal account that perhaps the sceptics are right after all. In the NDE some kind of hallucination – possibly nature's way of softening the moment of death – is taking place. Moody himself counters this argument with substantial evidence that a large number of recorded NDEs have taken place when there was a completely flat EEG.[16] "The sheer number of these cases tells me that in some people NDEs have happened when they were technically dead. Had these been hallucinations, they would have shown up on the EEG." The difficulty with this solution, however, is that at the current level of technology an EEG does not give a precise reading in every instance. As Moody himself concedes, "brain activity can be going on at such a deep level that surface electrodes don't pick it up." What impresses me much more is the remarkable fact that while NDEs vary widely in their tone and content, as we have seen, there is nevertheless *a common core* of experience running through them all regardless of time or place. It strains credulity in my view to suppose that hundreds of thousands of experiences, all of them hallucinatory, would still manage unanimously to convey such a profound sense of otherworldliness and of having somehow transcended death. I find this all the more cogent when the results of such experiences are almost uniformly positive – loss of the fear of death, commitment to greater love and understanding, and commitment to a greater spiritual, though not necessarily religious, awareness and lifestyle. One other significant point should be made. As Zaleski makes clear, "for every pathological condition presumed [by the critics] to cause near-death visions, one can find subjects who were demonstrably free of its influence; therefore no single psychological or physiological syndrome can account for near-death experience."[17]

There is one final objection I want to look at before summarizing our findings. It deserves attention both because of the prestige and popularity of its chief proponent and because, at first sight, it has about it an aura of great plausibility. I'm referring to the views of astronomer and keen debunker of all paranormal phenomena, Carl Sagan. In the concluding chapter of his book *Broca's Brain*, titled "The Amniotic Universe," Sagan uses the symbolism which has gathered around the universal experience of birth to explain away the cluster of experiences reported by those who have had an NDE.

In his view, not only the NDE but almost every major religious concept, from death and rebirth to the primal Eden and the Fall, derives from our unconscious memories of the womb, the birth passage, the emergence into light, and being swaddled and nursed. Religion, from his extremely polemical point of view, is nothing but the vague recollection of profound experiences at a time when we are utterly helpless and inarticulate.

As noted, there is a immediate appearance of verisimilitude

about this. Yet, to coin a phrase, the more you scratch the surface of it the more surface there is to scratch. Without attempting to deal with Sagan's theory as it affects the whole of religion, let me simply set out the problems I have with it *vis à vis* the topic in hand, the NDE.

First, birth, unlike the classical NDE, is an experience of moving from a place of safety, warmth, and total intimacy out into the exposed and separated world of individual existence. However dependent and close to the mother, the baby begins to experience the pain of existence right from the start. With the first breath often comes a cry. Any accounts of birth experiences I have encountered in the relevant literature all stress the element of trauma and pain that attends the moments of our leaving what Sagan calls "the amniotic universe." This is not what the NDE is about.

Second, so far from being "blurred perceptions" or "vague premonitions," as Sagan describes our perinatal memories, reports of the NDE describe a great sense of clarity surrounding both perceptions and the recall of them later. In fact, as we have seen, many liken normal, waking perception to "dreaming" compared with the reality and vividness of what they have gone through.

Third, Sagan deliberately ignores or plays down the extraordinary transformational power of the NDE. Nothing he says, in my view, comes close to explaining why it is that the majority of people who've had a near-death experience find themselves so profoundly moved and changed by the events of their NDE. Something numinous or totally "other" seems to have happened to them.

Sagan, a media-wise, militant sceptic, may be a scientist but he can hardly be viewed as completely objective in his claims at this point. He is a leading member of the American Committee for the Scientific Investigation of Claims of the Paranormal. It was founded in 1976 by Sagan, Isaac Asimov, and others to combat media promotion of anything purporting to be mysterious or unexplained – from the Bermuda Triangle to Von

Daniken's alien astronauts. There is nothing wrong with any of that except that, in their enthusiasm to expose "pseudo-science," Sagan and company sometimes get carried away and sweep with too wide a broom. They end up at times espousing not science but scientism, the view that *only* the empirical, scientific method can yield true knowledge. There are few things less scientific than that!

Obviously, if death is indeed a kind of new "birth" into an entirely different dimension of reality and being, it would not be surprising if attempts to describe it were to parallel those attendant on our emergence into the light of this world as infants. But the differences, at least to this investigator, seem to be much greater than the similarities.

Summary

After his NDE, Carl Jung wrote: "What happens after death is so unspeakably glorious that our imaginations and our feelings do not suffice to form even an approximate conception of it."[18] This view is almost universally held by both those who experience NDEs and the positive NDE researchers. But, of course, we are here still in the arena of faith and not of scientific proof. In her review of Moody's *The Light Beyond* in the IANDS *Journal of Near-Death Studies*, Judith Miller, Ph.D., chides Moody for not stating his faith in more positive terms and for not challenging traditional scientific paradigms.[19] Moody, the acknowledged "leader on the cutting edge of this field," begins the book by saying: "We are no closer to answering the basic question of the afterlife now than we were thousands of years ago when it was first pondered by ancient man." In other words, since the evidence provided by NDEs can't be replicated on demand in a scientific laboratory, none of the amazing stories is firm proof of life after death. What the matter comes down to in the end is the authority or weight we give to mystical glimpses or visions of realities other than the empirical world we live in.

Zaleski argues that, like the arguments for the existence of

God, the realities attested to by people who have had an NDE belong to a totally different sphere where the question is not so much, Can they be proven to be true? as, Do NDEs give insights which can be verified in one's own experience? She concludes: "We may find no difficulty in respecting the testimony of those whose lives have been transformed by a near-death vision, but we can verify their discoveries only if, in some sense, we experience them for ourselves."

I find the whole expanding exploration and research in this field to be one of the most exciting developments of our time. In my own thinking and research I find myself increasingly (though cautiously) positive about the validity of the NDE as a witness to invisible realities beyond. What carries most weight with me, as I have already suggested, is the consistency and clarity of the stories themselves, together with the undeniable evidence of dramatically changed lives. I know from my own pastoral experience the truth of what researcher Dr. Bruce Greyson has said. Psychiatry or therapeutic counselling often takes years to bring about only slight changes in people's outlook and behaviour, but "the NDE regularly brings about a total transformation almost overnight."

3

♦

Channelers:
The New
Spirit
Mediums

HISTORY WAS MADE ON NORTH AMERICAN TELEVISION IN 1967 when the American medium, or psychic, the Reverend Arthur Ford, held a seance on TV. The affair made headlines across the continent because Ford's participant, or "seeker," was none other than Bishop James A. Pike, unquestionably the most controversial bishop in the Anglican communion in modern times. Because he had publicly announced his doubts about the Virgin Birth, the Holy Trinity, and other orthodox teachings of his Episcopal Church, Pike had come close to facing a heresy trial, and in 1965 he was forced to resign as leader of the Episcopal Diocese of California. He remained a bishop, however, and continued to make news as he probed Christian origins and leaned increasingly toward interest in the paranormal.

In February 1966, Pike's son Jim, aged twenty-two, committed suicide in a hotel room in New York. Pike was studying at Cambridge University in England at the time and, filled with remorse at having neglected the young man and his problems, he began consulting mediums.

The famous public seance, arranged by my predecessor as religion editor of *The Toronto Star*, Allen Spraggett, author of several books on paranormal phenomena, took place in the studios of CFTO-TV in Scarborough, Ontario. It was taped as part of a special two-hour program on Pike's ideas and stormy career and aired on September 17. Ford went into a trance and professed to make contact with Pike's son, Jim Jr., through his own habitual "spirit control," who went by the name of Fletcher. (Fletcher had been a childhood playmate of Ford's who had died at an early age.)[1]

Ford, wearing a blindfold, mentioned several persons from Pike's past, including his son's grandfather who "was with [him] on the other side." Not only did the son speak to Pike, but there were also brief messages from the others – most notably from Pike's predecessor as Bishop of California, the Right Reverend Karl Block. Pike told Block how much he admired him and added that he hoped Block had not been too upset by some of the changes he had introduced. Block told him: "No . . . You did a magnificent job and you have magnificent work yet to do." The key point of the affair, however, was the statement, purportedly from Jim Jr., assuring Pike that he was in no way to blame for what had happened.

Voice: "Jim says he wants you to definitely understand that neither you nor any other member of the family have any right to feel any sense of guilt or have any feeling that you failed him in any way."[2]

This most reassuring message, accompanied by some bits of information that the medium, in the bishop's view, "could not have possibly known," persuaded Pike that Ford had really conversed with the dead youth, and in subsequent interviews he gave great credence to the belief that bona fide mediums could indeed make use of spiritual "entities" to bridge the gap between the dead and the living. *The New York Times* and other papers quoted him as saying he truly believed he had spoken with his son: "To me, this is the most plausible explanation of the phenomena that occurred."

When Arthur Ford died at the age of seventy-five, however, the secret of his ability to cite dates, names, and obscure bits of information about those whom he was allegedly contacting was finally revealed. Among his belongings were vast files of obituary notices and other clippings on the relatives of the people he gave "sittings" for. He always took a briefcase filled with such material along with him when travelling to see new clients. Spraggett, who initially had been completely taken in by Ford himself, later wrote a book describing how Ford used this research in the Pike seance and other similar frauds.

The unfortunate bishop, one of the brightest and most colourful churchmen of his or any other day, (he was the only bishop in church history known to have had two ex-wives and his current wife all mourn him at his funeral), did not have the magnificent future predicted by Ford. He died horribly, not long after the seance, of thirst and exposure in the Judean wilderness while trying to reach the Dead Sea caves. His third wife, Diane, who accompanied him, escaped the tragedy. The search for Pike went on for several days and made headlines around the world. He was eventually found dead at the foot of a cliff over which he had fallen in a heat- and thirst-induced delirium. In death as in life he made front-page news.

The sad truth is that it would take almost a library of books to contain the full accounts of all the past deceptions and frauds perpetrated by would-be spiritualists and psychics. Their number is legion. Most of them, of course, have not had the panache – or the publicity – of an Arthur Ford. Significantly, considering the staggering nature of their claims, one is almost always struck by the extraordinary triviality and triteness of what they report. I agree with Colin Wilson's comment that most of this stuff is banal, "oddly boring and disappointing." It's not just that what the spirits have to say is so inconsequential, he notes, it's that it usually "sounds like the ramblings of an uninspired Sunday School teacher."[3]

For the origins of spiritualism, Wilson's treatment in his book, *Afterlife*, is as good as any. For our purposes here, we can be fairly brief. Necromancy, as it is called by scholars, the belief system which has as its chief focus the establishment of communication with the dead, existed among most primitive peoples, and there is evidence of it in the Hebrew Bible, where it is repeatedly condemned. In its modern form it dates from the occult experiences of the Fox family in 1848 in the U.S.A., from where it soon spread to England and Europe.

The Fox affair began with some poltergeist-like rappings and knockings at the Fox home in Hydesville Township, near Rochester, New York, in March of that year. At first, it was the two girls, Margaretta, fourteen, and Kate, twelve (who, incidentally, were born in Canada), who found they could get the "spirit" behind the knocking to imitate their commands and rap on cue. Then Mrs. Fox, joined eventually by curious neighbours, found it was possible to ask questions by means of a kind of code – rap twice if the answer is yes, once for no. By this means it was established that the house was haunted by one Charles Rosma, a peddler who claimed he had been robbed and murdered there by a earlier tenant. Curiously, the sounds only happened when the children were in the home. The children were then separated and sent to stay with relatives, but the allegedly supernatural noises followed them and, later, when the Fox family reunited and moved to Rochester, the manifestations began to occur there as well. Publicity grew apace, and very soon many others began to report similar phenomena. Seances multiplied, and before long mediums were popping up everywhere across the country. "Table-moving" or "table-turning" became a common form of social activity both in the United States and in Britain and France. By 1888, however, both the Fox girls, whose antics had sparked the entire movement, publicly confessed that the whole thing – at least as far as their part in it was concerned – had been a gigantic hoax.[4]

Today's channelers, it seems, know and care little or nothing for any of the historical background, even though they seem to be nothing more than the mediums of the past under a fresh name. There are, however, slight but significant differences. For example, many channelers are concerned not so much with contacting dead persons as with dispensing arcane wisdom and guidance from other planes. While they usually claim to make use of various spirit guides or "entities" – sometimes a single name is given to a cluster of entities – many of them hold that their ultimate inspiration is the spirit of God or of "the gods," and that they provide ways to understand one's relationship to the divine Mind.[5]

Largely because of Shirley MacLaine's books, media appearances, and multiplying seminars, channeling has become so popular that today you can even take night-school courses in it at otherwise staid, academic institutions. While MacLaine herself doesn't claim to be a channeler, she promotes the whole process and is reportedly making a small fortune from her seminars alone, which are regularly attended by 1,000 participants at $300 a head. Channeling has become a big business, and not just for the leading figures in the New Age movement but for hundreds of lesser lights in every city and town on the continent. People flock to channelers for the kind of comfort and reassurance they once looked to doctors, clergy, or psychiatrists to give.

One might be tempted to dismiss the whole phenomenon as relatively harmless on the grounds that if people want this kind of thing and are willing to pay for it, it's nobody's business but their own. However, since we are engaged in an inquiry into whether there is any reason to believe in life after death, the matter cannot simply be left there. Two questions remain: Are these channelers actually in genuine contact with the deceased or other spirit beings? And what kind of messages are being conveyed to the eager and often very vulnerable people who are the recipients of this information or advice?

Having researched this fertile field, including listening to hours of tapes of sessions with channelers and interviewing both channelers and those who avail themselves of their services, I can say with all seriousness that I have seldom encountered such a mish-mash of weird speculations (solemnly taught as Gospel truth) and downright nonsense in a lifetime devoted to the study of religio-spiritual matters. There is so little regard for evidence or documentation and there are so many obvious distortions that it is impossible for me to come to any other conclusion than that these people, in spite of claims to the contrary, have very little passion for objectivity and truth. This is evident in, for example, the wholly uncritical acceptance of such unproven legends as that of the lost civilization of Atlantis, the belief that the whole human race is the result of genetic experiments by extraterrestrials from uncharted planets, the certainty of UFOs, and so on.

I am not saying that all channelers are fakes, hucksters, or patently insincere. That would be unfair and is beyond the bounds of normal proof in any case. Nor is it my conclusion that just because I find the kind of "evidence" being produced to be unconvincing there is therefore no communication taking place, and no spiritual beings or spirits around to be contacted. Indeed, given the popularity of this phenomenon and the sense of certainty of its proponents, it is very tempting to seize on the witness of the channelers and their devotees as a genuine reason for believing in life after death. My difficulty is that, however others may see it, I find that channeling presents far more problems than it solves.

Shirley MacLaine's best-selling books are filled with wild assertions about what the Bible says, what Einstein and other scientists say, and yet there are no solid facts or references to back up any of it. Anyone trying to check these alleged quotations or statements will find that they either don't exist or have been so wrenched from their context as to be totally different. We get a real clue to the kind of approach I'm referring to when we read her own words in *Out on a Limb*.[6] On information received from channelers: "Wherever the information came from didn't matter as much to me as the sense it made. Maybe it was a psychic's subconscious talking; maybe they were just good actors. But even if that were true, the morality of their message was unmistakable." MacLaine's most characteristic reply when questioned about any of her New Age beliefs, from UFO sightings to clairvoyance, is: "We all create our own reality." Or, "That's my reality anyway." As Henry Gordon remarks in his 1988 exposé book, *Channeling into the New Age, The Teachings of Shirley MacLaine and Other Such Gurus*, who can reason or argue with this kind of lack-logic? Once we all create our own realities, all discourse about what is or is not true becomes totally meaningless. Anyone can say whatever far-out or ridiculous thing takes their fancy and not fear rebuttal.

It's not just Shirley MacLaine who does this. I have to say it is characteristic of all the channelers I have met or researched to date. Such unmitigated pomposities, such unproven and unprovable spoutings on everything from the origins of humanity or the "true" interpretation of the Bible to the purpose of life have seldom, in my opinion, been so gravely uttered to such gullible audiences. As Isaac Asimov has said, history continues to show that "even more powerful than the instinct for self-preservation is the will to believe."

What is risky about a lot of this material, however, is that it can easily end by messing up people's minds and actually destroying families. Henry Gordon cites a graphic case of this. When MacLaine was a guest on the "Larry King Live!" TV show on September 17, 1987, a caller complained that his family had been "blown apart." He said his wife had been suffering acute depression and went to a channeler, who, by means of her "entity," told the woman that her husband had murdered her in a past life and then had run off with their teenaged daughter. She immediately left her husband and disappeared. He hadn't seen her in two years. He went on to comment that he thought his wife "was looking for a crutch to avoid dealing with the realities of life."[7]

I could match this story with several similar ones that readers have written to me in response to my newspaper columns on reincarnation and hypnotic regression into alleged past lives. In fairness, it must also be said that the misuse or overly fanatical pursuit of almost any set of ideas, religious or otherwise, can readily result in personal or social harm.

What I find most dangerous in the beliefs that often go along with channeling, however, is the New Age theory, based upon a misunderstanding of the teaching of Dr. Carl Jung about evil, that the truly spiritual person is beyond good and evil. This argument for amorality cropped up continuously in the channeling material I examined. For example, one of the best-known channelers of today, J. Z. Knight, who has been highly endorsed by Shirley MacLaine, operates with an "entity" whom she calls Ramtha, an alleged 35,000-year-old warrior from the lost civilization of Atlantis. Ramtha, whose very name set MacLaine to weeping when she first heard it, says that God is neither good nor evil. He is without morality and judges nobody for anything. Thus, there is no such thing as evil. Nothing is wrong or taboo for you – not even murder – because it may be that your soul needs this experience to grow in understanding. We all need to experience everything to broaden our experience of life and become fully realized.[8]

I read these statements of Ramtha's on November 8, 1989. In *The Toronto Star* of that same date there was a story about the sentencing of a California serial murderer called "The Night Stalker." Richard Ramirez, a drifter from El Paso, Texas, went on a five-month rampage in 1985. He was convicted by a jury in Los Angeles of thirteen murders in addition to thirty other crimes, including multiple rapes. One of his victims was a four-year-old girl. Ramirez, an avowed Satanist, had gouged out the eyes of one victim and brutally mutilated others. When sentenced to death in the gas-chamber, the murderer was defiant and said he was beyond good and evil and a servant of the devil. He vowed he would be revenged. Charles Manson, we must remember, also believed he was beyond morality. Obviously it would be both grossly unfair and untrue to suggest there is any connection between MacLaine or any of her ilk and the demented thinking of a Ramirez or a Manson. Nevertheless, we need to be mindful of the risks here.

MacLaine herself has never to my knowledge claimed to be above good and evil, yet it is implicit in her often-repeated belief that each of us *is* God. (This, of course, is quite different from the Jewish, Christian, or Muslim belief that God is *in* us or that we are *in* God.) She is fond of telling the story of how she once found herself alone, dancing on a beach and shouting "I am God!" When the Bible tells us to love God, she claims, this means self-love since we ourselves are divine. But once you are God, traditional moral values don't just change, they vanish before the almighty "I" or "Me." The well-nigh inevitable result of this kind of thought process leads to individual and social chaos.

Summary

The incredible number of admitted frauds and the almost unbelievably trivial nature of the information provided about "the departed" by the old-style spiritualist mediums leads me to difficulties with their claims of evidence of life after death. In the case of the New Age channelers, fraud is much harder to establish because their messages are not generally subject to empirical refutation. It is next to impossible to argue with someone who claims to be speaking the thoughts of a disembodied entity when the subjects under discussion are lost civilizations, alien intelligences from hidden planets, or various kinds of spirit "vibrations." As for evidence of life after death, in spite of all the insistence on communication with spirit "entities," there is nothing solid on which their claims stand. My own view – at least at this point – is that the channelers are either delving into their own or the group's unconscious fantasies, or that they are what MacLaine calls "good actors."

What may be at work here, although the followers of this aspect of New Age thought would be horrified to be told so, is the very same thing that is evident wherever religious fundamentalism is rooted and growing. The need being filled in both cases is that of a deeply anxious public wanting simple, black-and-white answers to personal and social problems at a time of deep spiritual unrest. There is a longing for magic, for instant solutions. The followers of both camps seem to have the same inability to cope with ambiguity and uncertainty, so they opt for those who will give them either the certainty of an infallible book, such as the Bible or the Qur'an, or the certainty of an otherworldly spirit guide. It may seem like a comforting route to go, but from what I have seen, unfortunately it tends to be attended by little evidence and by large risks.

Finally, let me add that there is no doubt whatever in my mind that channeling "works" in the sense that certain individuals can and do sometimes find a new sense of worth, meaning, and self-confidence when they consult a channeler. A great spiritual search is going on at this moment in history and there would be no such thing as the channeling explosion if it were not addressing specific needs with some measure of success. In a confusing and confused world, where traditional faiths seem under fire and unable to bridge the gap between their dogmas and the needs of ordinary people, where the individual can so easily get lost in the shuffling of forces beyond his or her control, where materialism seems to exclude all else, to be addressed by voices or guides from the other side can be of considerable solace. One is given a sort of "instant spirituality," an appropriate remedy from a culture that has an instant solution for everything else. One is assured of an infinity of possibilities for one's future, of wider dimensions than mundane living, and of the certainty of bliss to come. In fact, channeling today functions rather like the spiritualism of the last century; it is a kind of protest against a secularist worldview. It operates as a substitute religion, one that is very personal and much easier than traditional spiritual disciplines. I believe the traditional faiths could learn a great deal about themselves and their own failure to speak meaningfully to contemporary men and women by paying much greater attention to this aspect of the whole channeling phenomenon, instead of simply criticizing or condemning it.

4

◆

Reincarnation

"YOU CAN RELIVE YOUR PAST LIVES" THE TABLOID'S THREE-inch, black headline screams. "Expert gives step-by-step instructions . . ." One of the most popular features of New Age thinking is the very ancient theory that we have already lived many lives and will continue to do so in the future. This process, it is believed, goes on until we have learned all the lessons God (or life itself) has to teach us and are sufficiently enlightened to be released from the cycle of rebirth. We are then fit for the Presence of God, union with universal Mind, or the oblivion of nirvanic bliss. The law of karma, the spiritual equivalent of physical cause and effect in the scientific world, governs the kind of sufferings or blessings experienced in each successive life. Free will enters into it, of course. According to the mainstream theory in the West – and there are many variations depending upon the particular religious or philosophical approach taken – there is free choice about how one deals with specific aspects of our karma. The matter of where, to which parents, and in what circumstances one is reborn is widely believed to be a matter of choice. Advice, however, may be given by exalted masters or other higher spiritual beings in the plane between lives.

Until quite recently, it was possible to think of belief in reincarnation as something rather exotic, belonging to the great religious traditions of the East but foreign to western thought. A visit to the nearest bookstore or a glance at the tabloids at the neighbourhood supermarket will quickly dispel such a notion. Recent public opinion polls reveal some quite remarkable statistics. According to the 1981 Gallup poll on religion in the United States, some 38 million Americans (23 per cent) profess to be believers in reincarnation. A more recent Gallup poll of Canadian views on an afterlife shows that nearly one-third of the population (29 per cent) believe you are reborn into another life here on earth after death. Most of this can be seen as the result of the enormous impact over the past three decades of eastern religious ideas upon western society. But there are deeper causes, too. The decline of Christianity in the West and the spiritual vacuum created by this have provided a fertile ground for alternative answers to the most basic questions of all.

Belief in some form of reincarnation or in the transmigration of souls is one of the oldest, most universal religious phenomena known. It came to the West originally from India by way of Pythagoras and Plato, but it is found in almost every culture and tribe on earth, from the Inuit of the Arctic to the Aborigines of Australia. Since a significant portion of the whole of humanity throughout history has held it, including some of the best minds, both ancient and modern, ever to address the mysteries of human existence, reincarnation is not something to be lightly dismissed. I have some sympathy with those, for example, who have criticized Hans Küng, the renowned Roman Catholic theologian, for doing precisely this in his otherwise clever book, *Eternal Life?*[1] On the other hand, the fact that many millions of people still believe in reincarnation – or any other doctrine – or that celebrities such as Shirley MacLaine cite it as a definite ingredient in their obviously successful life philosophies doesn't prove it to be true either.

Speaking of proof, or at any rate of evidence, for reincarnation, one of the things which makes this whole matter particularly interesting at this time is the large number of people coming forward to report that under hypnosis they have actually revisited and relived their past lives. Serious hypnotherapists as well as innumerable quacks make a lucrative living by counselling and guiding people today on the basis of what is alleged to have happened to them in previous existences. In response to invitations in my column, readers by the score have written to me giving firsthand accounts of their own experiences in this regard. For example, a hypnotherapist, who says this story is only one of more than thirty cases he has on record, wrote the following:

A young married woman once came to see him about her dread of sleeping in the dark. She had been to many doctors but to no avail. Under hypnosis she regressed to a previous life where she was known as Anna. She lived at a specific address in Heidelberg, Germany. She was then thirteen years old. The year was 1943 and her family was Jewish. She vividly recalled the Nazis coming, putting her in a van with many others, then pushing her along a narrow corridor into a very dark room. "She became hysterical under hypnosis and cried bitterly saying, 'What are they going to do with us?'" The therapist was then able to assure her that although she had been killed and her body destroyed, her soul was indestructible. She would soon be living in another body. She described her in-between life – known in *The Tibetan Book of the Dead* as taking place in "the Bardo" – as very peaceful and surrounded by angelic beings of light.

The therapist went on to write: "Having found the ground of her fear of darkness, I suggested that this fear belonged to Anna, Anna was in the past, and the past was no longer with her. She was then able to sleep in the dark with no further fears."

Incidentally, this same hypnotherapist claims to have written to the Heidelberg address and to have confirmed that a Jewish family had indeed once lived there. The father was a music teacher, there were children, and the teacher's name was Arthur, just as the patient (as Anna) had said.

The occult or New Age sections of bookstores now overflow with books detailing similar narratives. However, although one is assured, as in the case of Anna, that proper research was done and that the record confirms things were exactly as described in the trance, a truly objective outsider will find nothing but endless frustration in trying to pin any of it down satisfactorily. I have read and examined as many of these as I could, and while one encounters some quite unusual stories I have seen nothing yet that amounts to convincing evidence or proof of a single incident.

Certainly the work of Dr. Ian Stevenson, Carlson Professor of Psychiatry at the University of Virginia Medical School, must be mentioned wherever reincarnation is discussed today because of what he has to say about contemporary hypnotic regression into past lives. For an enthusiastic review of his research the best and most concise source is the 1984 book *Reincarnation, A New Horizon in Science, Religion, and Society*, by Sylvia Cranston and Carey Williams.[2]

Cranston and Willams, to their credit, quote some remarks of Dr. Stevenson's from the October 1976 newsletter of the American Society for Psychical Research.[3] Stevenson notes that many people write to him asking for hypnotic regression to previous lives or to investigate material arising from such experiences. He then comments: "Many persons who attach no importance whatever to their dreams . . . nevertheless believe that whatever emerges during hypnosis can invariably be taken at face value. In fact, the state of a hypnotized person resembles in many ways – though not in all – that of a person dreaming. The subconscious parts of the mind are released from ordinary inhibitions, and they may then present in dramatic form a new 'personality.' If the person has been told by the hypnotist, either explicitly or implicitly, to 'go back to another time and place,' the 'new personality' may be extremely plausible both to the person having the experience and to others watching . . . In fact, however, nearly all such hypnotically evoked 'previous personalities' are *entirely imaginary* [my italics], just as are the contents of most dreams."

Stevenson goes on to say that such experiences may include some accurate historical details, but these are usually derived from information the person has acquired through reading, from radio and television programs, or from other sources. "He may not remember where he obtained the information, but sometimes this can be brought out in other hypnotic sessions designed to search for the sources of the information used in making up the 'previous personality.'"

Coming from such a prestigious source and from one who himself seems convinced, for other reasons, of the reality of reincarnation, this is a powerful antidote to many of the often bizarre claims made in the name of past-life regression. It should be noted as well that Stevenson has some words of caution for those who experiment with this kind of hypnosis: "There are some hazards in this procedure of regression to 'previous lives.' In a few instances, the previous personality has not gone away when instructed to do so, and the subject in such cases has been left in an altered state of personality for several days or longer before restoration of his normal personality."

Professor Geddes MacGregor, professor emeritus of philosophy at the University of Southern California and an Anglican (Episcopalian) priest for over forty years, believes in reincarnation. His 1978 book, *Reincarnation in Christianity*, is one of the most reasonable I have read on the subject. However, MacGregor, though friendly to the doctrine, also has major reservations about using alleged past life recall as a proof. He notes that many such cases have turned out to be completely bogus and says, "The literature on the subject is considerable; the results, though they leave many unsolved puzzles, are inconclusive."[4]

More and more doctors and psychologists are expressing concern over the uncritical acceptance by some members of the healing professions of alleged past life recall as a means of healing. Mark Albrecht, in *Reincarnation, A Christian Critique of a New Age Doctrine*, quotes Alexander Rogawski, former chief of the Los Angeles County Medical Association's psychiatry section: "Indeed, the past-lives movement is cashing in on the disillusionment with conventional therapies, fear of death and the current interest in the occult. But all the therapy's popularity proves is that suckers are born every minute and customers can be found for anything."[5]

The doctor's blunt words were originally spoken to reporters from *Time* magazine, and appear in the October 3, 1977, issue. In the same article, Dr. Lucille Forer, a member of the board of directors of the Los Angeles County Psychological Association, said that most of her contemporaries were sceptical about hypnotic regression to past lives as a therapy. She warned that a good therapist may be able to use material brought up from a patient's subconscious, but that leading a person to believe that past lives were being tapped could be dangerous: "A person could develop psychosis if the fantasy material was extreme. He could feel guilt about what he thought were past acts. I would warn anyone who wants to do this sort of thing to do it with a trained person who can handle any problems that might arise ... People are looking for shortcuts that don't exist."

Professor Ernest Hilgard, director of the Hypnosis Research Laboratory at Stanford University, views claims of past-life regression as complete nonsense. He is on record saying that hypnosis is a very dangerous tool in the hands of amateurs. He adds: "New identities claimed during trance are not uncommon and are very easy to produce. Invariably they're related to long buried memories, and anybody who makes claims to the contrary has not based them on scholarly judgements."[6]

One possible explanation for those cases where the contents of the hypnotic trance do seem particularly vivid or can be checked out in some detail is the phenomenon of cryptoamnesia. There are millions of details stored in our subconscious minds and many, if not the majority, became stored there without our having been aware of them. The British psychiatrist Anthony Storr contends that recall of past lives is actually an example of this cryptoamnesia, a purely imaginary construction using sub-conscious memories of some long-forgotten historical novel, film, or magazine article. He comments that "most of us have a grade B movie running in our heads most of the time."[7]

The famous, or if you prefer notorious, Bridey Murphy affair of the 1950s still stands as an additional caveat to those who wish to gallop off in this particular direction. For a full account of this apparent hoax I refer the reader to Colin Wilson's book, *Afterlife*.[8] It is a long, complicated, and in many ways fascinating story. In essence, Virginia Tighe, the wife of an insurance sales-man in Pueblo, Colorado, was persuaded to undergo hypnotic regression by Morey Bernstein, a Pueblo businessman who had found he was naturally proficient at putting people into a hyp-notic trance. Under hypnosis, Tighe began to speak in Gaelic and said she was Bridey Murphy, born near Cork, Ireland, in 1798. In a series of tape-recorded sessions, she talked in great detail of her life as the wife of a Belfast lawyer who taught at Queen's University in that city. She had died in 1864. Bernstein wrote a book, *The Search for Bridey Murphy*, and it became front-page news. Mrs. Tighe appeared on national television in the United States.

Various events then occurred to debunk her story, not the least of which was the coming forward of Tighe's Irish nanny who had helped care for her to about age two. She recognized the baby-game songs she had sung to Mrs. Tighe as an infant, some even including the name "Bridey."

As we have already had occasion to observe, there is nothing stronger than the will to believe, which is such a prominent characteristic of our time. Far from being an age of unbelief, this is an age of unmatched credulity and willingness to accept almost anything, from the significance of numbers in one's life (numerology) to healing with crystals to contact with aliens on UFOs. Evidence is the last thing on many people's minds.

I had a remarkable example of this recently in a lengthy interview with a successful businessman. This was a man who told himself at the age of twenty that he would be a millionaire by the time he was thirty-five. He is now just over fifty and a millionaire several times over. However, he has become deeply involved in reincarnational belief over the past few years and now believes he has had a succession of past lives. Even though he is aware of the warnings of Stevenson and others in the field, he nevertheless remains unshaken in his conviction that, for example, he was a young man in Jerusalem at the time of Christ, that Christ once touched his head as he stood at the front of a crowd as He passed by, and that he was crucified soon after Jesus himself. This person is totally reasonable in every other way, yet he is adamant in the belief that every major figure in his life today – both friend and foe – has been connected to him in a repeated cycle of previous lives. In this respect, he is typical of many hundreds of thousands of North Americans today.

Stevenson, who is, as we have seen, extremely sceptical of claims about most hypnosis-induced, past-life experience, nevertheless is impressed by the phenomenon of children who suddenly and quite spontaneously speak in some language other than that spoken in their home or immediate background. He is equally impressed by the more than two thousand cases he has investigated of young children in both East and West who seem to have spontaneous and fairly precise "recall" of places, people, and even incidents that it would appear they could not have experienced. This phenomenon seems to defy normal explanation.[9]

There is little to be gained by reproducing specific examples of this from Stevenson. Some of the cases he relates are quite extraordinary and I have no reason to doubt the authenticity of what he reports. But, as with the case of that common experience called *déjà vu*, or the case of child prodigies such as Mozart, who wrote a sonata when he was four and an opera when he was only seven, the theory of past lives is by no means the most obvious or most plausible explanation. There is a whole range of possibilities.

Dr. Stevenson himself admits that in addition to reincarnation there could be several other explanations for the detailed, spontaneous recall he has been able to observe in the children he has studied. For example, it could be caused by telepathy, clairvoyance, or even spirit possesssion, the influence of some discarnate personality. This has been suggested by none other than an orthodox Hindu Swami, Sri Sri Somasundara Desika Paramachariya of South India. The swami, a believer in reincarnation, has written an open letter to Stevenson denying that the hundreds of cases from India the doctor cites are any proof whatever of the reincarnation doctrine. He wrote: "All the 300-odd cases reported by you do not in fact support the theory of reincarnation . . . They are all spirit possessions, ignored by the learned in south India."[10]

Whatever one may think of that particular approach, it is undoubtedly true that the full mysteries of the human mind, particularly human memory, remain largely uncharted territory. Some of the most recent discoveries of neurologists and other researchers, however, point to the probability that memories reside in the "soft disks" of our DNA (deoxyribonucleic acid). In other words, along with the rest of our genetic coding, perhaps tracks or imprints of experiences of the family, clan, or tribe are also stored. These DNA impressions, especially in our youth, can flash into consciousness much as do the images of dreams.

There is also the matter of RNA (ribonucleic acid), which our DNA uses to direct the activities of individual cells. One thoughtful reader of my weekly columns responded to the incident of "Anna," which I have already quoted, with an interesting letter. She is a registered nurse and not long ago attended a conference on prenatal psychology. At one lecture, a professor who has been studying the nature of our inherited RNA and its role in long-term memory storage put forward a theory.

"Nobody," he said, "knows where long-term memory, body memory of movements needed to perform tasks, or a baby's pre-verbal memories are stored." Using the analogy of silicon chips and their use in computers, he suggested that "protein chips" in the RNA could hold much more information, extending back through one's ancestors and eventually linking all humanity in a unified family. Bits would be inherited from all sides – some verbal, some visual, some perhaps pre-verbal – which might explain those times when we experience vague feelings of having been somewhere before but are unable to express where or when. Perhaps just hearing or seeing a certain sound or image, or smelling a particular scent could trigger this information and bring it to consciousness.

Other explanations for what now seems to masquerade as past-life recall would include Carl Jung's concept of the "collective unconscious," which he postulated is common to us all and holds the great archetypes of our memories as humans. And then there is the whole phenomenon of extrasensory perception, ESP, with which some seem more endowed than others but which may well operate at times unconsciously in us all.

Some Problems with Reincarnation

Despite what may be said by either the supporters or the opponents of reincarnation in general, there is absolutely no way of proving or disproving the theory at this time. One can simply look at all the various arguments for and against and come to a reasoned stance of acceptance, disbelief, or open-minded scepticism. If it is true, then of course there obviously is life after death – many lives in fact. If it is not, we would have to look elsewhere in our search for clues. Having given it much thought ever since first encountering the theory while reading Plato at Oxford as an undergraduate, and having read as widely as possible in the current literature, I have become personally convinced that the arguments against it weigh more heavily than those for.

First, the theory does not deliver at the very point where it is most highly touted as the most satisfactory explanation. I am referring to the moral issue of divine justice, or theodicy. The argument that the law of karma – "As a man soweth so shall he surely reap" – explains all the manifest injustices of life is one that is made repeatedly in the reincarnational literature I have studied. We keep coming back, or rather our souls do, in thousands of rebirths until all the necessary lessons are learned. The good news, in this view, is presumably that this one life here and now is not our only chance. Each of us gets another, and another – in fact, as many chances as we need to "get it right." Nobody will ever be lost or damned, because there are endless opportunities to atone for past misdeeds and to learn true virtues.

There is a surface appearance of plausibility about this that has attracted many, including some very bright people. I think in particular of the late Reverend Leslie Weatherhead, of London, England, who to my mind was one of the greatest preachers of this century, and who came to accept reincarnation in his later years. When one thinks about it at length, however, it seems to me that some rather large contradictions arise.

In spite of all the recent emphasis on past-life recall, it is central to the orthodox theory of reincarnation that one forgets one's previous lives. "The cumulative pain might be too great otherwise," we are told. In the Platonic myth, for example, souls drink from the river of forgetfulness (Lethe) before they can be reborn. But if the vast majority of us cannot remember our previous incarnations, where is the justice in having to suffer for mistakes committed in them, or in benefitting from good deeds we cannot know? If I have absolutely no memory of a particular action, punishing me or rewarding me for it accomplishes nothing.

The problem is made worse by the fact that in certain versions of reincarnational thought the personality of the individual does not survive each death and rebirth; only the soul goes on from body to body. But if there is no memory and no continuity of personality, what sense does it make to say that any one of us actually survives death at all? If you die as one person and come back as another, why should the second have to pay for the sins of the first? If Hitler, for example, were to come back as John Jones the farmer, with no memory of his abominations and a wholly different personality, how is justice served by the said John Jones having to endure untold hardships or horrors?

I have serious doubts about the value of a belief that tells me I have lived many times before when I haven't the slightest glimmering of a memory of any of it. It's fine to say we're in a kind of cosmic school, where we learn successive lessons about life and gradually purify ourselves. But if I can't remember a single thing from all of this, of what use are these lessons and who is the "I" who is supposed to be the student? I know it is argued that while we forget the details of past lives (unless there is a hypnotist around) the really important lessons are retained as changes in the inner nature of our souls themselves. But since memory is an essential part of what makes me me and you you, I cannot see in what sense we remain the same person through repeated reincarnations, or what possible good it does us to be told that we have lived before.

I spoke about this criticism to Dr. Joel Whitton, a noted Toronto psychiatrist and author of the popular book *Life Between Life*, a study of "the Bardo," or in-between state of those who have died and are about to be reborn.[11] Dr. Whitton noted there are various views of karma, all the way from the older "an eye for an eye" belief, where one gets back in successive lives exactly what one has handed out, to that of the alchemists who taught that it simply refers to the process whereby the point of any given event or experience in each incarnation is, What am I supposed to learn from it for my overall growth? Whitton suscribes to the view that for the most part the lack of memory of previous lives is a good thing, because "with an average of twenty or so lives behind us, as some authorities hold, there would be just too much pain involved in remembering it all." He added that most exponents of reincarnation in the West – and the Lamaist Buddhists of Tibet – believe that while names, outward circumstances, and so forth do change, the essential person remains throughout each life lived. "Tom," he said, "would continue to be recognizable as Tom for those with the proper discernment."

My second reason for rejecting the theory of reincarnation is that, as adapted and reinterpreted in the West, it is linked inextricably to a myth of inevitable and eternal progress. But there is nothing to guarantee that the collective karma of the human race will ineluctably improve. On the contrary, given the way in which evil seems to be increasing rather than decreasing at present – the ecological crisis, the AIDS epidemic, the increase of torture as a state weapon, the growing gap between rich nations and poor nations, drugs, terrorism, and many other crimes against humanity – one could make a powerful case for the exponential growth of bad karma. The blithe belief that every day in every way things eventually get better seems wholly lacking in any reasonable foundation.

Third, I am quite aware that in the great world religions that hold reincarnation as a key doctrine it is accepted not because it suits their fancy but because of deep insights and convictions that this is the way the universe operates. But I must confess that the working out, over countless millions of years, of this cold, impersonal force called karma seems to me, at any rate, to reduce the cosmos and the "wheel of life" to a chilling, heartless kind of machine. Since it will all end one day in an equilibrium of the universe leading inevitably to another cycle of cosmic rebirth, one has to ask: What is the point of it all? If we have done it all and seen it all before, not once but perhaps a myriad of times, can anything be more boring or ultimately meaningless? One can agree with the advocates of reincarnation when they argue that surely one lifetime is too short to learn all the spiritual truth of which the human soul is capable. But that does not constitute proof of reincarnation. It only adds to the evidence already before us that belief in some form of existence beyond our life span on earth is truly universal.

5

♦

Dreams of
Death
and
Dying

MY FIRST ACQUAINTANCE WITH THE REMARKABLE DR.
Marie-Louise von Franz came when I attended a two-day symposium in Toronto, in the summer of 1987, at which we viewed a unique series of films called *The Way of the Dream*. The films, a documentary series produced and directed by Fraser Boa, a Canadian Jungian dream analyst, featured Dr. von Franz in her Zurich consulting room commenting on and interpreting the dreams of a wide range of people, from California surfers to skinheads in London and business executives in New York.

Like the many thousands who have given this series standing ovations in most of the major cities of Europe and North America, I was captivated by the depth of wisdom and insight displayed. Dr. von Franz is the foremost living successor of the Swiss psychiatrist, Dr. Carl Jung, who pioneered research into the world of dreams. "He discovered that dreams attempt to regulate and balance both our physical and mental energies,"

said Boa. "They not only reveal the root cause of inner dishar-
mony and emotional distress, but also indicate the latent potential for life within the individual." Dreams offer innovative
solutions to problems of daily life and creative directions for the
individual in his or her life journey. Jung came to realize that it is
often in our dreams that we gradually discover our own true
identity.[1] Dr. von Franz worked directly with Jung for over thirty
years, collaborating on at least two of his books. Like Jung, she
believes that our dreams are the "voice of nature within us" and
so cannot be manipulated. If one can see the meaning of their
symbolism – for the language of dreams is always symbolic – one
can get an objective view of the psychic reality within. Having
analysed more than sixty-five thousand dreams in a lifetime
devoted to this approach to healing the soul, she then wrote
what in my opinion is one of the most important books ever
written as far as the question of life after death is concerned, *On
Dreams and Death, a Jungian Interpretation*.[2]

In her introduction, Dr. von Franz notes that in the incredible
outpouring of books about death and dying that began soon after
the 1976 publication of Raymond Moody's *Life After Life*, and has
gone on apace ever since, very little has been said about dreams.
Yet, as her patients have revealed to her over the years, the unconscious, through dreams, speaks often and eloquently about death,
especially in the second half of life. In fact, she notes, compared
with near-death experiences, dreams are much more graphic, varied, and detailed. The imagery is much richer: "Compared with
dreams, near-death experiences appear schematic and more specifically culture-formed. It seems to me that the individuals experience something inexpressible in the death experiences which they
then elaborate in culture-specific images."[3]

We have already seen just how true this is in our discussion of
the NDE phenomenon. What the doctor is talking about is the
way in which there is a certain set pattern now expected in the
recounting of an NDE, and why someone from the American
Bible Belt, for example, will talk about "seeing" Jesus or angels
where a Hindu from India will "see" the Lord Krishna.

Dr. von Franz says that her analysis of the dreams of older people has provided a wealth of dream symbols that "psychically prepare the dreamers for impending death." Nature, or God, it seems, has a concern to prepare the individual for the ultimate and inevitable end of physical life. Yet, she notes, Jung himself emphasized that the unconscious psyche very obviously "believes" in a life after death. The dream symbols seem to indicate certain basic, archetypal structures existing in the very depths of the soul which behave "as if the psychic life of the individual . . . will simply continue." There are indeed dreams, as examples will demonstrate, that use vivid symbols to show "the end of bodily life *and the explicit continuation of psychic life after death* [my italics]."

Of course, von Franz is aware that sceptics will immediately pounce upon such statements and say that what we are dealing with here is the projection in dreams of our own lust for immortality. She refutes this objection by pointing out that Jung himself has shown quite clearly how dreams much more often portray a wholly objective psychic "natural event" that is quite uninfluenced by the desires of the ego. The best example of this, she says, is the case where the dreamer won't accept the truth of his or her impending death or is utterly unaware how close it is: "Dreams may even indicate this fact quite brutally and mercilessly, as, for instance, in the motif of the dreamer's clock which has stopped and cannot be started again, or the theme of the life-tree, which has been hewn down and is lying on the ground."[5] This point is of such great importance it is impossible to overemphasize it. The evidence which follows here cannot simply be shrugged off with the kind of easy criticism I myself so often hear whenever I mention life after death in my columns – "That's just wish-fulfillment speaking."

Nobody in their right mind wishes to die, either physically or psychically. As Dr. von Franz remarks, "The comforting message of the unconscious – that death is a 'cure' and that there is an afterlife – obviously cannot be interpreted here as a wish-fulfillment dream, for at the same time the end of physical

existence is also predicted, quite brutally and unequivocably."
She says that many people begin to dream of death from middle
age on. "Such dreams do not indicate an immediately impending death, but are rather to be understood as a *memento mori*."
They are reminders, paticularly when the individual has an
"overly youthful attitude towards life," that death is a reality,
and call the dreamer to some serious thought about it.[6]

The Dreams

The entire literature about death and dying from the dawn of
history is filled with references to plants – grass, grain, or trees,
for example – as symbols of the continuity of life after death.
This theme runs all through the myths of the ancient Egyptians,
the Greeks, and the Druids. Jesus spoke of the natural law that a
kernel of wheat must fall to the ground and die if the wheat is to
spring up to renewed, transformed life. He is referring plainly to
the spiritual truth of the need for the death of the individual as
the gateway to rising again.[7] In the Book of Revelation, which
we will examine later, the seer's vision of the next world is filled
with images of trees. There is the tree of life whose leaves are "for
the healing of the nations." Similarly in the Qur'an we find that
in the Islamic paradise there are many trees of precious stones,
especially the *tula* tree which has "its roots in the sky and its
light reaches into every corner of the world." From her many
thousands of dream analyses, Dr. von Franz testifies to the
recurrence of such vegetation imagery in the dreams of the
dying. In each case, the meaning clearly denotes the deep-seated
belief of the unconscious mind that life goes on beyond the
grave.

Here is the dream of a dying seventy-five-year-old man: "I see
an old, gnarled tree high up on a steep bluff. It is only half-
rooted in the earth, the remainder of the roots reaching into the
empty air . . . Then it becomes separated from the earth
altogether, loses its support, and falls. My heart misses a beat. But
then, something wonderful happens: the tree floats, it does not

fall, it floats. Where to? Into the sea? I do not know." The tree, which here clearly symbolizes the dying man, his life, and his potential for growth or what Jung called "individuation," teeters on the brink of the abyss and then falls. In other words, death is frankly faced and admitted. But then to his utter surprise, the tree floats. It is not destroyed but exists in an entirely new way.

The doctor then cites the dream of another man who died a few days later. He sees himself as on or in a sky-blue "air-liquid" that seems shaped like an egg. Then he feels he is "falling into the blue, into the universe." But suddenly he is caught and carried by what appears to be a little blue cloth. The feeling of falling into the universe is repeated, and part of him welcomes this, but again he feels himself "caught by cloths and by people who speak to me." The small cloths surround him and he sees a red staircase which then becomes a Christmas tree.

At first, the dream seems an enigma or sheer fantasy. But for one experienced in dream symbolism and the archetypes of the unconscious mind, it speaks lucidly of his psyche's belief in a continuing life beyond the grave. The dreamer feels he is about to fall to nothingness, to disintegrate. The cloths or "honorary garments" protect him from destruction. People reassure him of ongoing community. The tree – a Christmas tree, with all the lights and celebration that go with this image – symbolizes growth towards fuller spiritual or inner maturity. Thus, Dr. von Franz concludes, "The dream seems to say to the dreamer that in the Beyond he will continue to grow and to develop toward a higher degree of awareness."

The following dream is that of a young woman whose body had been taken over by cancer. Once it reached the brain, she was unconscious most of the time. The therapist, a colleague of Dr. von Franz's, continued to visit her regularly, sitting at her bedside in silence. Some twenty-four hours before she died, the patient suddenly opened her eyes and told of a dream she had just had:

"I am standing beside my bed in the hospital room and I feel strong and healthy. Sunshine flows in at the window. The doctor is there and says, 'Well, Miss X, you are unexpectedly completely cured. You may get dressed and leave the hospital.' At that moment I turn around and see, lying in the bed – my own dead body!"

Dr. von Franz's comments are significant. She says that while the unconscious is clearly stating that death is a form of cure and that the young woman's life will go on renewed beyond the grave, at the same time it is not indulging in mere wishful thinking. It announces the impending physical death of the patient with brutal clarity.

An old woman, earlier in the day on which she died, had a dream in which she sees a candle lit on the windowsill of her hospital room. Quite suddenly the candle goes out. "Fear and anxiety ensue as the darkness envelops her. Suddenly the candle lights on the other side of the window and she awakens."[8] The woman died wholly at peace because she was helped to see the dream's meaning. The candle in some mysterious way dematerializes and then materializes on the other side of the closed window. The meaning being communicated by her unconscious mind, according to von Franz, is that the "light" of the individual goes out at death but is miraculously renewed *on the other side.*

The dream of another elderly European woman, just before her death, reaches the same conclusion through different imagery. In this case, she has packed two suitcases for a journey. One has her working clothes; the other contains her diaries, her photographs, and her jewellery. She is aware that the first is for the "mainland" but the other is "for America." Dr. von Franz comments that the old lady's unconscious is making her aware that in dying she is on a journey where she will not be able to take along her everyday attitudes and her physical body, "But she can take along her inner psychic treasures." Obviously America is the symbol for "the Beyond," or life in the hereafter.[9]

Another dream, this one sent to Jung himself by an elderly man, recalls something of the dream of the man who felt himself falling into the universe and then being caught and given the vision of the Christmas tree:

"He meets two . . . guides who lead him to a building where he finds many people, among them his father . . . and his mother who gives him a kiss of welcome. He has to go on a long climb ending at the edge of a deep precipice. A voice commands him to leap; after several desperate refusals he obeys and finds himself swimming 'deliciously into the blue of eternity.'" Jung saw this dream as a preparation for coming death and wrote to the man to point out the Hindu belief that the dying rise upward to the cosmic *Atman* where they find "allness" or "increasing completeness."[10]

Summary

For now, we have examined enough specific examples of dreams to show how they can illustrate the belief of our deepest natures in some kind of ongoing life after death. As Dr. von Franz notes, all such dreams of people facing death "indicate that the unconscious, that is our instinct world, prepares consciousness not for a definite end but for a profound transformation and for a kind of continuation of the life process which, however, is unimaginable to everyday consciousness."[11] What's more, her research shows beyond dispute that the symbols that appear in dreams to convey this message, while greatly varied, "present a thematic or structural harmony with the teachings of the various religions about life after death." They use mythical images drawn not just from the world's great religions but from religions and cults going back to the earliest stages of civilization. None of this by itself proves beyond a shadow of a doubt that there is a life after death, but it is a fascinating, new, and it seems to me strong piece of evidence pointing in that direction. We must turn now to some equally intriguing material from neurology and from physics.

6

♦

New Light
From
Science

"What is one to say to the assertion that brain machinery has accounted for the mind, the spirit of man, and the idea of God?... It is a basic tenet of materialism. But, I find no evidence to support it in [my] studies of the human brain."
– Dr. Wilder Penfield, neurosurgeon and author.[1]

IN POLLING READERS OF MY COLUMN ABOUT THEIR VIEWS and experiences with regard to an afterlife, I received a number of sceptical letters ranging all the way from an agnostic position – "I simply don't know" – to adamant denial of any such possibility. The following excerpt is typical of the view put forward by the most rigidly opposed. It comes from a Bramalea, Ontario, businessman: "If you would just step outside your thoughts and look at the question logically you would quickly see that the belief in an afterlife is simply wishful thinking ... No, Mr. Harpur, there is no life after death ... When we die we are just as dead and gone as the cow that provided the roast beef for lunch. The cow has simply returned to its elemental parts and that is what will happen to both you and I when we depart this life. Our thoughts are just so much electro-chemical reaction and they will be gone too . . . Sorry to be such a wet blanket but that's the way it is."

I am tempted to stop here and critique the dogmatism and faith aspects of "that's the way it is" and to ask this respondent how, if our thoughts are "just so much electro-chemical reaction," he can ask me to "step outside them." I mean, who is it who is doing the "stepping outside"? But I'll let that pass for the moment because I want to show that this reader has more or less stated the classical position of rationalistic doubters. To do that, the simplest way is to quote from the brilliant agnostic, Lord Bertrand Russell, in his book *Why I Am Not a Christian*:

"All the evidence goes to show that what we regard as our mental life is bound up with brain structure and organized bodily energy. Therefore it is rational to suppose that mental life ceases when body life ceases."[2]

The nineteenth-century biologist Thomas H. Huxley made a similar point when he said, "The thoughts to which I am giving utterance and your thoughts regarding them are the expression of molecular exchanges."[3]

Russell devotes a complete chapter, "Do we Survive Death?" to the question of life after death, but his chief argument against the proposition is the materialistic one that the mind or consciousness is merely a function of brain "machinery" and so must perforce cease when the brain dies. Because of his total acceptance of what is now being called "The Old Story of Science," Russell believed we are nothing but the result of purely mechanical, chance causes, "the outcome of accidental collocations of atoms." Thus he was able to say that "no fire, no heroism, no intensity of thought and feeling, can preserve an individual life beyond the grave." This led to his now famous, if somewhat mournful, dictum: "Only on the scaffolding of these truths, only on the firm foundation of unyielding despair, can the soul's habitation henceforth be safely built."[4]

There is a major problem, however, for this kind of objection to the belief in an afterlife today: it is based on a scientific worldview that has now been completely revolutionized and transformed. People who still argue that the mind is simply a matter of brain function or that matter is the sole and ultimate reality are wholly out of touch with developments in physics, cosmology, and neurophysiology – the study of the human brain and nervous system. The best, brief introduction to this area of knowledge is the striking work *The New Story of Science*, with a preface by the great neurosurgeon Sir John Eccles. It's written by two Americans, Robert M. Augros and George N. Stanciu. I can do no more here than to sketch the main outline of the argument, but its importance cannot be overemphasized. Scientists are obviously not in the business of attempting to "prove" a life after death. What is significant is that, because of their new insights, the old, so-called scientific or rationalistic "proofs" that the grave is the final end no longer bear scrutiny.

Here's why I say this. The old view of science held, with Newton, that atoms were the ultimate particles of matter – hard, impenetrable, and, as the original Greek behind the word suggests, uncuttable or indivisible into smaller particles. Matter, space, time – these are the Newtonian ingredients of the cosmos, all of them obeying unalterable laws, such as gravity. The scientist, as observer, stood, as it were, outside looking on as he did his measurements and experiments. But since 1903, when Russell first penned the words quoted above from *Why I Am Not a Christian*, incredible changes have taken place. First of all, Einstein's theory of relativity led physics to abandon the ideas of both absolute space and absolute time. The observer is not apart from, but is *a part of* the world of physics. Time and space are relative to the point at which the observer takes his or her stand. "Einstein showed that space-time and the laws of motion can be defined only by reference to an observer and his physical conditions."[5]

Then a similar revolution occurred in the realm of particle physics. Instead of being a hard, ultimate piece of matter, it was established by Ernest Rutherford in 1911 that an atom consists of an inner nucleus surrounded by a host of invisible electrons. This led eventually to the overthrow of Newtonian atomic theory and the development of quantum mechanics by thinkers such as Niels Bohr and Werner Heisenberg in the 1920s. Two things happened here. In quantum mechanics it was realized that the old idea of the scientist as unobserved observer "looking on," already put in question by Einstein's theory of relativity, had to be completely scrapped. The mere act of observing electrons, for example, was found to interfere with their behaviour. The observer becomes a participant in the world he is trying to observe. As Augros and Stanciu remark, "In some strange sense, this is a participatory universe."

The second significant aspect of this discovery that atoms are balls of energy rather than bits of indestructible matter is that it led to the current view of material reality by physicists as "a cosmic dance of energy" rather than as some kind of stuff or substance.[6] That's why modern physicists often come close to the language of mysticism when they try to describe the underlying basis of the cosmos. This is a theme we will return to in a moment. For now, we turn to look more closely at the role played by the human mind or consciousness *vis-à-vis* the universe.

In the Newtonian model, mind played no important part in the physical realities of the universe. With relativity and quantum mechanics, however, it is an essential part of the whole. Thus, Augros and Stanciu can state: "Physics in the twentieth century has gradually replaced materialism with the affirmation that mind plays an essential role in the universe."[7] This raises immediately the question of the nature of mind. As we have seen, in the old view, mind was nothing more than a function of the physical brain. To be wholly made up of matter meant to be totally subject to mortality and decay, as both my respondent above and Bertrand Russell have made clear. The only thing that is eternal in that view, as the pre-Socratic philosopher Democritus noted over two millennia ago, is matter itself.

But it is at this point that twentieth-century neurophysiology comes in. Sir Charles Sherrington (1857–1952), who was in many ways the founder of contemporary neurophysiology, said that, as a result of his research on the human nervous system and the brain, he had to conclude that "A radical distinction has . . . arisen between [physical] life and mind. The former is a matter of physics and chemistry; the latter escapes chemistry and physics."[8] Sherrington came to the conviction that our humanity has two fundamental elements, matter and mind. Sir John Eccles agrees: "Conscious experiences . . . are quite different from any goings-on in the neuronal machinery."[9] The biologist Adolf Portmann, in his book *New Pathways in Biology*, puts it this way: "No amount of research along physical or chemical lines can ever give us a full picture of psychological, spiritual or intellectual processes."[10] In other words, while the mind depends on the physical brain as its tool or base in this life, it is nevertheless something different from and greater than the brain itself. In his watershed book, *The Mystery of the Mind, A Critical Study of Consciousness and the Human Brain*, the distinguished Canadian neurosurgeon Dr. Wilder Penfield notes that the mind seems to act with an energy all its own. It makes decisions and puts them into action by employing the various mechanisms of the brain, but it is something more than these mechanisms themselves.[11] Thus, as the authors of *The New Story of Science* point out, "expecting the mind to be found in some part of the brain, or in the whole brain, is like expecting the programmer to be a part of the computer."[12]

If the mind is not simply a matter of "electro-chemical reaction," as our Bramalea businessman insists, the whole basis of his argument falls to pieces. What the neuroscientists are now saying reveals that the mind, as Penfield puts it, "may be a distinct and different essence" from the body altogether.[13] Reading Penfield's reflections, not just in *The Mystery of the Mind* but in his essay "Science, the Arts and the Spirit," in his book, *Second Thoughts*,

as well as in his other numerous articles and books, one is struck
by a remarkable irony or paradox. Penfield admits quite candidly
that he began his career and struggled for years to fulfill his
intention of proving that "the brain accounts for the mind." All
his research, however, brought him to the inescapable conclusion
that the materialistic view of the mind was wholly untenable.
"The physical basis of the mind is the brain action in each
individual. It accompanies the activity of his spirit. But the spirit
is free . . . No brain mechanism has yet been demonstrated that
directs the action of the mind."[14] Carrying the logical consequences of this kind of finding into the realm of our special
interest, Eccles says: "What a thrill it is to discover that the
scientist too can legitimately believe in spirit." Since the mind
and will are non-material, it then becomes possible for such
scientists to argue that they are *not subject in death to the disinte-
gration that affects both the body and the brain* [my italics]."[15]

Christian theologians, in my view, as well as those in most
other faiths, have not yet taken these new developments in
physics and in neuroscience as seriously as they ought. Those
interested in a rational approach to the belief in life after death
will get more insight in this area from the work of Carl Jung and
his disciple, Marie-Louise von Franz, than from official religious
sources. In *On Dreams and Death*, von Franz has a chapter on
the "subtle" or astral body and one on Jung's "new hypothesis,"
in which she introduces these new findings of physics and
neuroscience to a rationale for an afterlife. She discusses the
widespread belief in China, wherever Hinduism has spread,
among primitive peoples, and among many Christians who
believe in a resurrection of the body, that each person has not
just a physical body but also a subtle body which survives
death. In theory this body, which has many names – a spiritual
body, a sidereal or "star" body – is made up of a finer, more
intense energy than the physical body. Given the way physics
now sees that even the coarsest of material substances is ultimately made up of a "cosmic dance of energy," von Franz argues
that it may one day be shown that the psychic energy of the soul

or mind-spirit is part of a continuum which underlies all three aspects of our humanity – mind, subtle body, and physical body. She goes on to point out that Jung himself formulated this kind of hypothesis in a letter to a friend.[16]

Jung defined the psyche or inner self thus: "Psyche = highest intensity [of energy] in the smallest space." He likened the human brain to a kind of "transformer station" in which the exceedingly intense energy of the mind – "transcending, for instance, the velocity of light" – is changed or transformed into frequencies or "extensions" suitable for our use in our earthly, space-time mode. This seems to me to be an even more potent analogy for mind-brain relationship than that of the computer as brain and the mind as the programmer.

The point being made by Jung and von Franz is that we may be dealing here with a form of energy that gradually changes or moves from the *physically* measurable – as in the measuring of brainwaves by an EEG – to the *psychically* immeasurable. Von Franz concludes: "The subtle body in this sense would then be a form of the psyche that would indeed remain close to the body but would also possess a certain minimal mass and extension in time-space." She quotes the physicist Fritjof Capra to underline the point already made that to speak of mass and extension can no longer be thought of in the crude terms of the "Old Story of Science": "In modern physics, mass is no longer associated with a material substance, and hence particles are not seen as consisting of any basic 'stuff,' but as bundles of energy."[17]

Once you conceive of matter in this way, von Franz rightly says, the idea of a body that is transformed into an intensity which is no longer visible in space and time becomes quite a rational concept. This whole mode of thinking has, it seems to me, not just enormous relevance to the renewal of religious thinking about the resurrection of the body, it also offers a radically new approach to the rationalization or understanding of such paranormal phenomena as apparitions or ghosts.

In our normal human condition, light is the highest perceivable form of energy intensity. It constitutes our ultimate limit.

That is why near-death experiences, as well as the language of all religions, are filled with references to light. *"Deus illuminatio mea,"* "The Lord is my light," says the Psalmist. The phrase "Light of Light" is one of humanity's highest attempts to describe or define the Deity. But today we know of energies more subtle and more powerful than light. Many modern physicists, Fritjof Capra for instance, have gone so far as to postulate vast universes of energies of other frequencies, which not only underlie our own but in a sense interlock with it. There are, in this view, many dimensions of reality or being all going on simultaneously around us. We experience one, the physical, empirically, another, the psychic, through imagination, intuition, and insight. But there may be others as well which we do not have either the "eyes" or "ears" to discern. It's a little like knowing that the air all around us is filled with transmissions of dozens of channels of television and radio programming – a veritable maelstrom of sounds and images – and yet, without a radio or a television, we are unaware of any signal whatsoever.

The material or physical universe, on this new scientific line of reasoning, could be a double of a subtler, psychic universe. The latter, Jung believed, is possessed of a transpersonal knowledge, a knowledge he sums up in his idea of a collective unconscious from which the various great archetypes of our human unconscious arise. Considering all of this, God, in my view, would be the author and source of the eternal universe behind, beneath, and through all the others, the ultimate consciousness and energy of the whole. The Circle whose centre is everywhere, whose circumference is everywhere as well.

◆

PART TWO

THE RELIGIOUS WITNESS: *Christianity*

7

◆

The
Witness
of
St. Paul

THOSE WHO HAVE LITTLE OR NO ACQUAINTANCE WITH FOR-
mal New Testament studies may be unaware that the letters of
Paul were written before any of the four Gospels. In fact, the
earliest letter of Paul was written at least fifteen or twenty years
before the earliest Gospel, Mark's. Thus, the first written
account of the Resurrection of Jesus comes not in the Gospels
but in Paul's first letter to the young Christians at Corinth,
about 50 A.D.

For the purposes of our study it is of great importance to
recognize that in chapter 15 of I Corinthians, Paul is setting out
the most primitive form of the tradition about eyewitnesses to
the Risen Christ. He adds authenticity to his account, not just
by using the technical words of his time for the careful handing
on of an oral tradition, but by noting that the majority of those
eyewitnesses cited are still living at the time of writing. In other
words, he is inviting the readers not simply to take his word for

it; they can check it out with those who were there when the various appearances occurred. He believes his claims can be verified. Added to all of this, he tells us, is his own personal, mystical encounter with Jesus on the road to Damascus. For Paul, this life-changing experience, turning him from an arch-persecutor to a leading protagonist in the Church, was the final clincher. Because this whole chapter is the firmest historical documentation for the belief in the Resurrection of Jesus, and because it sets out in very vivid detail Paul's thinking about the nature of a "bodily" resurrection for humanity, it ought to be much more familiar to the general public, Christian and non-Christian, than it has been or is. For this reason, and since I will be commenting on parts of it to clarify my own views on authentic Christian teaching about a future life, I want to let readers see for themselves just what it is Paul had to say. What follows is my own translation of the original Greek text:

"Brothers [and sisters], I am making known to you the Gospel which I once preached to you, which you received, and in which you stand; through which also you are being saved – that is, if you are indeed holding my words steadfastly and have not simply believed in a reckless fashion.

"For, I handed on to you at the beginning the tradition which I myself had received: that Christ died for our sins, according to the Scriptures, that he was buried, and that he was raised on the third day according to the scriptures. And that he was seen by Cephas [Peter], then by the Twelve. Then, he was seen by more than five hundred of the brethren at one time, of whom some have died but the majority are alive to this day. Then, he was seen by James, then by all the apostles. Last of all, he was seen by me also; it is as if I were somebody who had an untimely birth. My reason for saying this is that I am the least of all the apostles. I am not worthy to be called an apostle because I was a persecutor of the church of God.

"But, I am what I am by the Grace of God. For, his Grace towards me has not been in vain. I have toiled more vigorously than all the rest – yet not I, but the Grace of God that was with me. However, whether it was I or the others, so we go on preaching, and so you came to faith.

"If Christ is being proclaimed as one who was raised from the dead, how is it certain dissenters among you are saying that there is no resurrection of the dead? If there is no resurrection of the dead, then Christ was not raised up either. And it follows that if Christ was not raised up, then our preaching is empty and your faith is vain, too. We are discovered to be false witnesses of God because we have borne testimony that God raised Christ – whom he did not raise up if indeed the dead are not raised. For, if the dead are not raised, Christ has not been raised either. And, if Christ be not raised, your faith is void and you are still in your sins. What's more, those who have died in Christ have perished utterly. If we have hope in Christ only in this life, we are more pitiable than all others!

"But now has Christ been raised from the dead as the firstfruits of those who have died. For since death came by a man (Adam), so too the Resurrection comes by a man (Jesus). For, as in Adam all die, so too in Christ shall all be made alive, but each in his own order; Christ is the leader in this, then those who belong to Christ at his coming again.

"Then comes the consummation when he will hand over the kingdom to the Father; when he has abolished all rule, authority, and power. For he must reign until he has put all his enemies under his feet. The last enemy to be destroyed is death itself. 'For He has put all things under his feet,' the Scripture says. But when it says that all things have been subordinated to him, it is manifest that He who is the Agent of this subordination [God] is not included. When He has subjected all things unto him, then the Son himself will be made subordinate to Him that has made all things subject to him – in order that God may be All in All.

"Otherwise, what will they do who are having themselves baptized on behalf of their dead [loved ones]? If there is no way the dead are raised, why are they being baptized on their behalf?

And why do we live in danger [as Christians] hour by hour? I swear to you as you are my pride in Christ Jesus, I die daily. If, humanly speaking, I fought with wild beasts when I was at Ephesus, what good did it do me if the dead are not raised? 'Let us eat, drink, and be merry, for tomorrow we die!'

"Don't be made to err: bad companions corrupt good character. Wake up to righteousness and don't go on in sin; for, some [there in Corinth] are ignorant of God's ways. I say this to shame you."

Paul then goes on to explain how resurrection is possible:

"But, someone will say: 'How are the dead raised? With what kind of body do they come?' Foolish person! Whatever you sow is not made to live unless it dies first. And what you sow is not the body that will come into being but a naked seed – perhaps of wheat or of some other plant. But, God gives it a body according to His will, and to each seed a body of its own. All flesh is not the same; there is human flesh, a flesh of beasts, of birds, and of fish. And there are heavenly bodies just as there are earthly bodies. But the glory of the heavenly is one thing; the glory of the earthly is another. There is one glory of the sun, but another of the moon, and another of the stars. For one star differs from another in brilliance.

"So, too, with the resurrection of the dead. It is sown in decay, it is raised up in immortality; it is sown in dishonour, it is raised up in glory; it is sown in weakness, it is raised up in power. What is 'sown' is an earthly or animal body, it is raised up as a spiritual body. There is a natural body and there is a spiritual [or psychic] body. Thus, it is written: 'The first man, Adam, became a living creature; the last Adam [Christ] became a life-giving spirit.' But the spiritual body is not first; rather, the natural body is first, and then comes the spiritual. The first man was of the earth, earthy; the Second Man was from heaven [the spiritual sphere]. Such as was the earthy, so too are those that are earthy. As was the heavenly, so too shall the heavenly be. And, just as we have borne the appearance of the earthy, so too shall we bear the likeness of the heavenly.

"I tell you this my friends: Flesh and blood cannot inherit the Kingdom of God. Nor can decay inherit immortality. Look, I am declaring a mystery to you: We shall not all die, but we shall all of us be changed, in a moment, in the twinkling of an eye, at the final trumpet sound. For the trumpet shall sound and the dead shall be raised up immortal, and we shall be changed. For this perishable body must be clothed with that which does not perish, and this mortal body must put on immortality. Then shall come to pass the saying that is written: Death is swallowed up in victory. Where, oh death, is thy victory? Death, where is thy sting?

"The sting of death is sin; and the power of sin comes from the law. But thanks be to God who keeps giving us the victory through our Lord, Jesus Christ. So, beloved brethren, be steadfast, immovable, always abounding in the work of the Lord. For you know that your labour is never in vain in the Lord."

The Resurrection of the Body

I do not believe that Paul was infallible; it is certainly not something he ever claimed for himself. In fact, he has a habit of making a sharp differentiation between those occasions when he has a specific "word of the Lord" to back what he is saying and when he is simply speaking on his own. There are many places where a modern understanding of issues (for example, the role and calling of women in the Church), is more spiritual than his culturally conditioned approach. But, granting his enormous intellect and his obvious, balancing, mystical insights, I believe that what he has to say about resurrection commands the greatest respect.

On a personal note, I remember well how as a student of the humanities and particularly philosophy at Oxford I went through a long, dry period when I simply could not say certain parts of the Creeds. My philosophy don, an avowed atheist, had been giving me a difficult time in tutorials as he echoed the kind of mocking sentiments about life after death that we see Paul contending with in the Book of Acts. Thus, when it came to the statement in the Creeds about believing in the resurrection of the body I simply stood mute. It was only when I found myself in my rooms one evening rereading this passage from I Corinthians that I really understood for the first time what was being said.

Paul is not talking about the resuscitation of corpses when he speaks either of Jesus' Resurrection or of that of any other person. All the nit-picking objections of my tutor and similar sceptics were totally beside the point, I discovered. It didn't matter whether or not we were talking about those who have been tragically lost at sea, blown to smithereens in war, consumed by the flames of cremation, or hacked to pieces in the obscenity of murder. The fate of the actual physical body, according to Paul, is irrelevant to the resurrection of the body – or, as I prefer to render it, a bodily resurrection.

Paul meets the query about what kind of body the risen dead will have by the metaphor of the dying and rising wheat. The seed (our physical body) dies and rots away. But new life appears and springs up because "God gives it a body according to his will . . . to each seed a body of its own." In the case of humans, he says, our physical body decays in the grave, but we are raised in a spiritual body. The Greek is instructive here. Paul calls our physical body the *psychikon soma* (a psychic or natural body) while the new resurrection body is called the *pneumatikon soma* (a pneumatic or spirit body). His logic is unassailable because he notes correctly that ordinary flesh and blood, which is corruptible, cannot inherit immortality. God, who remains the prime actor in Jesus' Resurrection, giving him a new and glorious body fit for eternal life, similarly acts to clothe us with the spiritual body needed for the life to come.

What is particularly interesting in this account is that it so closely parallels what modern investigators of the paranormal insist upon. They have various ways of expressing it, but such terms as astral body, sidereal body, subtle body, or etheric body are all attempts to distinguish between our physical selves and a bodily reality which transcends them. It is a body still recognizably ours and intimately connected with what has gone before, but, exactly as in the case of the stories of the Resurrection body of Jesus, it is freed from earthly limitations. It is precisely the sort of body one would need to move into a more spiritual world – the world of not just many but of infinite dimensions.

Treasure in Earthen Vessels

Paul did not know the historical Jesus, but his conviction that at his famous conversion on the road to Damascus he had a real encounter with the Risen Christ is absolutely fundamental to his writing. What actually happened at that time, as with any profoundly moving, mystical experience, is difficult to describe with any hope of precision. But that something momentous occurred there cannot be doubted. When a man as brilliant and passionate as Paul changes suddenly from persecuting Christians to witnessing at great personal cost to the Resurrection of a crucified "Lord," there has to be a sufficient cause.

Paul, we know, belonged to the group within Judaism that believed in the doctrine of bodily resurrection. He was a Pharisee, and resurrection was a major point of difference between Pharisees and the other major religious party, the Sadducees. In fact, like Jesus before him, he occasionally made use of this contentious difference to set the two groups at loggerheads and thus deflect their attacks on himself. But it is a far cry from a general belief in this doctrine to an acceptance of Christian claims that God raised up Jesus from the dead.

Paul's encounter with the Risen Christ is described three times in the Book of Acts. Interestingly, each of these accounts differs in some minor details, and there are one or two major contradictions. For example, in Acts 9:1ff, Paul says those travelling with him heard the voice that spoke, saying, "I am Jesus, whom you are persecuting," but that they saw nothing. In Acts

22:6-16, Paul says the others saw the bright light that shone "from heaven" but that they "did not hear the voice of him that spoke." Thus, the question is raised rather sharply as to whether this experience was objective, that is, exterior to Paul, or whether it was subjective, an inner happening. That it was quite different from the appearances of the Resurrected Jesus to the original disciples is evident not just from the obvious differences between the two types, but from Paul himself.

We have already seen how he refers to his experience as unusual: "Last of all, he was seen by me also; it is as if I were somebody who had an untimely birth." In his letter to the young Christians of Galatia, Paul speaks of his conversion meeting with Christ thus: "When it pleased God to reveal his Son *to me* [my italics]." The King James Version says "in me" rather than "to me" and, indeed, this is what the Greek original says, *en emoi*. In this perhaps we can again see a reference to the inward or subjective nature of what Paul experienced. But beyond this, we cannot go.[1]

The whole episode has to be understood, however, in the context of Paul's extraordinary psychic and extrasensory gifts. Scholar and rationalist though he was, he was more than at home with the so-called paranormal, whether it was non-medical healing, speaking in tongues (glossolalia), or out-of-body experiences. He tells us himself that he was given "a plethora of mystical revelations." Speaking of various "visions and revelations," he describes a curious out-of-body event that, if one didn't know its source, could well seem like something from the *National Enquirer*:

"I knew a man in Christ more than fourteen years ago [he obviously means himself] – whether in the body or out of the body I cannot tell, God knows – who was snatched up into the third heaven. And I know that this man – whether in the body or out of it I don't know, God knows – was snatched up into paradise and heard unutterable words which it is not permitted for humans to speak."[2]

Unlike the tabloid articles of today, however, Paul does not go on to give us any details. In fact, he tends to bring these experiences up only to play them down again as if they were a source of embarrassment. But, I wonder whether Paul's total certainty about the future bliss that lies beyond the grave is based, at least in part, upon his own experience of what he terms paradise. This would throw light upon his eloquent and emphatic Creed-like affirmation: "As it is written, Eye has not seen nor ear heard, neither has it entered into the heart of man, the things which God has prepared for them that love Him."[3] It may also lie behind his other soaring passage, which has meant so much to so many down the centuries. Here it is in my translation from the Greek: "For now we see as it were riddles reflected in a mirror; but then face to face. Now I have partial knowledge; but then I shall know even as also I am known."[4]

While Paul never takes an escapist view of life, one in which we can let this world and its problems or our personal conduct "go to hell" because heavenly rewards are all that matter, there can be little doubt that it is eternal life in the realm beyond death that constitutes for him the fulfilment of human existence. Our present body is a clay pot or vessel into which the treasure of God's light has been poured. This "outer man" grows older daily, but our true inner, or higher self is daily renewed. "For we keep looking not at the things which are seen but at the things which cannot be seen. For the things that can be seen are for a moment, but the things unseen are forever."[5]

Changing the imagery, he likens our physical body to a tent and says that when it is destroyed we "have a building from God" – an eternal body "in the heavens." At times, he says, we feel the burden of our mortality weighing us down and we groan or sigh as we look forward to a life to come. It's not, he rushes to state, that we are anxious to escape this life, but that we yearn for the day when the physical body with all its weaknesses will be "utterly swallowed up by life."[6] Unlike the Platonists and their successors, he doesn't conceive of a pure state of being for the soul or higher self. Always he insists upon our being "clothed" by a new, spiritual body. "For, having been clothed, we shall not be found naked." The same thought is powerfully conveyed in Paul's letter to the Philippians, where he seems to come close to the Platonic idea of this world versus the real world of the eternal, but where he again insists upon the fact that any future life will be an embodied one: "For our citizenship is in heaven whence we await our Saviour . . . who will transform our lowly body into the likeness of his glorious body."[7]

While there are some basic constants in Paul's thinking about life after death, the biggest mistake anyone can make is to try to impose an overall, totally consistent theology or schema upon what he has to say. He really lacks what we would call an elaborated eschatology or doctrine. In one of his earliest letters, his first one to the Thessalonians, he seems to be expecting the imminent return of Christ and talks about those who "sleep" (meaning the dead) being raised first, and then "those who still remain alive" will be snatched up to meet the Lord. This seems to imply a belief in a waiting period for those already dead and so, presumably, a kind of intermediate state where the deceased exist without a body. But later, in II Corinthians, he states quite boldly that there is no waiting period at all because "to be absent from the body [is] to be present with the Lord."[8] This latter position, that the day of resurrection is always *now* because it is outside space and time, is the one I feel makes the most sense.

One final note: In Paul's letters, the ultimate fate of the unrepentant is death in the sense of complete annihilation or nothingness. As in the Gospel and letters attributed to John, there is no fiery hell or torment. In several places he suggests that those who persist in not wanting God and in saying no to His grace and mercy are ultimately let go and simply perish. But, at the same time, however paradoxical it may seem, he frequently expresses his conviction that the whole of creation will one day be reconciled to God. The kind of loving God experienced and trusted by Paul will, in the end, let none of his creatures be lost.

8

◆

The
Teachings
of
Jesus

ANYONE WHO READS THE NEW TESTAMENT OR SEARCHES
elsewhere for a consistent body of doctrine that could readily be
packaged and labelled "Jesus' Doctrine of Survival beyond the
Grave" is in for a complete disappointment. The wise reader will
do well to beware of those who profess to have discovered such a
neat set of teachings. The Bible as a whole offers no tidy, logical
theory of life after death, and Jesus' views are part of the Bible's
overall, at times openly contradictory, *mélange* of messages.

However else one understands the historical Jesus, he not
only was often addressed as a rabbi he also taught very much as
a rabbi, using pithy aphorisms, paradoxes, similes, and parables.
This is not the style of a Greek philosopher. The Greeks arrived
at their belief in an afterlife through a philosophical approach
that took the immortality of the soul as a given. However, the
doctrine of an immortal soul (as utterly distinct from the total
person) is nowhere found in either Old or New Testaments.

Eternal life and the resurrection of the body are *gifts of God* because of His faithfulness and love; they are not a natural possession of the human animal, at least according to the Bible. In Jesus' teaching, they come not through intense intellectual accomplishment but in the response of faith and trust characterized by that of a little child.

In any case, Jesus taught by imagery and not by following the linear, left-brain thinking so typical of our western world since Gutenberg and the invention of book printing. From our point of view, the content of this kind of communication often seems inconsistent, but it stems from a wholly different way of coming at truth – a belief that spiritual truth is hammered out between paradoxes, that it is best illustrated by means of stories, that it is something to be grasped as much or more with the heart (intuition, imagination, and emotion) than with our purely rational mind. Nevertheless, having said all that, it is still possible to discern some very basic directions in Jesus' thought on this matter. Like the Pharisees, he believed in the resurrection of the body and in a life after death in the presence of God. To elucidate this further, we need to look at two key concepts.

The Kingdom of God

As related in my book *For Christ's Sake*, I can never forget the sense of illumination and of liberation that came when I fully realized for the first time that Jesus' main message and sense of mission had very little to do with saving us from sin and with proclaiming himself as a third person of the Trinity (that is, as absolute Deity) and everything to do with proclaiming the reality of the Kingdom of God. The opening verses of Mark, the earliest of the four Gospels, make this absolutely clear. Jesus came preaching the *euaggelion* or "good news" of God's Kingdom. The entire focus of the parables and other sayings is upon the Kingdom of God, also known by the pious synonym "the Kingdom of Heaven." (Pious Jews used "heaven" as a way to avoid saying the name of God.) Jesus announced by word and deed that no matter what outward appearances may seem, God is in complete and ultimate control of human affairs. God reigns, nurtures, heals, and finally delivers humanity into an entirely fresh dimension of being and wholeness.

It is essential to notice that the primary emphasis of Jesus' teaching about the Kingdom is not about some kind of escape from this present world with its great joys, its grievous sufferings, and its enormous challenges. Rather, his call is for a radical trust in God now, in the present moment. The Kingdom is the offer of God's loving presence with and within us today. "The Kingdom of God is within you or in your midst," he said. It is a reality of any human community where right relationships or justice prevail; it is present in the form of a judgement and a challenge to action wherever injustice exists, as for example in South Africa or Central America, or indeed in the midst of the homelessness and poverty in our great cities.

Belonging to the Kingdom is not a matter of trusting some deity "above all things" or somehow "out there." It is about a God who is the ground and depth of the entire cosmos, and hence of every one of us. This Kingdom or Presence of God in power is both a current reality and a future or "eschatalogical" event. In Jesus' teaching, one enters this Kingdom now by childlike trust – not in dusty dogmas or in rigid creeds, but in the living God. Yet, at the same time, because of the very trustworthiness of this Presence, there is the assurance that one day the Kingdom will come in all its fullness. What Jesus taught his followers to pray for – "Thy will be done on earth as in heaven" – will indeed be done. Sickness, pain, and death will have no more reign over humanity in this teaching. Significantly, the most prevalent metaphor of this future bliss is that of a great wedding feast. The truth described in this image is that life in the future Kingdom (itself a metaphor) will be richly celebrative, communal, and filled with all the sense of newness, adventure, and creativity that only a wedding can signify.

Already we can get a foretaste here of what that "heaven" will be like.

Eternal Life

The first three Gospels, while constantly using the image of the Kingdom of God when Jesus speaks of God's presence and our relationship to the spiritual order, have one other important way of expressing this same reality. Though they use it rather sparsely, it becomes the dominant note in the fourth Gospel, that attributed to John. I'm referring, of course, to the phrase "eternal life." When the rich young man, in Mark 10:17ff, comes running to Jesus, we are told that he fell at his feet and asked him excitedly, "What must I do to inherit eternal life?" This expression, which occurs only a couple of times in Matthew, Mark, and Luke, appears some fourteen or fifteen times in John. The reason for this is not hard to find. We know that the fourth Gospel was aimed at sophisticated, Hellenistic Jews and gentiles. For these readers, the phrase "the Kingdom of God," with all its Hebraic background, would have had a very unfamiliar ring, so John uses it only a couple of times. Paul totally avoids its use in his own writings for the very same reason. He too uses the term eternal life – for example in Romans 2:7 – but he has other ways of expressing the same concept. Anyone interested in good communication obviously has to speak the language of the intended audience. The early Christians thus felt no inhibitions about dropping the imagery favoured by Jesus and replacing it with their own. The phrase "eternal life" made perfectly good sense in Greek, and John fills it with all the meaning that he was convinced flows from a right relationship with God, oneself, and others through Christ. John's Jesus, (who is in so many striking ways different from the Jesus of the first three Gospels), teaches that to follow him, to trust in his revelation of the nature of God, to keep his sayings, is to be at one with God – as he knows himself to be. All of this is to have eternal life.

The Problem

The great difficulty about such an expression in English, however, is that while it appears self-explanatory it doesn't quite get
the meaning of the original Greek, and consequently has done
more, in my view, to put intelligent people in our culture off the
Christian view of life after death than any other single thing! The
same can be said of the synonym often used in the King James
Version, "everlasting life." Both expressions strongly suggest a life
very much like this one only going on and on *ad infinitum*.
Coupled with a literal understanding of other Bible imagery
about celestial choirs, harps without number, and streets paved
with gold, it has conjured up a mental image attended by colossal
boredom, if not outright horror. If that is what the afterlife is
going to be like, a great many people would like the opportunity
of saying, "No, thanks all the same." As Robert Service said in the
last line of his poem against the concept of immortality, "Please
God, spare me your great hereafter."

But the Greek words *aionios zoe* mean literally "life of the age,"
that is, of the age to come. In other words, the New Testament at
this point is not talking about an infinite extension of temporal
life but a wholly different quality of life – life as it was meant to
be, life as we have known it in rare glimpses, perhaps, not so
much life going on forever but rather the life of an eternal *now*. It
is a kind of life that might be endless but is actually beyond or
outside of time altogether. It is what T. S. Eliot was writing about
when he talked of "the intersection of the timeless with time."
It's the kind of fullness of living we get hints of in rare moments
here when God, or the life force, or however we care to express it
makes us feel "in time, yet out of time," at one with the universe,
ourselves, and others. It may be at the birth of a child, or when
we are in love, in deep meditation, or when we experience
nature in some profound way, or perhaps when we thrill to
music, art, or some other vision of great beauty.

Eternal life supremely means sharing in the life of God. Once again, as with the Kingdom of God, eternal life is not something pushed off into the future or an excuse for turning one's back on this earth, on this time-oriented existence, this reality of living. Rather, the life of the age to come is something one embarks upon here and now. Awareness of what we really are – the offspring of God – and of where we are ultimately going to be – in the realm where God will be known face to face – means a radically new quality of life at this very moment, a sense of being wholly present or alive as never before. We may not always feel like it or always hold firmly to this belief from an intellectual standpoint. We will not be spared the normal vicissitudes of earthly life. But John's Jesus assures the readers that it remains a reality all the same. It is, he says, God's will that everyone who puts their trust in him "may have eternal life." It is thus a present possession as well as a future hope.

I believe Carl Jung sums up best what is intended by all of this when he writes in his memoirs, "The decisive question for man is: is he related to something infinite or not? That is the telling question of his life. Only if we know that the thing that truly matters is the infinite can we avoid fixing our interests upon futilities, and upon all kinds of goals which are not of real importance . . . If we understand and feel that here in this life *we already have a link* with the infinite, desires and attitudes change. In the final analysis, we count for something only because of the essential we embody, and if we do not embody that, life is wasted [my italics]."[1]

The story of the raising of Lazarus in John's Gospel, chapter 11, is probably not historical. I say this not to be controversial, nor because of some dogmatic, liberal assumption that miracles are by definition impossible or unbelievable. The story seems improbable to me because such a stupendous event, especially if, as John insists, it was the last straw that precipitated the final decision of the authorities to have Jesus done away with, is hardly likely to have escaped the earliest Gospel tradition. Yet none of the other Gospels includes it, nor is it anywhere mentioned by Paul in his letters. But the passage is spiritually important for Christians. This is particularly so since it leads up to the unique saying of Christ, attributed to him because his own resurrection is already well in the past at the time of writing, that he himself is "the resurrection and the life." This saying, so integral a part of the Anglican, Episcopal, and other churches' funeral services, says in full, "I am the resurrection and the life. Whosoever believes in me [meaning, in the message I bring], even if he dies, yet shall he live. And everyone who believes in me shall not die unto the age to come." The meaning is clear. To trust in the living God whom Jesus reveals means that one may die physically but he or she will never perish spiritually. To die a physical death will be negated by being raised up through the power of God mediated by His Son, Jesus Christ.

Many Mansions

There is one other passage in John's Gospel that merits some mention. It contains the saying of Jesus that in the house of the Father there are many "mansions." Jesus says he is going to prepare a place for his followers that they may be with him always. The word in the Greek at this point for "mansions" is transliterated into English as *monai*. This means, quite literally, stopping places, way stations, or resting spots where one may refresh oneself on a journey before travelling on again. The Judaism of that period believed in various compartments or dwelling-places in the life to come. But it is important to notice that in this saying of Jesus the sense is not that of any static, permanent rest – for many people, suggestive of endless ennui – but of centres of recreation and renewal as the resurrected person progresses ever onwards towards greater freedom, knowledge, and enlightenment. The Bible's view of eternal life is definitely not about instant perfection of some kind but about growth and adventure beyond any earthbound expectations.

9

♦

The Gospels
and the
Resurrection
of Jesus

SCHOLARS ALMOST UNIVERSALLY AGREE THAT THE EARLI-
est Gospel, Mark's, was written some thirty years after the death
of Jesus Christ. Thus, the sayings and events of Jesus' life and
ministry recorded in Mark and the other three Gospels circulated for a full generation in an oral form. It is possible that there
was a collection of some sayings and parables written in Ara-
maic at an earlier point, and there is a strong possibility that
what is called "The Passion Narrative" – the story of the betrayal
and crucifixion – may also have been written down at an earlier
date. But the literary form known as a Gospel, which collated,
edited, and structured this diverse oral and written tradition,
came into existence, as we have already seen, well after Paul's
testimony in his first letter to the early Christians at Corinth.

I have discussed the Gospel accounts of the Resurrection
elsewhere, and other theologians, such as Hans Küng in his
book *On Being a Christian*, have treated the topic with such

thoroughness that it is unnecessary to cover the same ground in detail here.[1] Nevertheless, the matter is so central to our subject and so crucial for an understanding of the grounds for Christian belief in life after death that certain key elements must be examined here at least briefly.

Mark's Gospel

The ordinary reader, particularly if he or she has read only the King James Version of the Bible, is probably unaware that the most ancient and authentic Greek manuscripts of Mark's Gospel end abruptly at chapter 16, verse 8. What appears after that, verses 9 to 19, is called the "Longer Ending of Mark" and is obviously an attempt by a later hand to fill in an embarrassing gap. The reader can check this out personally by reading Mark 16 in the King James Version and then in any of the more modern translations such as the Revised Standard Version or the New English Bible. The much more ancient Greek texts upon which our modern, scholarly translations are based were simply not available to the scholars who created the King James Version. Here is how Mark ends according to the best available Greek text today:

"And when the Sabbath was over, Mary Magdalene and Mary the mother of James and Salome brought spices to come and anoint him. And very early in the morning, just after sunrise, on the first day of the week, they came to the tomb. And they said among themselves, 'Who will roll away the stone for us from the door of the tomb?' And looking ahead, they saw that the stone had been rolled away: for it was extremely large. Then, entering into the tomb, they saw a young man seated on the right side, clad in a white garment; and they were quite amazed. But he said to them, Don't be frightened; you seek for Jesus of Nazareth who was crucified. He has been raised up; he is not here; look, this is the place where they laid him. But go your way; tell the disciples and Peter that he is going before you into Galilee. You will see him there even as he told you. And, they came out and fled from the tomb; for they were seized by trembling and were beside themselves. And they said nothing to anyone, for they were afraid."

Several things stand out sharply. As in all the Gospels, the women are first to the tomb and the first to recognize that something quite unexpected, something immensely portentous, has occurred. (John, however, unlike the others, says that Mary Magdalene came to the tomb alone that first morning.) Luke and John have two angels at the tomb, Mark has a "young man," and Matthew says there was one angel. Mark's young man tells the women that Jesus will appear to the disciples in Galilee, a statement Matthew echoes. However, if you look at the account in Luke you will find that in it there are no recorded appearances of the Risen Christ in Galilee at all. Matthew describes but one (in a passage which is obviously a creation of the early Church), and in John the only such appearance is in an appendix added to the Gospel at a later date.[2]

We begin to get a feel for some of the various contradictions and discrepancies that mark the four accounts of Jesus' Resurrection when you lay them side by side. While such differences rule out any attempt by critics to argue that the Gospel writers colluded or conspired to "cook" their stories and make them match, thus adding to their general credibility (after all, witnesses to any happening rarely agree in all details), nevertheless, it is obvious that we can never have the sort of precision about the first Easter that many Christians somehow blindly assume.

What is really startling is the way in which Mark's account ends with the sheer terror of the women and their failure to tell anyone. It is, of course, possible that the original papyrus or vellum manuscript was torn off or spoiled in some way, and that Mark did go on to the kind of happier conclusion later supplied for him in the Longer Ending, but we don't know that for certain. The other point that should be made here is that although Mark and the others record that the tomb was empty, they nowhere attempt to describe the Resurrection itself. Scholars know this, but many church members seem unaware that none of the Gospels describe the actual event of Jesus being raised from the dead. This restraint on their part – since surely it must have been tempting to have depicted some tremendous epiphany or an intervention by hosts of angels – once again adds to one's respect for the overall veracity of the story.

Clearly, whatever happened was not an event like any other. If, as Christians believe, God raised Jesus from the dead, what happened was never described because it was, in principle, something that lay quite beyond our normal senses or abilities to comprehend. It was quite literally indescribable – a *miraculum*. Perhaps this is the real message behind the stark terror of the women in Mark's primitive narrative. He gives us no appearances, nothing save the journalistic description of the women themselves as they struggle to cope with the shock of thinking the unthinkable.

The Appearances in Matthew, Luke, and John

None of the Gospels describes the appearance of the risen Jesus to Peter alone (Luke merely mentions it in passing), although this is fundamental to Paul's account of the appearances in I Corinthians. Similarly, Paul apparently knew nothing of the tradition about the tomb being empty since he never speaks of it; indeed, it does not seem to have formed any part of the earliest preaching. Nevertheless, Paul does agree with the Gospels in that, for him as for Matthew, Luke, and John, the stories of the appearances of the resurrected Master form the bedrock of Christian certainty. There is absolutely no way to reconcile all the various appearance stories, in spite of what fundamentalists and others may claim. However, certain features should be noticed.

In Matthew, the appearances are attended by both fear and doubt on the part of the disciples, but they are able to approach Jesus, grasp his feet and pay reverence.[3] Obviously, he is recognizable. He speaks to them and bids them characteristically not to be afraid. In Luke we have the unique story of the two disciples who are walking back to the village of Emmaeus, just outside Jerusalem, when they meet a stranger. Later, invited in to eat with them, the stranger asks a blessing over the bread and distributes it to them. At this point, "their eyes were opened and they knew him." Jesus then suddenly vanishes from their sight. This passage may or may not be historical. If it were a historical event, it would undoubtedly have been part of the earliest tradition and so known to Paul and to the other evangelists. It seems more likely that it is a theological construct. That is, here we have the Risen Lord making himself known in the breaking of bread – at the eucharist. In other words, it is part of the author's belief that if you want to know the Risen Christ you can do so at the celebration of the Lord's Supper or Holy Communion. Jesus is present there and opens the eyes of those with the faith to "see" him.

Luke's version of the appearance to all the disciples cites their fear that they are seeing a disembodied ghost or spirit. Jesus tells them to look at his pierced hands and feet and then invites them to touch and handle him: "A spirit doesn't have flesh and bones as you see me to have." He then eats a piece of fish. We are reminded here of the appearance to the disciples in John's Gospel when Jesus invites Thomas to allay his doubts by thrusting his finger into the holes in his hands and feet and by thrusting his hand into his wounded side. I agree with those scholars, such as Professor F. W. Beare and others, who find the references to eating and to being touched somewhat crude and at variance with Paul's earlier contention that Christ's Resurrection body was of a more subtle or spiritual nature. And it is interesting in this connection to note that John, who does write of both the suggestion to Thomas of touching and of the Risen Jesus eating, also has the apparently contradictory story in which Mary Magdalene in the garden is forbidden to touch her Master "because I am not yet ascended."

What is influencing these narratives, no doubt, is the criticism by some early opponents of Christianity that Jesus was not raised up from the dead in some bodily way but that all that was seen was a ghostly wraith or pale spirit. The ancient world held a wide variety of beliefs in the survival of some kind of spirit or soul after death. What was unique about Pharisaic Judaism and Christianity was the belief that there would be a resurrection of the total person – not just the soul but a transformed bodily reality as well. The seeming contradictions in the appearance accounts are the result of trying to bear witness to these two truths: one, that the resurrection is a spiritual event, and two, that it is also a bodily event – the physical body is there but radically changed. Thus, the Risen Christ is apparently able to be in more than one place at once: he can pass through closed doors, he can appear or vanish at will. He is at times instantly recognizable; at others, even someone as close to him as Mary Magdalene has difficulty knowing who it is. In other words, in his risen body Christ can somehow control how and by whom he is perceived.

A Final Word

Sometimes preachers and others talk as though after the Resurrection anyone in the vicinity could have observed the Risen Master walking about or talking to his various followers. This was obviously not so. All the Resurrection appearances were to disciples, to his own circle of friends, with the exception of Paul, and we have already seen how he alone "saw" Christ on that occasion. There was something mystical, something paranormal, and beyond our everyday, empirical experience about "seeing" the resurrected person once known as Jesus of Nazareth. Everything about all of these appearance stories – despite contradictions and problems – resonates with the awareness that something quite new and different is being encountered. Jesus had, it was believed, entered into a new and higher plane of being. And, having done so, he had become the exemplar or forerunner of a destiny intended for all humankind.

10

◆

Hell

I HAVE DELIBERATELY NOT DEVOTED A CHAPTER TO THE concept of heaven because the subject matter involved has already been covered by our discussion of eternal life and will be touched on again in Part Five. Nevertheless, it is important to state here that the popular notion of heaven has been almost as great a stumbling block to belief in a life beyond the grave as the concept of a burning hell. The imagery and other descriptive embroidery is so crassly materialistic and the accompanying worldview so naive that the average thinking person can easily conclude the whole subject is one for children or for lovers of pure fantasy.

Some of the most familiar and best-loved hymns in our churches abound in descriptions of heaven that are frankly embarrassing to the modern mind. It is clear enough for the most part that the author's intention is not literal but symbolic. However, the cumulative effect of generations of believers singing these uncritically, coupled with the absence of any positive attempt to give alternative explanations, has meant that in popular thought heaven is perceived to be boring and banal. Nobody today is interested in some form of existence whose highlights consist of a steady diet of milk and honey – "Jerusalem the golden, with milk and honey blest" – walking around on pavements of gold, playing harps to accompany angelic choirs, or lying prostrate before the throne of God "to gaze and gaze on Thee." It is often stated by conservative theologians and preachers that the greatest coup of the devil has been to persuade people he doesn't exist. But it is a far greater devilish success to have so many people thinking that the final goal and consummation of all human striving is either incredible or boring!

There are few ideas in the entire history of religion that have caused more misery, cruelty, or misunderstanding than the concept of a fiery hell. There is no place where insistence upon a crude literalism has done more lasting damage to the human psyche. It is not just a question of the terror suffered by sensitive individuals down the ages because of fear of everlasting torment, either for themselves or for their loved ones. This is bad enough in itself. But the idea of a place of fiery, eternal punishment awaiting the damned has crucially warped our western understanding of God.

Since it is a fundamental spiritual law that the worshipper becomes like the object of his or her worship, the worship of a deity assumed capable – for whatever reasons – of eternally tormenting billions of people has led to disastrous results. The Inquisitors, in torturing and burning the "enemies of God," were simply emulating their Master! It is no accident today that the most vigorous supporters of an ever-increasing nuclear arsenal, including the Strategic Defence Initiative (known popularly as "Star Wars") are right-wing fundamentalists and their ilk in both Canada and the United States. If you believe in a God who has prepared a literal hell for his enemies, it is an easy jump to argue for strategies that may include the incineration of most of humankind.

One of the earliest memories of my boyhood is of preachers at a little Gospel Hall we attended ranting and raving until the perspiration rolled down their faces and the hairs at the nape of my neck stood on end. Their endless theme was the horror of hell and the need to escape its awesome clutches by being "saved." They were following a time-hallowed formula of holding sinners over the flames in order to persuade them to "get right with the Lord." One of their most common tactics was to point at various members of the congregation and ask, "What if you should die tonight? What if a car should strike you dead on your way home from here or a heart attack call you before your Maker? If you haven't been born again, my friend, prepare to spend a godless eternity in the fires of hell." This was strong stuff and it was no wonder that when the altar call came every youngster in the place and most of the adults answered it – regularly.

This kind of preaching still goes on today. Not just on television, where electronic evangelists flail away, but in countless churches everywhere. If you ask these preachers of the Gospel why they proclaim hellfire and eternal damnation, they have a single, simple answer, "Because it's in the Book." Since indeed it is not only "in the Book" but deeply embedded in the art and literature of our entire culture, no study of life after death can avoid it. One has only to read Dante or Milton, or visit the Sistine Chapel at the Vatican, to comprehend the visceral grip that the popular idea of hell holds on our western imagination. Where did it come from? Did Jesus believe in it and preach it? And what is its validity for us today?

Old Testament Beliefs

The earliest descriptions of life after death in the Old Testament are somewhat vague and partake of concepts widely held by all the Semitic peoples of the ancient Near East. The oldest of all is expressed in such descriptions of death as "being gathered to one's fathers." This phrase, found in Babylonian records as well as in the Hebrew Scriptures, is evidence that people then believed that at death the family circle was joined. Indeed, there was widespread worship of ancestors in that culture and the dead could be invoked for guidance. This art, called necromancy, is generally frowned upon in the Old Testament, but several passages make it plain that it was part of the popular cult in early times. The classic example, of course, is when a distraught King Saul disguises himself and goes to the Witch of Endor to "bring up" the prophet Samuel from the dead to give him counsel. When Samuel appears, he asks Saul, "Why hast thou disquieted me, to bring me up?"[1]

The dead could not only be invoked, they were viewed as needing food and other necessities. The placing of food on graves or even with corpses was widespread all over the ancient world. There is an inscription of the Assyrian King Ashurbanipal (who died in 626 B.C.) in which he says, "The rules for making offerings to the dead and libations to the ghosts of the kings my ancestors . . . I reintroduced. I did well unto god and man, to dead and living."[2] There is no attempt to reason out exactly where or how these ancestors lived, but they were alive and still powerful.

There is, however, another strand of thought which overlaps the ancestor cult and has elements common to all early Semitic mythology. It was particularly strong in Babylonian religion, and the forced exile of the Jews into Babylonian territory in about 590 B.C. confirmed its hold upon early Judaism. This has to do with She'ol, the underworld place of departed spirits. The earliest mention of She'ol comes from the eighth century B.C. and references abound in the Old Testament. For example, when Joseph's brothers sell him into slavery and lie to his father, Jacob, that he was killed by wild beasts (showing him the torn and bloody coat of many colours as "proof"), Jacob mourns and cries, "I will go down into the grave unto my son mourning."[3] The word here translated as "grave" is the Hebrew word *She'ol*, and the old man speaks of "going down."

The derivations of the word *She'ol* are still debated by

scholars, but the prevailing opinion is that it comes from a root word meaning "to be hollow." It is variously described as a hollow place under the earth or as a walled, subterranean city where there is neither hope nor joy of any kind. The dead feed on dust and murky waters in a shadowy existence that is but the palest reflection of anything that could be called life. The best way to describe this is the summary in the *Oxford Dictionary of the Christian Church*: "The notion reflects an undeveloped and shadowy belief in the future life which was gradually superseded by the more defined beliefs of later Judaism."[4]

In She'ol there is no thought of punishment or reward. Unfortunately, the translators of the Authorized Version sometimes render the word as "hell," as in "Thou wilt not leave my soul in hell . . ."[5] This falsely creates the impression that the Jews believed in a fiery place of punishment from the beginning. In fact, as we shall see, it was a very late development indeed.

While the She'ol belief implies a kind of future life, it was at best an unsatisfying, ill-defined doctrine. The shades in She'ol had no sense of God's presence: "For the grave [She'ol] cannot praise thee, death cannot celebrate thee: they that go down into the pit cannot hope for thy truth."[6] The Psalmist, in fact, is continually making the point that God should keep him alive, "for in death there is no remembrance of thee: in the grave [She'ol] who shall give thee thanks?"[7] The dead are those whom God "rememberest no more: and they are cut off from thy hand."[8]

The idea of hell as a place of fiery punishment for the wicked appears for the first time in Jewish writings in the second century B.C. To understand it properly one must comprehend the various pressures and influences at work. The conquests of Alexander the Great (who died in 323 B.C.) had spread the Greek language and culture over the whole of the ancient world. The Jews themselves were under Greek rule from the time of Alexander to the middle of the second century B.C. Some scholars, most notably F. W. Beare, argue that the popular concept of hell owes its origins to this source. He points out that it was no less an authority than Plato himself who first gave full-scale promotion to the idea of a hell of torment for evildoers in the life to come. "Hell was a Greek invention," he says.[9] But I agree with those who feel Beare overstates the case. In addition to Greek ideas, Jewish thought was influenced by other, more congenial concepts from ancient Persia. In the religion of Zoroaster, the conflict between good and evil, light and darkness, was to culminate in the resurrection of the dead, a fiery judgement, and then the creation of a new world where there would be no more crying or pain. It is easy to see how these ideas appealed to Jewish theologians of the time when you think about the specific problems of justice and oppression they were trying to solve.

It became impossible, as belief in the personal, caring nature of God developed, to continue to accept the She'ol view of life after death. Here and there, in hints and guesses at first, we find expressions of a growing conviction that to be true to himself God's concern for his people must transcend death. In the midst of his terrible sufferings, Job at first is afraid he will go down into She'ol and be no more remembered. The injustice of this, however, and his intense faith in God's mercy and faithfulness gradually bring Job to a daring leap of faith. He utters those words which have come down the centuries as part of the burial service of the Anglican Church, and which I have myself so often read at funerals: "For I know that my redeemer liveth, and that he shall stand at the latter day upon the earth: And though after my skin, worms destroy this body, yet in my flesh shall I see God."[10]

Professors W. O. E. Oesterly and T. H. Robinson in their classic work, *Hebrew Religion*, have commented on this text: "There is no general or formulated doctrine of the resurrection of the dead here. Yet, there is the conviction that, for Job at least, death is not the end . . . There is no thought of eternal life, no suggestion of heaven, but there is an assurance which will inevitably lead to these doctrines."[11] Similarly unformulated glimpses of the way this doctrine was beginning to emerge can be found in several places in the intimate, devotional prayers of the Psalms as well as in one of the most moving passages in the Old Testament, Isaiah 53. In describing the martyrdom of the suffering servant of God, the author clearly implies that God will vindicate him and raise him to complete the work he gave him to do.

However, in addition to wrestling with the issue of God's justice and mercy *vis-à-vis* the individual, there was the even more profound dilemma of God's dealings with the nation as a whole. The long-held belief in the political reality that God would one day smite Israel's enemies and restore the throne of David had to undergo a radical change in the face of inescapable, hard facts. As one foreign conqueror succeeded another in grinding the Jewish nation under its heel, there was widespread disillusionment and despair. How could God really be not only Israel's God but Lord of all the empires of the earth when he permitted his people to suffer such ignominy and repeated defeat?

The answer to this appeared in what is known as apocalyptic literature. The word "apocalypse" comes from Greek and means a revelation of secrets, in this case particularly secrets concerning the future. These writers solve the problem of God's justice by postulating a day of divine intervention when all his promises to Israel would be fulfilled. Jewish apocalyptic literature, written from about 200 B.C. to 100 A.D., includes the Old Testament Book of Daniel and such writings as the Book of Enoch, the Book of Jubilees, the Testaments of the Twelve Patriarchs, the Secrets of Enoch, and the Assumption of Moses. The classic Christian apocalypse is, of course, the Revelation of St. John the Divine, although there are passages of apocalyptic writing in the Gospels, most notably Mark, chapter 13, and elsewhere in the New Testament. A verse from II Peter 3:10 is typical of the genre: "But the day of the Lord will come as a thief in the night; in which the heavens shall pass away with a great noise, and the elements shall melt with fervent heat, the earth also and the works that are therein shall be burned up."

In the Sibylline Oracles, a collection of Jewish and Christian writings from 140 B.C. to 70 A.D., we read: "Then fire shall come upon the whole world . . . the whole world shall hear a rumbling and a mighty roar. And He [God] shall burn the whole earth."[12]

Christian apocalyptic literature borrowed heavily from Jewish writings and cannot be understood apart from them; Jewish apocalyptic writings, in turn, owed much to Persian sources. For example, the judgement of Israel's enemies becomes the final judgement of all people, the conflagration and burning become cosmological in scope, the establishment of God's Kingdom becomes the creation of a new world. This is behind the statement in Revelation: "Behold I saw a new heaven and a new earth: for the first heaven and the first earth were passed away."[13] There is no consistent teaching about a fiery hell in any of this apocalyptic material, just as no overall schema is adhered to. The writings share common elements, common imagery, but the details differ considerably. Sometimes resurrection is followed by judgement and punishment by fire; sometimes resurrection comes at the last and affects only the good. In some writings there is the idea of an intermediate state after death and before resurrection in which the good go to paradise, the evil to a place of torment. Then comes eventual final judgement leading to either lasting bliss or never-ending pain.

The two Old Testament passages that give undisputed evidence of the growing Jewish belief in the resurrection of the body both come from this kind of thinking and can be dated with certainty to the second century B.C. The first is from Isaiah 26:19 and reads: "The dead men shall live, together with my dead body they shall arise. Awake and sing, ye that dwell in dust [that is, in She'ol]: for thy dew is as the dew of herbs, and the earth shall cast out the dead." The second is from the apocalyptic work Daniel. In chapter 12:2 we read: "And many of them that sleep in the dust of the earth shall awake, some to everlasting life, and some to shame and everlasting contempt." It would be wrong, however, to take any of this language too literally. As we have noted before, religious language is necessarily picture or image language, the attempt to utter the unutterable. That this punishment was not actually seen as never-ending can be understood from a third-century A.D. rabbinical treatise which says: "After twelve months their souls become extinct . . . and they turn to ashes."[14]

Some readers will want to learn more about apocalyptic literature while others may feel this is already more than they needed to know. But, it must be said in the plainest terms that this is the context for the references to hell in the New Testament and is the intellectual inheritance of Jesus himself. You cannot appreciate isolated sayings attributed to Christ in the Gospels without at least a nodding acquaintance with this complex of religious ideas.

The Gospels

I have discussed at some length in my book *For Christ's Sake* the obvious fact that Jesus was very much a child of his age.[15] However you understand the doctrine of the Incarnation you have to take his humanity with full seriousness. We should expect what indeed we find, that Jesus' own words reveal much of the imagery and metaphors involved in apocalyptic thinking. He believed in the resurrection of the body, a final judgement, and the imminent coming, by divine intervention, of the last days. But a closer examination of the Gospels throws some startling light upon his actual beliefs regarding hell and "eternal" punishment.

The idea of a fiery hell of punishment occurs only once in the earliest Gospel, Mark, once in Luke, and not at all in John's Gospel or the Johannine Epistles. Matthew, written about 80 A.D., some twenty years after Mark, is the chief source of sayings attributed to Jesus on this theme. Professor Beare suggests, "For Matthew, it seems to have had a morbid fascination."[16] The sole reference to hell in Mark deserves a closer look. It comes closely after the striking, and much neglected, saying of Jesus that he who is not actively engaged against us (the disciples and their cause) is "on our side." Here is the passage as it is rendered by me from the currently approved Greek text:

"And whosoever shall offend [cause to stumble] one of these little ones that believe in me, it is better for him that a millstone were hanged about his neck, and he were cast into the sea.

"And if thy hand offend thee, cut it off: it is better for thee to enter into life maimed, than having two hands to go into Gehenna, into the fire that never shall be quenched. And if thy foot offend thee, cut it off: it is better to enter lame into life, than having two feet to be cast into Gehenna. And if thine eye offend thee, pluck it out: it is better for thee to enter into the Kingdom of God with one eye, than having two eyes to be cast into Gehenna, where the worm does not die and the fire is not put out."[17]

It is unfortunate that the translators of the King James Version used the word "hell" here (and even "hell-fire" for verse 47) because that is not what the Greek original plainly says. The word actually used, and repeated, by Mark is "Gehenna." Gehenna is the transliteration into Greek of the Hebrew *Gehinnom* or Valley of Hinnom (sometimes called the Valley of Ben Hinnom) and refers to a deep gully immediately southwest of the old City of Jerusalem. It was considered accursed by the Jews because it had been used for human sacrifices to the god Moloch by the Canaanites in the pre-conquest days.[18] By the time of Jesus it had long been used as the city's garbage dump, a place of burning and decay and therefore a vivid symbol of desolation, destruction, and loss.

Once you realize this, it becomes abundantly clear that Jesus is using contemporary imagery as a striking way of highlighting the fact that important issues are at stake. Sacrifices must be made by those who would be disciples, but they are worth it because the alternative is to endure a haunting sense of loss. In trying to avoid the discipline of discipleship one risks desolation, or being cast on the refuse heap. There is absolutely no warrant here for the later, terrifying doctrines of the Church about hell. The proof, if more is needed, that Jesus is speaking symbolically here can be had by asking oneself whether Jesus is really calling on people to go ahead and mutilate themselves by literally cutting off arms and hands or gouging out their eyes! The one reference to Gehenna in Luke (also translated as "hell" in the King James Version) is similarly metaphorical.[19] The only other case where the word "Gehenna" appears in the New Testament is in the Epistle of James, where it is used in a purely figurative sense that has nothing whatever to do with eternal punishment. The King James Version says:

"And the tongue is a fire . . . and it is set on fire of hell [Gehenna]."[20]

Matthew, who as we have seen is darkly obsessed by the themes of judgement and "furnaces of fire," has his own reasons for piling on images of terrible punishments to come. Modern scholarship has shown how the particular situation in the life of the early Church that this Gospel was written to address made strident polemic against the Pharisees and the synagogue inevitable. The author, facing bitter rivalry between the vigorous Judaism of his time and the emerging Christian community, often heightens elements in the older tradition to the point where they no longer represent the actual teaching of Jesus at all. Thus, as many scholars have noted, even where Matthew puts sayings about fiery torments in Jesus' mouth we can see they do not fit the context and, in some cases, war against it. Frank Beare, in his classic commentary on this Gospel, queries "whether this imagery of a hell of fire was used by Jesus at all. Apart from Matthew, it finds almost no echo in the Synoptic tradition."[21] When you add to this the silence of the Johannine literature on the topic and the fact that Paul never mentions it, the case for Jesus' sanction of such a concept weakens to the point where it is no longer sustainable. (Paul speaks instead of the consequences of unbelief as "death" or "destruction" or "annihilation." See Romans, 6:21, 23; Philippians, 3:19.)

The Apocalypse

Apart from Matthew, the main source of subsequent thinking and teaching by the Church about a fiery hell of everlasting torment is the Book of the Apocalypse, better known as Revelation. Before citing examples from the text itself, a brief introduction is called for.

The Book of Revelation is not just the last book in the New Testament, it was the last book to be included in the canon of authoritative New Testament writings. Most lay Church members, never mind outsiders, are unaware that this book was long regarded as questionable by the early Church, and its place was hotly debated for several centuries. It was particularly rejected by the Church in the eastern part of the empire and it was omitted from the Armenian and Syriac versions of the New Testament in their original form.

Although it claims apostolic authorship and was originally thought to be the work of St. John the Apostle, it was (and still is) evident to anyone who reads Greek that its barbarous style has nothing in common with the other works ascribed to John. Moreover, the author nowhere claims to have been an eyewitness of Jesus' ministry and refers to the twelve Apostles in a very reverential and removed manner, which is incompatible with one who belonged to the group himself. He says he was in exile on the bleak, volcanic-rock island of Patmos, just off the coast of Asia Minor (modern Turkey) "for the word of God." That, and the obvious context of his visions, received "in the Spirit," has led scholars to believe he was a Christian who had been banished during the reign of the Emperor Domitian. The date of the work, accordingly, cannot have been earlier than that reign – 81 to 96 A.D.

While many contemporary fundamentalist Christians and sectarians now have a field day explaining the book as a blueprint for present and future world events – including the much-heralded Day of Armageddon – the imagery and references all make perfect sense *in the context of that time.* In an hour of persecution, when it was feared that the hated Emperor Nero had literally come back to life as Domitian, the author uses the apocalyptic mode to name the "beast" or anti-Christ under a symbolic or coded message. The near-psychedelic nature of the visions and imagery suggests that they may have been caused by prolonged fasting and sensory-deprivation. According to the tradition, the author lived in a cave and was forced to work in a marble quarry. This comment is by no means meant to imply, however, that divine inspiration was not also involved – as I hope to make plain later. Tourists visiting Patmos today are shown both the cave and the ancient quarry as the chief highlights of an otherwise desolate spot.

In exile, on a bleak, volcanic outcropping which itself suggested the end of the world, and in despair over the apparent triumph of evil in the form of Roman oppression and cruelty – Domitian had assumed the mantle of a despot and demanded that public worship be given him as *Dominus et Deus,* Lord and God – the author sees world cataclysm and a supernatural victory as the only just solution. Not unnaturally, his indignation and his desire to see the fate of the wicked expresses itself in images of fire without end.

The classic passages occur near the end of the book. In chapter 19, we read that the false prophet and the beast are taken and thrown into a lake of fire burning with "brimstone" (sulphur). The following chapter describes how the devil is also thrown into the lake of fire, where all three "shall be tormented day and night for ever and ever." The most horrendous passage comes in chapter 21:8: "But the fearful, and unbelieving, and the abominable, and murderers, and whoremongers, and sorcerers, and idolaters, and all liars, shall have their part in the lake which burneth with fire and brimstone: which is the second death."

The article on hell in *The Oxford Dictionary of the Christian Church* rightly comments: "From such texts as these, often understood overliterally, the popular idea of hell was derived."

From what has already been said above, it should by now be obvious that these verses are definitely not to be taken literally. What's more, they have little in common with the teaching of Jesus or the compassionate nature of God as revealed by him.

Subsequent Developments

One thing stands out in our survey of the roots of the doctrine of hell: there is no overall, consistent paradigm or metaphysical system worked out in the Bible. The ancient Hebrew mind was not given to philosophical or metaphysical abstractions; it thought in concrete images. As Oesterley and Robinson point out, "The forms most characteristic of the Hebrew genius are the lyric and the short prophetic oracle, instinct with life, throbbing with emotion, but rarely the product of deep and conscious reflection. Among such a people we must not look for any elaborate or deeply conceived metaphysic."[22] Thus, it is a mistake to try to impose a tight structure or pattern and say, This is what the Bible teaches about hell. The other contributing factor to this (to me) less than satisfactory imprecision is the way in which the Bible itself was formed. When you have a collection of some sixty-six writings or "books" written in different places by widely differing people at different epochs as much as several centuries apart, you must expect to find a development or process rather than a precise doctrine formulated neatly for all time.

This accounts for the way in which various groups and denominations in the history of the Church have been able to seize upon different strands in the tradition and thus develop a whole range of sometimes conflicting views. In his book *Early Christian Doctrines*, J. N. D. Kelly remarks that there was "great uncertainty, not to say confusion" over the details of the fate of the soul after death in all the writings of the early Fathers."[23] People like Origen, Gregory of Nyssa, and Gregory Nazianus took a "soft" view of the meaning of hell, while others, including the great preacher John Chrysostom (347-407 A.D.) took a harsh, literal view. However, by the mid-fifth century "the stern doctrine that sinners will have no second chance after this life and that the fire which will devour them will never be extinguished was everywhere paramount."[24] Those who are familiar with the way other doctrines, for example, the teaching about the divinity of Jesus, developed during this same period will realize that what later came to be believed by all or nearly all was not necessarily always an accurate reflection of the original meaning of the biblical texts.

Summary

There is no consistent teaching about the fate of the "wicked" or the unrepentant in either the Old or the New Testaments. Nor, considering the figurative language used to describe hell, is there justification for the traditional, popular view of a literal place of eternal, fiery punishment for the "damned." The Jesus of history never taught such a doctrine, and it desecrates the name of the God he came to reveal to preach and teach that he did. This conclusion will not please those conservative Christians who hate to be disturbed by the facts, but it seems to me inescapable on the basis of the evidence.

Frequently in his teaching Jesus used the argument that if we as earthly parents long to give good gifts to our own children how much more must "your heavenly Father" desire to give good gifts to those that ask.[25] If I, as a father, would never torment and punish a child for an hour, let alone a day, how blasphemous it is to suggest that a loving God would punish his "children" for eternity! This is not a God to be worshipped but one to be shunned and abhorred as a sadistic monster.

Yet if, as I have argued earlier, religious language is often metaphorical, what is the reality to which the metaphor or imagery of hell points? It is clear throughout the Bible that the holiness and justice of God, counterbalanced by his mercy and grace, always stand in judgement upon human thoughts, motives, and actions. Given this, it makes sense that at the end of life there would be some kind of judgement passed upon us. As we have seen, even the most optimistic view of the contemporary near-death experience holds that there is moment of review, or a kind of "tribunal," where the dying person sees the full meaning and direction of his or her life.

I believe, as we shall see more fully later, the evidence indicates that this judgement is a kind of self-judgement induced by finding oneself in the presence of God or of the Light. To see for the first time, perhaps, the full implications of what we have done and the way we have at times fallen short of our true humanity will be a kind of suffering or hell. To the extent that they were really a part of the teaching of the historical Jesus, this is what the stern imagery of his warnings was pointing to. Thankfully, this fleeting, though deeply humbling experience is not the whole story. It is the beginning of the road to growth into fuller life and maturity.

Postscript:

Since writing this chapter, I have come across a passage in Origen (185-254 A.D.), the brilliant Alexandrian Bible scholar, in which he roundly criticizes those who foolishly read the Scripture passages about life after death in a crudely literal fashion. Each sinner, he says, kindles his own fire and his or her vices "form its fuel." Professor J. N. D. Kelly comments: "In other words, the real punishment of the wicked consists in their own interior anguish." Moreover, Origen goes on to state emphatically that all such punishment must have an end. In his view, all things will ultimately be restored. In the end, all humanity and even the devil, he says, will return to wholeness – not by coercion but through persuasion and instruction. At the last, they will recognize their own true good and be reconciled with God. Origen thus preserves human free will on the one hand and God's merciful goodness, as well as justice, on the other.[26]

11

◆

What about Purgatory?

THE FAILURE TO REALIZE THAT ALL LANGUAGE ABOUT GOD is in the end metaphorical – a phenomenon most obvious in the traditional teachings about a fiery hell – crops up again when we examine the notion of Purgatory. Purgatory, from the Latin verb *purgare*, to cleanse or purify either physically or spiritually, is traditionally believed to be the place or state of temporary punishment "where those who have died in the grace of God [Christians] are expiating their venial faults and such pains as are still due to forgiven mortal sins," before being admitted to the Vision of God. The early Christian Fathers were faced with a problem. It was fairly easy to say that obviously holy people who died in the arms of Mother Church were immediately ushered into the presence of God and granted the Beatific Vision after death. And the fate of those who were notorious sinners or pagans was quite clear also; they went to hell. But, what about the great throng of those who had been nurtured in the Church and its sacraments but had then fallen away? What about others who were practising Christians but, as St. Augustine said, were too much entangled with the things of earth to be fit to see God or enter His Presence? Using the same religious symbols and ideas (largely derived from Persian sources) that had shaped the doctrine of hell, the concept of a time of spiritual cleansing before the full Beatific Vision seemed to make good sense.

The main scriptural source was a passage in the Apocrypha (late Jewish writings, which were part of the Greek version of the Old Testament but were not part of the Hebrew Bible itself). In 2 Maccabees 12:39-45 we read how Judas Maccabaeus is said to have "made propitiation for them that had died that they might be released from their sin." There is nothing whatever about Purgatory, however, in the New Testament. Some scholars down the centuries have taken the saying of Jesus about the sin against the Holy Ghost being the one thing that can't be forgiven "either in this world or the next" as implying the possibility of expiation for *other* sins after death.[1] But this is not the obvious meaning. To suggest that a person's sins could be forgiven beyond the grave is not the same thing as insisting that there is a temporal place or state of suffering where such sin must be consumed or "paid for." In any case, Jesus was not making a doctrinal statement about life after death in the verse cited. To say that an offence against the Holy Spirit is beyond forgiveness here or hereafter is simply a characteristic way of stressing how serious this sin is.

One other similarly figurative passage, this time from Paul, has been used to support the belief in Purgatory.[2] Paul is talking about a time when every deed or "work" will be tried by a kind of fire. Some works will be abiding; others will not stand the test. The person will suffer loss, he says, but "he himself shall be saved; yet so as by fire." If you take this phrase in the context of the whole metaphor which Paul is using here – that of a master builder who lays a foundation and then has others build various edifices upon it – you quickly see that nothing is further from his mind than setting down a basis for a doctrine of Purgatory, or indeed making any definitive statement about a future life.

Nevertheless, it is clear that the early theologians of both the Eastern Church and the Latin Church of the West used a belief in Purgatory to justify prayers for the dead and to answer the question of how visibly imperfect people could be made ready to behold perfection. St. Clement of Alexandria says that those who repent on their deathbed but have no time to do works of penance will be sanctified in the next world by "purifying fire." This thought was developed further by Origen and others, such as St. Cyril of Jerusalem and the great preacher St. John Chrysostom. In the West, St. Ambrose taught that the souls of the departed await the end of time in different dwelling places, their fate varying with their deeds. St. Augustine, the greatest mind of all in the early Church – though capable of horrifying statements on such subjects as women or slavery – clearly taught that purifying suffering and pains are an absolute certainty in the life to come. This teaching was taken over later by St. Thomas Aquinas and other scholastics who held that whatever its beneficial power, the least pain in Purgatory is "greater than the worst on earth."[3] The pain, however, is relieved, according to Thomas, by the certainty of salvation, which brings the souls of the faithful departed a great peace.

Aquinas and his contemporaries taught that those in purgatorial pain may be helped by the prayers of the faithful, and especially by masses said on their behalf. Aquinas based this belief on his firm commitment to the idea of the Communion of Saints, that is, the belief that the Church militant here on earth and the Church of the faithful departed enjoy a spiritual unity. The practical result, however, was to extend the control of the Church beyond the grave to the souls of the dead. The abuse of this power through, among other things, the sale of indulgences (forgiveness of sins) and many other distortions led to the protest of Martin Luther and the beginnings of the Protestant Reformation in Europe.

The sixteenth-century Reformers, basing their doctrines on

Scripture alone, rejected the doctrine of Purgatory and taught that souls are freed from sin by faith in Christ and, if saved, go directly into God's Presence. The Thirty-nine Articles of Religion set out in the Book of Common Prayer by the Anglican scholars of the Reformation state this view quite bluntly. Article XXII reads: "The Romish doctrine concerning Purgatory, Pardons, Worshipping and Adoration as well as of Images as of relics and also Invocation of Saints, is a fond thing vainly invented, and grounded upon no warranty of Scripture, but rather, repugnant to the Word of God."

While I find myself in agreement with the Reformation theologians on the absence of any firm scriptural foundation for the Roman Catholic and Eastern Orthodox insistence upon Purgatory as a place or state of refining punishment, I believe from my studies that in throwing out the idea completely, Protestantism and Anglicanism lost the truth to which the imagery of Purgatory really points. What is missed, I am convinced, is the deeply intuitive sense that whatever the life after death may be it is not one of instant perfection. The doctrine is an imperfect and even crude attempt to witness to a belief that life beyond the grave involves growth into an ever greater spiritual maturity. Hans Küng seems to me close to the mark when he argues that there is really no need, nor justification, for a special place, event, or time frame for this. What is intellectually required is a belief that our encounter with God after death will be "profoundly humiliating, painful and therefore purifying."[4] Küng sees Purgatory as a symbolic way of speaking of "encounter with God in the sense that it judges and purifies, but also liberates and enlightens, heals and completes man."

In summing up, then, I repeat: the purgatorial concept of fire and pain must be understood as an allegory. The reality is a matter of spiritual and mental awareness of one's shortcomings in the Presence of God. To be aware of this and to be in that Presence is to find gradual wholeness and holiness. The fire is the symbol of the pain that any such growth in consciousness requires. While it is comforting, as well as natural, to pray for the deceased, their well-being depends not upon our efforts – or expenses – but upon the all-encompassing mercy of God.

Limbo

Finally, a word about a much misunderstood concept, limbo. Latin theology, with its love of systematizing and categorizing everything no matter how slim the evidence, postulated that in addition to Heaven, Hell, and Purgatory there must be another "place" for those who don't otherwise fit the scheme. Thus they spoke of a region on the borders of Hell known as "the hem of Hell" or limbo. Here again there were held to be two divisions, the *limbus patrum*, in which the Old Testament saints were thought to stay until Christ's Second Coming and the redemption of the world, and the *limbus infantium*, the eternal place and state of infants who died unbaptized, and so unregenerate, but innocent of actual sins. Such infants were said to be excluded from the Beatific Vision of God, but, at least in the opinion of St. Thomas Aquinas, they enjoy a fully natural happiness.

Earlier, St. Augustine, perhaps led on by his polemics against the Pelagians, taught firmly that, since all who die unbaptized are still tainted by original sin, these infants necessarily must suffer some degree of "positive punishment."[5] Needless to say, there is absolutely no warrant for such a sadistic view in any of the Scriptures. It is repugnant to common sense and our own moral judgement. In fact, it is the sort of nonsense which, if true, would render us more moral and compassionate than God. Sadly, the teaching regarding limbo, hardly ever heard now in official Catholic teaching, has caused enormous suffering down past centuries among the uneducated and illiterate masses. It is one aspect of the Church's teaching about life after death that ought to be repudiated officially as unworthy of credence, now or ever.

12

◆

Muddying
the
Waters

WE RETURN NOW TO SOME PROBLEMS TOUCHED ON BRIEFLY
in our discussion of the concept of a fiery hell – those posed by
the very last book in the New Testament. Without question, the
Book of Revelation, as interpreted by self-professed experts on
"prophecy," has spawned more confused, speculative nonsense
than any other book in the Bible. Because of a total unwillingness
to acknowledge the peculiar, cultural-specific nature of this work,
combined with a stubborn determination to force literal meanings upon highly symbolic terminology, fundamentalists of various warring schools have twisted the text to fit patterns never
intended by its author. The amazingly popular, doomsday-style
books of the American Hal Lindsey are a part of this.

Scholars, and indeed anyone willing to use their reason
and do even the most basic reading and research, particularly
those who take the time to read Revelation – recognize that the
book makes no claims to prophecies about events in the

late-twentieth century. All the elaborate attempts to see the European Common Market, China, the Soviet Union, and other modern states cited as major players in a drama leading up to a nuclear Armageddon are simply a deluded exploitation of our contemporary fears. The point is that we know the kind of book this is and the kind of social and religious conditions which gave rise to the literary genre to which it so clearly belongs. It is a Christian version of the style of writing known as "Apocalyptic," popular in Judaism in the two centuries before and in the period immediately after the birth of Christianity. As we have seen, it is the product of persecution and of despair of ever seeing God's justice done to his people *in this present life.* Thus it predicts an immediate, dramatic, divine intervention by God, the punishment of the wicked (oppressors) and the inauguration of eternal blessings for the righteous.

Apocalyptic writing makes abundant use of colourful imagery and quite unashamedly sets events *which have already happened* in the future to throw new light upon their inner meaning. This was part of the coding, familiar to contemporary readers but open to misunderstanding by the naive or those with a preconceived fixation about the "inerrancy" of anything that appears in the Bible. What's more, apocalyptic books were regularly ascribed to prestigious personages from the past in order to ensure their being read and taken as fully authoritative.

For example, the Book of Daniel in the Old Testament was not written by Daniel. We know from its style and other similarities with second century Jewish apocalyptic writings, plus the fact that it is written in Greek, not Hebrew like the rest of the Old Testament, that it came into being centuries after Daniel. Similarly, while the Book of Revelation may have been written by a man named John – one of the commonest male names of the period – it was certainly not written by the Apostle John. Nor was it written by the John to whom the Gospel and epistles are ascribed in the New Testament. There is absolutely no way anyone who knows Greek could suppose that all these works were penned by the same hand.

I suggest to those still reluctant to follow where the argument has taken us so far that they take a look at the ending of Revelation. As he sums up, the author once again follows a convention of his day – one that applied not just to apocalyptic writings but to all sorts of other documents as well. In Revelation 22:19, he issues a stern warning that if anybody tampers with his book and cuts out parts of it God will damn him or her by cutting them out of "the book of life." I have heard evangelical preachers use this text to reinforce their own very subjective interpretations of this and other biblical books. They utterly ignore the fact that this kind of warning was written into pagan documents from all over the ancient Near East at that time. There were no copyright laws, no guarantees that once a book left the author's hands it wouldn't be altered to suit the tastes of whoever acquired it. Consequently, you sent your work out complete with a curse on anyone who would dare to change it!

One of the clearest examples of this from antiquity is the paragraph added to the Greek translation of the Old Testament – commonly called the Septuagint, because there were allegedly seventy-two translators – in the third century B.C. The Epistle of Aristeas tells us that when the work was finished "the whole company . . . bade them to pronounce a curse in accordance with their custom upon anyone who should make alteration either by adding or changing or omitting anything."

Most likely, Revelation dates from the period of persecution of the Church under the emperor Domitian (81-96 A.D.). The "Number of the Beast" undoubtedly refers to the infamous Nero who inaugurated the first persecution of Christians, and Domitian himself is regarded as a "second Nero" or *Nero redivivus*, back from the dead. The author, banished to the arid, volcanic rock of the Island of Patmos, is wholly consumed by the conviction that all his visions and proclamations bear on the immediate future – the world of the Roman Empire in the twilight hours of the first century A.D. There is absolutely nothing in what he has to say that cannot be explained in that immediate context. In fact, although the modern literalists persist in ignoring it, the author does his utmost to stress that the entire point of his prophecy is that it is about to come to pass then and there. His opening line plainly states that all his words will be fulfilled swiftly, and the theme is echoed throughout the whole document.

I refer the reader to any scholarly, modern commentary on Revelation for a detailed exegesis or interpretation of its contents. What is important to stress is that the language is that of myth and symbol. It conveys a meaning, certainly, but not that of the literal or surface rendering. Some of the concepts are quite conventional to apocalyptic writing in general, and quite out of step with what is taught elsewhere in the New Testament by Jesus, Paul, and other key sources. For example, all the material about a first resurrection and a second resurrection is borrowed straight from the Jewish apocalyptic tradition and is without any corroboration or backing from the rest of the New Testament.

This is also true of the passages – fruitful of endless disputations between various kinds of fundamentalists today – that deal with a millennium or thousand-year reign of Christ on this earth, a belief known as Millenarianism. I doubt very much whether any other single idea has ever caused so much division and acrimony among Christians through history as this one. Yet it was never taught by Jesus or by Paul, it appears in only one book out of twenty-six in the New Testament, and was clearly borrowed by the author from stock teaching in non-Christian sources. Millenarianism is thus an alien concept to the mainline teaching of Christianity about a future life. As the *Oxford Dictionary of the Christian Church* says: "Though Millenarianism has never been formally rejected by orthodox Christianity, it may be doubted whether there is adequate justification for it either in Scripture or in Christian tradition."[1]

Nevertheless, in spite of all that has been said so far, or, rather, in light of it, the Book of Revelation contains much that is sublime in relation to our understanding of Christian beliefs about the afterlife. If we realize that the author, in describing the world to come, is doing the best he can within the limits of human vocabulary, and that it is a fallacy to confuse metaphors and images with the realities being described, there are some very inspiring words here indeed. For example, who could fail to be moved by "And I saw a new heaven and a new earth. For the first heaven and the first earth were gone and there was no more sea. And I saw the holy city, the New Jerusalem, coming down from God out of heaven, prepared like a bride for her husband. And I heard a great voice coming from out of the throne saying, Behold the dwelling of God is with humanity and he will tabernacle among them, and they shall be his people and God himself will be with them. And He shall wipe away every tear from their eyes, and there shall be no more death, neither grief nor crying nor pain any longer . . . And He that sat upon the throne said: Behold I am making all things new."[2]

Equally haunting are the words that begin the final chapter of the book: "And He showed me a river of the water of life as shining as crystal proceeding forth out of the throne and God and of the lamb. In the midst of the plain and on either side of the river there was the tree of life, which bore twelve kinds of fruit . . . and the leaves of the tree were for the healing of the nations. And there shall be no more curse." Only the foolish would take this literally. There is no "throne" with a river flowing out of it. But the promises here of eternal life and of healing so powerfully expressed under the imagery of the tree of life and the flowing, crystal waters resonate with mystical truth. The throne is the author's only way of communicating his conviction that God reigns, and that because of this, life and wholeness are the ultimate destiny of humankind.

Elsewhere in this book, the author describes the New Jerusalem, his favorite metaphor for the life beyond, in the familiar terms of streets of gold and walls of amethysts, sapphires, and other precious jewels. He, too, is responsible for the traditional hymnbook imagery of harp-playing crowds in white robes and endless, angelic choirs. Down the centuries, unfortunately, such caricatures of eternal bliss have become so familiar through religious art and language that they still are the first associative ideas to spring to most people's minds when the words "heaven" or "afterlife" are mentioned. If it is too late to convince contemporary men and women that none of that was ever meant to be taken literally – that the author of Revelation simply used the most precious things he knew to describe the indescribable – then it would be better to scrap the imagery altogether and begin again. That is the topic for chapter fourteen. First though, I want to look at whether the Bible supports a belief in reincarnation.

13

◆

Reincarnation
and
the Bible

NEW AGE THINKERS HAVE MADE A NUMBER OF ASSER-
tions concerning the doctrine of reincarnation and its alleged
confirmation in the pages of the Bible. Some of these statements
appear contradictory, as we shall see. Others are based upon
"facts of history," which, on closer examination, turn out to
have no foundation. Since, however, the stature of some of
these experts is beyond dispute and the mass appeal of others is
established through the media, it is essential to examine the
matter more closely.

In Shirley MacLaine's best-selling book *Out on a Limb*, a
character called David is explaining the theory of reincarnation
to her:

"'But David,' she said, 'why aren't these teachings recorded in
the Bible?'

"'They are,' he said. 'The theory of reincarnation is recorded
in the Bible. But the proper interpretations were struck from it

during an ecumenical council meeting of the Catholic Church in Constantinople sometime around 553 A.D. called the Council of Nicea. The council members voted to strike those teachings from the Bible in order to solidify Church control.'"[1]

This passage and its sentiments are repeated in MacLaine's writings and crop up continuously wherever the New Age gospel is proclaimed. But it simply bristles with problems. The Council of Nicea, of course, was held in Nicea in Asia Minor and not at Constantinople. It was in the year 325 A.D., not 553. There *was* a council held in Constantinople in 553 called the Second Council of Constantinople. However, neither at Nicea nor Constantinople – nor indeed at any other recorded ecumenical council – were passages relating to the doctrine of reincarnation or any other theory expurgated from the biblical text.

Without question there were early Christians – most notably the Gnostics – who believed in the transmigration of souls, and pronouncements were made condemning it by theologians and councils. One of the reasons that the brilliant Alexandrian, Origen (c.185 – c.254 A.D.) was driven from the priesthood and regarded as a heretic was over his espousal of a form of this doctrine. (Incidentally, it was Origen who is reported to have had himself emasculated in an over-literal application of Jesus' words: "And some have made themselves eunuchs for the sake of the Kingdom.") But arguments based upon a supposed deliberate attempt to conceal the "true" teachings of Moses or Jesus on this theory are simply false. Since the most influential (and by far the easiest to read) exposition of the grounds for believing in reincarnation today is Sylvia Cranston's and Carey Williams's 1984 book *Reincarnation, A New Horizon in Science, Religion, and Society*, I propose to look now at the case set forth there for the presence of reincarnational thinking in the Old and New Testaments.

The Old Testament

Cranston and Williams say that none of the three main branches of Judaism today "openly" teach reincarnation. They point out as well that the doctrine of the rebirth of souls is not developed in a systematic fashion in most traditional Jewish writings. They do, however, document fairly fully the indisputable fact that esoteric or cabbalistic Judaism – an ancient and important strain of mysticism and interest in the occult – has always believed in the doctrine. The most important modern figure in the revival of this movement was Gershom Scholem (1897–1982), the late professor of mysticism and cabbala at the Hebrew University of Jerusalem. His book, *Major Trends in Jewish Mysticism*, remains a classic for those who wish to pursue this aspect of Jewish tradition more deeply. Today it is within the Hasidic movement, which originated in Poland in the eighteenth century, that this particular teaching finds a central place.[2] It can be found everywhere in the Hasidic writings but is nowhere more movingly expressed than in Martin Buber's book, *For the Sake of Heaven*.

When this has been said, however, Cranston and Williams themselves concede that all this flows from extra-canonical literature, from Jewish mystical writings, and not from the Old Testament itself. In fact, they are unable to produce a single text in support of the teaching of reincarnation. As we have already seen, explicit evidence for a belief of any kind in life after death is extremely scant and undeveloped in the Old Testament. When it comes to the migration of souls there is total silence. The best that our two authors can say is that "nowhere in the Old Testament is reincarnation denied. In the Book of Job, Job plaintively asks 'If a man dies will he live again?' but receives no answer." This, of course, is an argument from silence, which carries little or no weight at all.[3]

The New Testament

In asking the question, Did Jesus and his Disciples believe in reincarnation? it has to be made quite clear that it is different from the question, Are there leading Christians today who hold this theory and who believe that Jesus and his earliest disciples did also? The answer to the latter is a very firm yes. Undoubtedly there have been, and are today, many, including some notable scholars, who remain church members while adhering to such a view. Cranston and Williams cite in particular the Anglican theologian Geddes MacGregor, author of several books on the subject, including, *Reincarnation in Christianity*.[4] But what about the New Testament evidence itself? It is one thing to believe in a doctrine; it is another to claim that this or that document actually teaches or upholds it.

At the outset, our two authors again propose the argument from silence: "It can be stated without qualification that Jesus in the four Gospels and St. Paul in the books of the New Testament attributed to him say not one word against the teaching of reincarnation."[5] But then they go further and proclaim (a position taken by nearly all New Age exponents, even though they paradoxically also hold that all references to reincarnation were purged by early councils) that in the Gospels "there are a number of places where reincarnation seems clearly expressed." The reason the record is not more "expansive," we are told, is because Christ's disciples misunderstood him and supposed the world was about to end shortly. The fact that nearly all New Testament scholars today agree that Jesus himself is the source of this expectation of an imminent doomsday is either ignored or unknown to Cranston and Williams. Indeed, much of the urgency which characterized all of Jesus' teaching would have completely evaporated if he himself had believed that there were countless lives ahead and that this present life was not "the accepted time" for a decision for God.

Our two authors go on to a type of *a fortiori* argument, which goes like this: If Christ is really the Son of God then he presumably has all powers, so why would he not have the power to be reborn again and again to save the world? This is unworthy of the generally quite intelligent and careful approach the pair uses. There is practically no limit to what one can "prove" taking such a tack. They argue that Jesus himself implied he had such power and indeed would use it when he said in the Gospel of

John, "I lay down my life for the sheep. And I have other sheep, that are not of this fold; I must bring them also . . . So there shall be one flock and one shepherd . . . No one takes it from me, but I lay it down of my own accord. I have power to lay it down and I have power to take it again."[6]

But there is not one word in any of this to witness to Jesus' belief in reincarnation. In John's Gospel, which is late (90–100 A.D.), we are reading not what Jesus actually said, but post-Resurrection theologizing of the early Church put into his mouth. In any case, he is simply saying that he seeks not just the "sheep" of the House of Israel (Jews), but gentiles as well. In saying he has power to lay his life down and to take it again, the author has Jesus affirm his sovereignty and his control over the events of the Passion and Crucifixion. I don't know of a single major New Testament scholar who would take this latter assertion in any other way.

As further evidence of their contention that Jesus himself taught that he had appeared on earth in previous ages and might do so again, Cranston and Williams then adduce another passage from John where Jesus is being taunted as setting himself up above "our father, Abraham." Jesus tells his adversaries, "Your father Abraham rejoiced to see my day and was glad." Surprised, they respond, "You are not yet fifty years old and hast thou seen Abraham?"[7] Jesus replies: "Truly, truly I say to you, before Abraham was, I am." Unfortunately, however, even if one were to take a fundamentalist view and hold that these are the exact words of the historical Jesus, they cannot be said to be valid evidence for reincarnational thinking. What is being claimed by the speaker is pre-existence as the Divine Son of God. This is in keeping with the opening verses of the Gospel about the Logos (Word of God) being "in the beginning with God." It has no reference to repeated rebirths. And there is no suggestion whatever that this pre-existent state is one shared with all humanity. Quite the opposite. It is the Son's uniqueness that is being stressed by the evangelist.

Admitting that even if their arguments to this point were solid they would still not necessarily apply to ourselves, our authors then ask whether the New Testament gives any indication that anyone other than Jesus has the power (or necessity) to be reborn. They believe it does. Returning to John, they quote the case of the man born blind.[8] Walking along with his disciples Jesus sees a blind man. His disciples ask him: "Rabbi, who sinned, this man or his parents, that he was born blind?" At first sight it does seem that the question indicates "there were only two explanations . . . either he had sinned before he was born, suggesting he had lived previously, or that his parents had been guilty of some transgression."[9] The two go on to build on this, saying that the fact the idea of pre-existence and possible reincarnation had entered the disciples' minds "appears to indicate it was a prevalent theory among the Jews at that time." But there is no evidence whatever that it *was* a prevalent theory. What is more, any evidence I have been able to discover points in quite another direction.

Certainly the Jews of that period believed that disease was the direct result of punishment for sin. The man was blind, therefore someone must have done wrong. We can understand this reasoning in the case of parental sin, but what are we to make of the suggestion that the man might have sinned prenatally? The truth is that in Jewish thought of the time it was quite possible to think of a person sinning prenatally as a fetus in utero. Commentaries on specific Old Testament passages of that era reveal it was believed that when, for example, a pregnant Jewish woman worshipped in a heathen temple the fetus also was guilty of the sin of idolatry! All the disciples are querying, then, is whether there was this type of prenatal sin by the man or whether his parents alone were to blame.

Incidentally, in his reply to the disciples' question, Jesus explicitly rejects the disease-as-a-result-of-sin doctrine. I can find nothing in his words here to suggest he held reincarnational views.

This brings us to what Cranston and Williams call "The Case of Elijah and John the Baptist." The prophet Elijah, who lived in the ninth century B.C., went up to heaven in a chariot of fire instead of dying in the normal manner, according to the Old Testament record. Much later, the prophet Malachi proclaimed that God would send Elijah back to earth before the final "Day of the Lord" – the end of all things. This was widely interpreted as meaning that before the Messiah came, Elijah would return to presage his arrival. The followers of Jesus, believing him to be the Messiah, naturally, then, were concerned to know what had happened to the forerunner.

Indeed, in the passage known as Peter's Confession, where Christ asks his disciples "Whom do men say that I am?" the reply comes, "Some say John the Baptist, others say Elijah, and others Jeremiah or one of the prophets."[10] In other words, some of his contemporaries took Jesus to be Elijah, come back from the dead.

The issue becomes explicit in Matthew, chapter 11. Here Jesus tells his disciples that John the Baptist is indeed "Elijah who is to come." Interestingly, according to John's Gospel, when John the Baptist himself was asked whether or not he was Elijah he denied it quite abruptly. What are we to make of the Elijah references? Cranston and Williams – in agreement with their sources – have no doubts. They are convinced that Jesus explicitly believed there is such a thing as reincarnation and that his words about Elijah and John confirm this.

But there are two overwhelming difficulties with their reasoning. In the first place, the belief in the return of Elijah was never thought of in terms of the orthodox reincarnational position that the spirit keeps coming back but as someone else. What the Jews believed was that Elijah would come back *as himself*. He had not died as other humans do and therefore God could send him back, not as a child, but as the fully mature adult he was when he died. Second, there is a literalist reading of the text here that betrays a complete ignorance of Semitic thinking and of the biblical use of typology. For a full understanding of this one should read Northrop Frye's book *The Great Code*.[11] For our purposes, however, it is sufficient to point out that when Jesus spoke of John the Baptist as "Elijah who is to come," he was in no way making a direct, one-to-one identification. This is not how typology works. What he was saying was that John the Baptist was playing the role of an Elijah, that he represented or stood for what was meant in the symbolism of a returning Elijah. To say "John is Elijah" is to speak in the same way as Paul does when he says Christ is a second Adam or as Christ himself did at the Last Supper when he took bread and wine and said, "This is my body . . . this is my blood."

I am surprised that such a scholar as Professor MacGregor would strain the text to the point where he takes all references to returning prophets as evidence that the theory of reincarnation was commonplace among the followers of Jesus. He says these questions "were characteristic of the way people were thinking at the time of Jesus."[12] Nobody doubts that it was held that great saints – and in the case of Nero, great sinners – might return, but there was no suggestion of a belief that they might be reborn as somebody new and different.

The story of the Transfiguration in Mark, chapter 9, with parallel accounts in Luke and Matthew, is also used by the authors as evidence for reincarnation in the New Testament. This time both Elijah and Moses are involved. The narrative is a familiar one. Jesus leads his inner circle of disciples, Peter, James, and John, up a high mountain. There he is transfigured before them and is seen talking with Moses and Elijah. Whether or not this episode is historical we can never know. Most liberal scholars would deny that it is. They would argue that the entire meaning of the event is theological. In other words, it is inserted into the text by the evangelist to express the early Church's deep conviction that Christ's teaching was in full accord with and in fulfilment of both the law (Moses) and the prophets (Elijah).

Undoubtedly, supposing it was historical, the theological import given to it would have been the same. But if it actually happened just as it is described – and there are modern accounts of Indian and other holy men which come amazingly close – does it provide evidence for reincarnation from the New

Testament? The enthusiasts think so, but similar arguments to those I have used above apply. Moses and Elijah are not reborn here, nor do they appear as entities other than they originally were. After the descent from the mountain, when they ask him about the coming of Elijah to precede the Messiah, Jesus tells them that Elijah, that is, John the Baptist, has come already and they (Herod) have done to him "what they wished."

In his book *Mystical Christianity*, the Reverend Thomas Strong, a contender for Christian belief in reincarnation, calls this incident "interesting" because it "indicates that reincarnation was accepted by the disciples, and Christ's reply confirms he also believes it."[13] My conclusions, after much study and thought, run totally contrary to his. You can only get reincarnation out of the New Testament if you have already determined to find it there before you start. This doesn't mean that the doctrine itself is not true; it does mean one should beware of those who too glibly assert that it's all there "in the Book" if you're willing to read between the lines.

I have spent some time on this because, as a former professor of the New Testament, I have direct knowledge and expertise in this field, and because so many unfounded claims have been and are still being made by New Agers about what the Bible "says" on this matter. The time for an honest appraisal and rebuttal of such glibly inaccurate affirmations is long overdue.

14

♦

The Christ Myth as the Ultimate Myth of the Self

"The biography of a spiritual teacher is not an account of historical facts . . . It is a symbol of the spiritual biography of that man, and all the elements of the biography are symbolic. Just through reading them properly you learn the message."
Joseph Campbell[1]

BY NOW ONE THING HAS BECOME ABUNDANTLY CLEAR. I AM convinced that the chief reason Christian teaching about life after death seems so remote and unreal to so many millions of people today is that the whole package designated by the word Christianity has been understood with a crude, mistaken literalism. A story and a whole range of symbols meant to relate us to our own, inner selves have been taken purely as historical facts about a distant, inhuman person who was a God-in-disguise. As Carl Jung argued, it makes Jesus Christ a monster figure to say that one can only become fully human in the presence of and through the death of one who is uniquely God-man.[2] In that view, we can never be what he was and is. He is so far unlike and removed from us as to be of little real help. Pretending to live a normal, human life, he really always had "four aces up his sleeve."

In *For Christ's Sake*, I argued that the underlying meaning of the Christ-myth is one of the deepest, oldest, and most universal religious ideas known to humanity: "That is the insight or belief that each one of us comes from God and lives, moves, and has his or her being in God; that each of us has a measure of His Spirit, an inner divinity, as an essential part of ourselves, and that we will one day be raised up beyond death to an eternal destiny with Him. At the unconscious level where all myths find their origin, the evangelists and early Christians saw in Jesus the prototype or 'pioneer' of our common calling and eventual future."[3] Our calling is to become what we are and to realize the divinity latent within us, God's gift of Himself/Herself. Our true humanity, I wrote, lies, paradoxically, in our divinity. To regain the power and dynamic of the Christian Gospel, the Church today has to rediscover the truth that whatever else the Christian message is about it is essentially a mythos or "truth in story form" of the Self in everyone.

Myth

We have become so used to a literalistic, historicist approach to religion in our western culture that the very mention of the word myth frightens many people. It immediately conjures up the idea of untrue legends, fairy-tales, misconceptions, or outright lies. But anyone familiar with the books or television lectures of the late Joseph Campbell or the writings of Carl Jung – or indeed with any in-depth study of religion – knows that myths are not just any kind of story or symbolism. Myths are symbolic portrayals of the basic energies and conflicts that make up the very essence of our lives. They portray vital truths that can be known or expressed in no other way because they point to realities which by their very nature are unseen yet enormously powerful. Myths are those stories that deal with the mysteries of life. As I wrote in an Easter column in 1989: "They arise from the unconscious in response to specific needs and experiences. Their function is to relate us to our own, innermost being, to other people, to nature and, ultimately to the Mystery we call God." Myths appeal to the heart, to the intuitive side of our natures. As Joseph Campbell puts it: "A symbol, a mythic symbol, does not refer to something which is known or knowable in a rational way. It refers to a spiritual power that is operative in life and is known only through its effects."[4]

The purpose of religious myths is not to entertain. It's to bring about a change of consciousness in each of us. As I noted in the Easter column, such stories "take us beyond our present, limited understandings and free us to be more truly ourselves – for others. The goal is not greater commitment to some dusty dogmas or more pious rituals, though these may all have their place. They have a much more practical and vivifying aim: to help us see our place in the cosmos and thus liberate us to live more intensely, more humanly."

When people today read the New Testament or study orthodox accounts of the Christian Gospel – not to mention when they watch the television preachers – they do so from a rationalistic, literalistic mind-set. Thus, they either dismiss the whole thing as unbelievable and, in any case, remote from their lives, or they accept the whole thing as historically factual and end up as slaves to a system of thought that makes Jesus an idol and themselves dependent, unthinking children, cut off from all others who do not share their dogmatism. Their own spiritual growth remains stunted. Their fundamentalist-style religion continues more as a part of the world's problems and conflicts than as an answer.

An incredibly potent thing happens, however, when we approach this material not as history or dogma about a person who lived two thousand years ago and who was the unique and only Son of God but as a paradigm or myth of the Self in each one of us today. It helps us to do this if, as Campbell, Jung, and others have argued, we place the Christian myth in relation to similar myths and symbols in other religions. I do not propose to do more at this point than to refer the reader to the whole library of books written by Campbell on this theme, but anyone with the time and interest can verify for themselves that the ideas of virgin births, dying and rising gods, ascending and descending saviour figures, blood atonement, or triune deities did not originate with Christianity. Campbell notes that at the end of the last century, the German anthropologist Adolf Bastian discovered in his research and travels that throughout the world the same mythological symbols occur: "death and resurrection, virgin births, promised lands and all this kind of thing. He called these 'elementary ideas.'"[5] Jung, who was interested in the question as to what it was in the human psyche that causes and supports such symbols on a universal scale, called them archetypes or archetypal images in the unconscious. They flow or arise from the very ground and depths of our being. What we have in Christianity is a particularly powerful projection or formulation of concepts hinted at or found elsewhere and at other times. With this approach in mind, then, I propose here to look afresh at the story of Jesus Christ.

The Virgin Birth

Luke and Matthew alone tell us that Jesus was born of a virgin. There is no need whatever to regard this as a historical statement, a literal fact. As with all stories of the virgin births of great personages of the past, the real meaning is symbolic or mythical. And there are several layers or nuances to this meaning. The Virgin Birth is not so much an event as it is a coded way of saying, This birth has enormous significance, it makes a vital difference to how human beings perceive both it and themselves. But that's not all. By insisting that the real father of Jesus was not Joseph – or some other man, perhaps Pantheros, a Roman soldier? – the evangelists are saying that there was a natural side to Jesus' humanity and there was a divine side or spark. If we probe further, however, and see this as part of the myth of the human Self, or of every man and woman born into this world, what this says at the most profound level is that each human being's birth is a miraculous happening. We have a physical-psychical nature from our mother's womb but we are also begotten of God. We have a divine origin or a latent divinity within ourselves as a result of divine intervention. This higher or more spiritual meaning is directly expressed in the prologue of John's Gospel where he says: "That was the true light which gives light to every human being as he or she comes into the world."

Joseph Campbell sees the mythic meaning of the Virgin Birth as the coming to awareness by the individual that he or she is more than a human animal concerned with reproduction and material things. It is "the birth of the spiritual as opposed to the merely natural life," the recognition that there are higher aims and values in living than self-preservation, acquisition of money and things, and the struggle for power or status.[6] It's a birth in the heart, or the idea of being "born again" that Jesus spoke of and which has been so misunderstood by fundamentalists today. So, the question posed to us by the Virgin Birth is not, Do you believe this literally? but, Have you experienced your own divinity within? Are you claiming your inheritance as more than a human animal – a fully human being? To put this another way: Has the Christ Principle been born in the manger of your consciousness? You don't have to be a Christian or a member of any church for this to take place.

Baptism and Temptation

Mark's Gospel begins with the ministry of John the Baptist and Jesus' baptism by John in the Jordan River. For the earliest tradition, then, Jesus' own coming to consciousness of God's Presence within and of his close relationship to that ultimate, creative energy at the heart of the universe whom he called

Father, happened at and was signified by his baptism at the hands of John. The other Gospels, most notably the Fourth Gospel, are uncomfortable with the idea that Jesus had to be baptized by John. They didn't want to admit any possible inferiority to the Baptist and they were anxious, as the tradition developed, to avoid the suggestion that Jesus needed to be cleansed from any sins. But it is obvious to New Testament scholars that Jesus, prior to his baptism, was indeed a follower of John the Baptist. "There comes one after me" – meaning, as a disciple of mine – "the latchet of whose sandals I am not worthy to unloose," says the Baptist in John's account.

At the Jordan, however, comes the moment when Jesus, having been washed by John, realizes he is his own man and that he is called to live out his own destiny. The voice from heaven, "This is my beloved Son. . ." is the mythical portrayal of Jesus' inner awareness that he is at one with the source of all being, that the divinity prefigured in the Lucan and Matthean stories of the Virgin Birth is alive in him. Thus, the baptism is also a call to commitment and dedication to that inner certainty. His real life's work has begun.

He departs to the wilderness to be alone and to contemplate in solitude what the implications of such "Sonship" truly are. He is a follower of others – parents, scribes, John the Baptist – no longer. The washing in the water is symbolic of this break with the past. Water always symbolizes consciousness and new beginnings. He has said no to nature's desire for domination and to the demands of the ego in its basic selfishness. It is a crisis point in his spiritual development, but its meaning is universal.

What happened to Jesus is what must happen to the Self in each of us if we are to tread the path that leads to becoming a human being and not just a human animal. The event speaks of the crisis to be faced by every man and woman. We must all come to consciousness of our higher nature and to the realization that the spark of divinity in us makes us one with the divine Source. We too are called to make a commitment to its ever greater realization in our lives through inner growth and loving service. The Christian rite of baptism, unfortunately, has been robbed of this richness and relevancy. It is generally something done to us in infancy and the tremendous, energizing power of the symbolism is reduced to "having little Johnny done." It becomes an excuse for a christening party and the healing potential evaporates in a liturgical mumbo jumbo heavily laced with talk of sin. It is really about saying yes to the higher Self within and the call of God to human maturity.

As soon as Jesus comes to this point, he is "driven" by the Spirit into the desert to be tempted. Once again, to see this as a matter of literal, historical fact concerned with the testing of a unique, divine being, God Incarnate, is to miss the whole point. It is to make the story totally irrelevant to modern men and women. If, however, we read it in the context of the myth of the Self, then Jesus' mystical experience – or rather what it symbolizes – becomes a powerful means of personal growth for us. The symbol of Satan in the narrative represents the conflicting energies at work in all of human life, and particularly wherever we are being challenged to make spiritual progress. Thus, in the drama portrayed in the three Synoptic Gospels, Matthew, Mark, and Luke, Jesus, alone with his soul and facing the implications of "Sonship" is tempted by Satan three times. This by no means should be thought of as the only time Jesus was tested during his earthly lifetime. The number three is itself symbolic and we are to understand that these three tests stand for or mean the whole experience of what it is like to struggle to be true to one's spiritual calling.

The first temptation is to remain at the level of the animal self, to use one's powers for purely economic or material ends. "If thou be the Son of God, command that these stones be made bread." Jesus' reply is significant: "Man shall not live by bread alone, but by every word that proceedeth out of the mouth of God." In other words, he acknowledges the importance of bread, or the basic animal needs of all of us. (Bread here, as in the Lord's Prayer, "Give us this day our daily bread," stands for all the essentials for our physical life.) But he insists that human beings have spiritual needs that must never be prostituted to the mere satisfaction of our ego. We live the higher life, the one that makes us truly human, by the words or principles that come from the divine source of all things. In our affluent western culture we suffer today from spiritual poverty because we have missed the meaning here. Drugs, violence, rootlessness, and a mindless search for diversions and pleasure are the symptoms of a society trying to live by bread alone.

The next temptation has to do with power – and not just political power, either. Satan takes Jesus up into a high mountain and shows him the kingdoms of the world. If Christ will but bow down and worship Satan, all this will be his. Christ answers: "Get thee behind me Satan; for it is written, Thou shalt worship the Lord thy God, and him only shalt thou serve." The will to power is not a temptation only of politicians. It belongs to leaders in all walks of life, from ecclesiastics to chief executive officers. To fail to see that it operates in all of us, however humble our station, is once again to miss the relevance of the myth for our own lives. We all are tempted to seek power – in personal relationships, in daily work, or in the search for recognition. Many of the ills of our society today – the oppression of women, the abuse of children – stem from a lust for or the misuse of power over others. The person truly seeking to be alive and to be a human being must struggle to worship – that is, put the ultimate value on – the energies and numinous Presence we call God.

The final temptation in Luke's account (these two are reversed in Matthew) is one whose full meaning has only come home to me while writing this book. The devil takes Jesus up to the pinnacle of the temple and says: "If thou be the Son of God, cast thyself down from hence. For it is written, he shall give his angels charge over thee, to keep thee. . ." At first sight, this seems to have absolutely nothing to do with men and women living in the twentieth century. But, as Joseph Campbell points out, this has profound, spiritual impact on our lives once we see it as a myth about the Self in each of us. The temptation is to think one is so spiritual, so called to the higher life, that one can defy one's basic, animal nature and live on another plane altogether. This would apply to those mistaken souls who take on a false or impossible asceticism; for example, those who take on obligatory celibacy when they have no charisma or special gift for it. Those who have no such commitment but cannot accept their sexuality because of a false belief that their spirituality is in conflict with anything so "earthy" partake of the same error. Jesus replies that to act this way is in fact to tempt God. We have to realize we are very much "in the body" and that to deny this is to invite physical and emotional harm. Campbell comments: "This is the great teaching of all the greatest teachers – not to disengage yourself from natural life and law, but at the same time, not to become bound to the world of sensory fact."[7]

Luke gives us the clue that this episode in Christ's life is a mythic portrayal of the deep ongoing struggle that faced Jesus – and so ourselves – throughout his life. He says that when the devil had ended these temptations "He departed from him for a season." But the key phrase is the one that concludes the narrative: "Jesus returned in the power of the Spirit into Galilee." Every time the soul successfully meets the kind of temptations or testings referred to here, there is a fresh surge of Spirit, an awareness of a flow of spiritual energy within. We are equipped to go forth to meet life and its reponsibilities renewed and empowered.

The Death and Resurrection of Jesus

In *For Christ's Sake*, I discussed the death and resurrection of Jesus at some length, and I will not repeat the details given there. It is time to look at these pivotal events from an entirely different perspective. There is no doubt in my mind that, from the mythical or spiritual standpoint, these key moments must be seen in the wider context of the universal archetypes of dying and rising gods found throughout the religious history of our race. One has to be mindful of the Egyptian myth of Osiris, of the dying and rising corn god of ancient fertility religions, and the various descents into the abyss of Greek mythology, to name but a few.

While the Christian story takes up the best in all of these and states the core truths in the most potent form yet known to humankind, it is by no means unique. What is different about it, however, is that it claims to be rooted in historical facts. After a lifetime of study, I take these basic facts to be facts indeed, although I am convinced the Church's orthodoxy has not always interpreted them correctly. But mere historical facts of themselves remain dusty and remote unless we see and experience in ourselves the dynamic, life-giving energy of the myth to which they point. In the suffering, death, and Resurrection of Jesus Christ, we find the mythical statement of the deepest truths about the spiritual journey of everyone. What good does it do us that a Jew of the first century was crucified, dead, and buried, and then raised to a new plane of existence by the power of God?

To answer this question, I repeat, we have to see behind these events the story of the human Self. The whole account of Jesus' willing acceptance of the cross – in some Gnostic narratives he goes to the cross joyfully, serene, and aware that he is saying yes not just to his fate but to the inevitable contradictions of life itself – is about how we as spiritual beings are to face the adventure of living. The cross stands for the continuing struggle to say no to the desires and demands of the purely animal self and to say yes to responsibility and the pain of spiritual growth.

As Scott Peck has made so beautifully clear in his best-seller *The Road Less Traveled*, all the great spiritual leaders, particularly the Buddha and Jesus, have made it clear that life is difficult. Neurosis stems from trying to deny or to escape this. True human-beingness is about facing this fact gladly. The spiritual life is necessarily one of discipline, of taking up one's cross. Campbell notes that even Nietzsche says that if you say no to a single important factor in your life – even if it is some deep source of pain or grief – you've unravelled your life because "life is a context of formally related and integrated contents."[8] This is not masochism or some stiff-upper-lip approach but a realism that in the end brings joy and maturity.

The cross, then, in Jesus' sayings about taking up one's cross and following him, is to be understood in this way. But when we come to the actual Crucifixion, the meaning is taken a step further. The ultimate "cross" for humans is our mortality, the fact that to be born is to suffer from a terminal illness. Peck says that life is about giving up things. We give up our youth, then our children, then our work. The final thing we must give up is our life itself. The point about the death of Christ on the cross is not that he suffered terrible torments. Thousands of Jews were crucified under Roman rule in Judea and elsewhere. The meaning is that he entered into the universal experience of death voluntarily because of his trust in God's faithfulness and in the power of love.

There are all kinds of important mythical factors at work in the New Testament insistence that Jesus was three days in the tomb.[9] For our purposes here it is enough to say that one of the points being made is that he was truly dead. It was not a case of swooning to be revived again as various speculative books have suggested over the years. The same point is behind the statement in the Creed that "he descended into hell." It means, quite simply, he really died. Then, in an event that no reporter or television camera could have discerned – which is why there is no eyewitness account in the Gospels of the Resurrection itself – God raised him from the dead. He had a new, transformed body just as the seed that falls into the ground and "dies" is resurrected in an entirely fresh form of being.

We have already examined the evidence for this and the nature of his appearances to the disciples. What concerns us here is that this is a parable or myth of the resurrected Self. As Paul insists in his classic expression of the meaning of the Resurrection for the rest of humanity, we are to be raised to experience new life precisely as Jesus was (I Cor. 15). Campbell says: "The cross symbolizes the earthly body, and what Jesus was doing was going through the cross to the father and transcendence. That's why he returns Easter Sunday radiant."[10] When Paul says that he no longer lives but "Christ lives in me," he is referring to his identification with this principle of dying to a merely materialistic or phsyical existence and rising to a life lived according to the values and call of the Spirit.

This whole myth, therefore, has relevance and power not just in terms of our final destiny at death but as a principle or norm of ordinary day-to-day living. The key question arising from the death and Resurrection of Christ is not, What do you make of an event that happened two thousand years ago? but, Are you and I constantly experiencing today what it is to die to the past and to rise again to what Paul calls, "newness of life"? That is the paradigm for the spiritual life whatever our personal faith or religion may be.

Summary

The Church has for centuries insisted that Christ is every person, and represents all of us. This, however, misses the profound truth of the myth that the reverse is also true. Everyone who comes to consciousness of their true nature as a physical-spiritual entity is Christ. It is not a matter of following or emulating some distant, historical figure. It is seeing oneself as wholly identified with the same truths and principles that moved and energized him. In a real sense, as Jung insisted, the individual is naturally "imbued with a latent divinity."[11] Like Christ, the idea of "two natures in one person" describes each of us. It is a description of the direction "of any human life, which is to say that psychic maturity resides in the discovery of one's native divinity."[12] All of this, in my view, makes the truths of the story of Jesus as relevant and vital to our lives as our very next breath.

◆

PART THREE

THE
RELIGIOUS
WITNESS:
Three
Christian
Sects

Introduction

In introducing this brief look at how three Christian sects look at life after death, I want to make it clear that I am not using the word "sect" in a pejorative sense. *The Concise Oxford Dictionary* defines a sect as a "body of persons agreed upon religious doctrines usually different from those of an established or orthodox Church from which they have separated." The three groups described here fit that description. The first two, Seventh-Day Adventists and Jehovah's Witnesses, arose from similar historical roots and have much in common, in spite of their marked differences. The third, Christian Science, though also "born in the U.S.A.," stands rather more by itself.

15

◆

The
Seventh-Day
Adventists

ADVENTISTS AS A RELIGIOUS MOVEMENT WITHIN CHRISTI-
anity are universally characterized by their emphasis on the
expectation of an imminent return of Christ to inaugurate the
consummation of the present world order. In other words, they
expect the Second Advent or coming of Jesus Christ at any
moment. Their origins can be traced to the early part of the
nineteenth century when extraordinary religious ferment swept
through much of the northern United States. As a denomina-
tion, they date from about 1831 and the teaching of a man called
William Miller in Dresden, New York. Having spent many years
in Bible study, particularly Old Testament prophecies thought to
predict the end of the world, Miller became convinced that the
Second Coming would take place in 1843-44. His movement
attracted numerous converts from the more staid, traditional
churches, and a newspaper, *The Midnight Cry*, became the chief
vehicle for spreading the Adventist message. Many tent-meetings

and conferences were held throughout the northeast as crowds
thronged in to get instructions on the impending millennium.

Very soon, however, particularly after the 1844 date came and
went without a sign of the promised Advent, the movement
split into a number of factions. Miller kept saying the end was
imminent, but others disagreed. It became impossible to get
unanimity on alternative dates; every factional leader had his or
her own views. And there were other, theological differences as
well, for example, over whether or not the soul itself is immortal. The original church, called the Evangelical Adventists,
maintained a more or less orthodox Christian position regarding the nature of the afterlife and gradually lost out to more
adventurous-minded sects. Today, the chief Adventist denominations are the Second Advent Christians and the Seventh-
Day Adventists. Since the latter are the largest and by far the
best-known, they afford the obvious example of Adventist-type
thinking for the purposes of our study.

As their name reveals, the Seventh-Day Adventists have
decided, on the basis of Bible study, that the Jewish Sabbath,
from sundown on Friday to sundown on Saturday, is the proper
day for rest and worship. Their beliefs are characterized by a
staunchly Protestant theology with a firm conviction that the
final, infallible authority in matters of faith is the Bible. Adult
baptism, by full immersion in water, is the norm. Independent
research has frequently confirmed that their well-known disciplines of abstinence from alcohol, tobacco, tea, coffee, and meat
have resulted in health statistics significantly better than those
of the general population in North America and other developed countries. There are some 40,000 Seventh-Day Adventists
in Canada, about 710,000 in the U.S.A., and the global figure
stands at about 7 million.

The Afterlife

Brian Lee, forty-two, is the director of public affairs, religious
liberty and communications for the Ontario Conference of

Seventh-Day Adventists. I talked with him about life after death on a bleak and blustery day in mid-January, 1990, and here is a verbatim account of that interview:

"We believe that at death a person goes into a sleep. The soul, by which we simply mean the life essence or energy, returns to God [is absorbed back into God] and the body, of course, returns to the dust. Things remain that way until Christ's visible return to earth. Then, those who are in Christ [faithful believers] are resurrected in a perfect body and, together with the living who are in Christ, they are caught up to reign in the heavens with Christ for a thousand years. [This is the promised millennium.] Those who died without Christ remain in the grave. At the end of the millennium, Christ again returns to earth with all the saints or faithful ones. Those remaining in the grave are resurrected, and Satan is loosed for a final battle between the forces of good and evil. Satan will be defeated, together with the wicked who fought on his side, and the earth will be consumed by fire and destruction. At that point, God will create a new heaven and a new earth, according to the prophecies, with a new Jerusalem as its capital. The saints will inhabit this renewed earth forever."

I asked Lee about final judgement and he said: "You are judged at the moment of dying. All who have loved God and lived in conformity with Christ's teaching will one day be saved."

He said that in the Adventists' view, you don't necessarily have to be an Adventist or even a Christian to inherit eternal life. It's a gift to all who love and obey God with their whole heart. There is no such thing as a fiery, eternal hell, in their beliefs. Those who are finally rejected are "extinguished completely."

What will the life to come be like? "It will be all that your heart ever desired, a renewed earth, renewed relationships – Paradise."[1]

16

♦

Jehovah's Witnesses

MOST PEOPLE KNOW LITTLE ABOUT JEHOVAH'S WITNESSES except that they refuse blood transfusions, are sometimes difficult to get shed of when they come knocking on the door, and can be seen standing resolutely, if somewhat forlornly, on street corners holding up a tract or magazine at odd hours of the day or night. As one parishioner said to me at the church door some years ago: "I don't know what they believe but I sure admire their zeal."

The religious organization known today as Jehovah's Witnesses (The Watchtower Bible and Tract Society) numbers roughly 3 million members in well over 200 countries. There are about 750,000 of them in the United States, and their struggles for religious freedoms not only there but in Canada, Great Britain, and in many African nations have been instrumental in securing the rights of all other religious groupings as well. They have been persecuted frequently in their 120-year history, particularly in fascist or newly independent states, because of their refusal to salute the flag, vote, or take part in any of the other rituals of loyalty traditionally thought to belong to citizenship.

While not totally pacifist, because they would fight for Christ in the final battle, Armageddon, they refuse to take up arms on behalf of the civil authorities. Their well-known stand against blood transfusions, based upon a literal reading of both Old and New Testament passages which forbid the eating of blood (see Genesis 9:4, Leviticus 7:26, Psalm 16, I Chronicles 11:17-19, and Acts 15:29) has been another key area of controversy. Though not much has been said or published about the fact, Jehovah's Witnesses were among the first victims of Hitler's infamous concentration camps.

The movement, like many other adventist groups, originated in the United States in the nineteenth century. A draper's son, Charles Taze Russell (1852-1916), left traditional Christianity because he could not reconcile the teaching about a loving God with the concept of a fiery, eternal punishment in hell for obdurate sinners. He drifted as an agnostic for a time before coming under the influence of the same kind of thinking that had led to the founding of Mormonism, the Seventh-Day Adventists, and other millenarian denominations.

Russell gathered a group around him in Pennsylvania in the 1870s to study the Bible prophecies about the Second Coming of Christ. They called themselves the International Bible Students and in 1879 began publication of *The Watchtower* magazine, which has a circulation today of over 10 million copies in dozens of different languages around the world. Publishing this, plus another magazine called *Awake!*, as well as numerous books and pamphlets, remains the key activity and service of the organization wherever it has spread.

Basic Beliefs

Russell and his successors believed that Christ would return soon to lead the forces of Jehovah (from *Yahweh*, the Hebrew name for God) against Satan and his minions in the Battle of Armageddon.

This would mark the end of the world order we have known and begin the millennium, or one-thousand-year reign of Christ on earth. At the end of the millennium, Satan will be let loose for a brief time for one more trial of the faith of believers, and then the total perfection of paradise will be instituted and last forever. As early as 1872, Russell believed that Christ would return secretly in 1874 and that the end battle would come in 1914. His convictions were set down in a small book, *The Object and Manner of Our Lord's Return*, which was widely circulated.

Russell's successor, "Judge" J. F. Rutherford (1869-1941), revised and developed his ideas, particularly stressing the concept of allegiance to Jehovah's theocratic Kingdom and opposition to all existing institutions, from traditional, organized religion to the apparatus of the state. Rutherford believed that the secret coming of Christ occurred in 1914 and that Armageddon could break out at any moment. It was he who first coined and promulgated the familiar Jehovah's Witness slogan: "Millions now living will never die."

The movement has been plagued from time to time by mass defections when various dates set for the return of Christ or Armageddon have passed without incident (1975 was once held as the certain date of the end until that too passed by quite harmlessly!). In Jehovah's Witness teaching, Jesus was not God nor part of a Holy Trinity. He was the perfect man, created by God for the redemption of the world. By his death he has atoned for sin and by being raised up in a spiritual resurrection he has opened the way to immortality for all who obey Jehovah. There is no distinctive caste of clergy in the Jehovah's Witnesses and the services in their Kingdom Halls are not so much concerned with worship as with instruction in the Bible, understood quite literally.

The Afterlife

Tibor Gribovsky, a forty-nine-year-old businessman, is an elder in the movement. Charles Dunn, sixty-five, is a friendly giant of

a man who makes a highly successful living as a country auc-
tioneer. Like Gribovsky, Dunn is a lifelong Jehovah's Witness. I
met with the two men for some time in order to learn firsthand
what the Witnesses believe about life after death.

"The first thing we believe is that death is real," they said.
"When you're dead, you're really dead. We don't believe in the
immortality of the soul because it's not in the Bible."

They went on to explain that "we don't have souls, according
to the Bible. We *are* souls. The soul is you, the essential person."
In their view, the dead know nothing and are held as a memory
in the mind of God. At death, the entire organism disintegrates
and is returned to the dust. The life force or energy returns to
God. But there are two classes of people, two resurrections, and
two kinds of eternal bliss. Taking a verse from Revelation, the
two men said Jehovah's Witnesses believe that there are 144,000
of "Jehovah's anointed," including the apostles and martyrs of
the earliest Christian era, who will be resurrected to a spiritual
life with Jehovah in heaven; of these, some 10,000 are still living.
Since they believe that Christ has already secretly returned (in
1914) those of the 144,000 who have died since then have gone
immediately to be with their God. This, they said, is the "first
resurrection." The general resurrection of all others who have
died before Armageddon begins – some time very soon – will
take place gradually over the millennium. During this period,
the earth will progressively be cleansed and returned to the
paradisal state of the first Garden of Eden. Those faithful who
live through Armageddon will remain and will be able to pro-
create until the proper population level is reached, according to
Jehovah's plan. Any who have resolutely and stubbornly
resisted Jehovah's call to obedience will simply be annihilated.
There is no such thing as hell or everlasting punishment. As the
dead are resurrected, they will be given a "second chance" to
align themselves with the divine will.

After the brief, final fling of Satan at the close of the thousand
years, those who have proved worthy will go on to live forever
on this by now perfected planet, this earthly paradise, where sin,

suffering, and sorrow will be no more. As the Bible says, "The lion will lie down with the lamb" and all of nature will be restored. Those sinners who have steadfastly refused salvation will simply be annihilated. Jehovah's Witnesses, since Jehovah is a "God of organization and order," will run the entire show under Christ's command. As Gribovsky and Dunn agreed, "Paradise is not a democracy!" Of death itself, they had this to say in summation: "Death is simply like falling asleep. So, whether you are a believer or not, there's really nothing to fear either way."[1]

17

♦

Christian Science

"THE PHYSICAL HEALING OF CHRISTIAN SCIENCE RESULTS now, as in Jesus' time, from the operation of divine Principle, before which sin and disease lose their reality in human consciousness and disappear as naturally and as necessarily as darkness gives place to light and sin to reformation. Now, as then, these mighty works are not supernatural, but supremely natural."[1]

These words from Mrs. Mary Baker Eddy, in the preface to her now-famous book, *Science and Health*, sum up the essential teaching of this movement. Born in New Hampshire in 1821 into a family with a strong Calvinist background, she suffered from various ailments throughout most of her childhood and early adult years. She then experienced what she believed to be a complete healing through an encounter with a well-known mesmerist or hypnotist, P. P. Quimby. As a result, she became greatly impressed with the power of the mind to heal both itself and the body. In a brief biographical sketch in her book *Retrospection and Introspection*, she tells us that as early as 1862 she had begun to write down and share with friends the results of her private study of the Bible, her "sole teacher." By the time Quimby died in 1866 she had discovered the "system" of thinking she named *Christian Science*.

Jesus Christ, she taught, was the first true Scientist. His mighty healings were wrought by following the natural laws of divine Principle rather than by some miraculous, external power. Suffering and death, according to Mrs. Eddy, are the effects of false belief in the reality of matter. For her, only the world of the Spirit is real. Thus, for the restoration of health, the proper course is not medical treatment but correcting one's thoughts. The patient must yield his or her illusions about the reality of sickness and matter and replace them with knowledge of the Truth.

In the glossary used in *Science and Health*, death is described as "An illusion, the lie of life in matter; the unreal and untrue . . . Any material evidence of death is false, for it contradicts the spiritual facts of being." Elsewhere in the book she again calls death an illusion, "for to the real man and the real universe there is no death process." In other words, then, death, according to Christian Science, is wholly unreal, an "error of thinking."

This radical approach to faith healing has been shunned by the main body of Christian churches as extreme and at variance with more orthodox Christian views on matter, sin, suffering, and death. It has even been satirized in an old limerick:

> There was a faith-healer from Deal,
> Who said, Although pain isn't real,
> When I sit on a pin and it punctures my skin,
> I dislike what I fancy I feel.

Mary Baker Eddy herself claimed thousands of cases of well-authenticated healings, and personal testimonies of healings still make up an important part of every Christian Science worship service today in more than three thousand churches in at least fifty-seven countries around the globe.

The chief reason for the initial impact of Christian Science was the fact that for a long time the traditional churches had simply ignored Bible passages on spiritual healing and the obviously deep connection between the mind and wholeness. In spite of its early success, however, the movement only really began to flourish after the founder's third marriage, to Mr. Eddy, an experienced businessman. In 1879 the First Church of Christ Scientist was opened in Boston, and, in 1881, the Metaphysical College was founded in that same city. During its first seven years, Mrs. Eddy personally taught some four thousand eager students.

Since the death of the founder in 1910, the organization has been run by a board of directors who hold office for life. Their leading asset, the *Christian Science Monitor*, is one of the world's most well-informed and responsible newspapers. There are some 1,800 Christian Science churches in the United States and 82 in Canada. The global figure stands at just over 3,000 churches. Church spokespersons told me that the church has a policy, originally set by Mrs. Eddy, of not publishing actual membership statistics. The reason she gave for this ban apparently was her fear, during the first, rapid growth of the movement, that people would get caught up by the allure of numbers. She reportedly wanted sincerity of purpose and the experience of valid healings rather than a mass of nominal members.

A Firsthand View

J. Don Fulton, a man I have known and respected for many years in my work as a journalist, is the chief spokesperson for Christian Science in central Canada. His offical position in the church is head of the Christian Science Committee on Publications for Ontario. I wrote to him and said how important it was for the purposes of this book to hear from an "insider." Then I listed a few, key questions on how he and his fellow members view death. He kindly gave me a written reply and here, as briefly as possible without changing any of his exact meaning, is what he had to say:

"The question of death is an important one. Obviously it affects the way life is lived – not just the future life, but our present life . . . Christian Scientists are human enough to be saddened when anyone dies, especially those we love, but Christian enough also to believe in life everlasting."

Fulton pointed out that his movement believes that death is neither "just lying in the grave" nor some kind of "instant propulsion to glory." In other words, there is a "working through and a progression" after death.

He writes: "I believe that until human life is fully redeemed, we will find ourselves after death with the same challenges, the same limited mortal sense of existence we had before death . . . Death is not a solution to challenges; it is not a friend. Paul characterized death as an enemy, the last enemy to be overcome. Death does not resolve things. What does resolve them is regeneration of our thought and heart. It is not the experience of death itself, but our reaching out to God that helps us to realize, know, and live more fully in accord with God. Willingness to learn and obey is the basis of our progress, and through God's grace I believe we will be helped onward."

Fulton says he is convinced that those who die without knowing God are given a "second chance." The Bible affirms God is love, and that this love is impartial and universal. Ultimately, nothing can ever separate any of us from this divine concern. God is life and He made man in His own image and likeness. "Therefore man can no more die than God can die. But this has to be spiritually discerned and proven step by step – or demonstrated in daily life, as a Christian Scientist might say."

Fulton said he is very much looking forward to heaven, but added: "I do not believe that heaven is a place so much as a state of consciousness, an awareness of God's presence comforting and guiding each of us, here and now. It's an awareness of the harmony, wholeness, and holiness that are ours as His beloved children. As Jesus taught, only when a false sense of self has been abandoned does one's life truly come rushing back, a divine gift of God. That new life, to me, includes an increasing sense of heaven, or God's presence, at hand."

◆

PART FOUR

THE RELIGIOUS WITNESS: *Other World Faiths*

18

◆

Zoroastrianism

Zoroastrianism is one of the world's oldest living religious traditions. Although today they number only about 250,000 worldwide, with some 4,000 in Canada – mainly in Toronto and Vancouver – Zoroastrians profess a faith that is estimated to be 3,500 years old and has had a profound influence upon Judaism, Christianity, and Islam. Much of Hebrew thought concerning the Day of Judgement, angels, the afterlife, and the nature of God as Light stems from this ancient source. Scholars believe Zoroastrian concepts lie behind some of the theology of the Essenes who produced the Dead Sea Scrolls (for example, the idea of a final battle between the Sons of Light and the Sons of Darkness). Similar thinking crops up again in New Testament references to the divine light, notably in the opening verses of John's Gospel. My own research leads me to the conviction that many other New Testament themes exhibit Zoroastrian parallels as well: a virgin-born Messiah, the coming of the Magi in Matthew's nativity story, the three days Jesus spent in the tomb, angels and demons, the importance attached to the figure seven, a flaming hell, a final battle of God and Satan, and the belief in a restored or new earth at the end of time.

Zoroaster, or Zarathustra as he is also known, lived in ancient Persia. His precise dates are a matter of considerable learned debate, with some experts opting for a relatively recent sixth century B.C. date and others for one as early as 1500 B.C. The majority of scholars, however, seem to be leaning today toward some time between 1200 and 1500 B.C. We know he lived at a time when many gods and goddesses were the objects of popular devotion. Personal ethics or conduct were largely irrelevant to these cults; priests alone were thought worthy of entering Paradise.

Married, with a family, Zoroaster at the age of thirty had a series of revelatory experiences that changed his life. It was revealed to him that there was but one God over all, the Lord of Light, Ahura Mazda. He immediately began to preach against the polytheism of his neighbours and to warn that, at death, there would be a day of judgement when Ahura Mazda would weigh the deeds done in a lifetime. Like all the other prophets to come after him, he was met with rejection and persecution. It took him ten years to make his first convert, a cousin. But eventually, his beliefs not only took hold of the population at large, they became the official creed of the Persian Empire. The Magi (the Wise Men of Matthew who came from the East) belonged to a priestly tribe which acted not only as royal chaplains but as missionaries for their religion throughout the realm. By the time of Jesus Christ, Zoroastrianism was the prevailing faith of much of the ancient Near East.

Cardinal Beliefs

Ahura Mazda, the Creator of all things, demands a deeply personal, ethical response from every human being. We are all part of a cosmic battle that goes on continually between Ahriman (Satan), the evil spirit, and the forces of Light. The Light, which is the ultimate symbol for the deity, will one day prevail, but meanwhile Ahriman does his best to tempt and mislead us. There is a strong emphasis upon personal responsibility and integrity, because of which Zoroastrians, or Parsis (pronounced Parsees) as they are called in India, have always enjoyed a high reputation for industry and honesty wherever they have spread. They have been enormously successful in business and the various professions, and it is worth noting that the first three Indians ever elected to the British Parliament were Parsis.

Their temples, today as in antiquity, are beautiful in their chaste simplicity. The focal ornament at the front is a font-like bronze or copper stand where the flame, "symbolizing Him Who Himself is that Eternal Light," always burns. One or two pictures of Zoroaster, who is respected but not worshipped, may hang on the walls. Little lamps, fed by vegetable oil – not candles, which might contain animal fats – sit on trays in front of the fire and may be lit as a form of prayer. In North America, the temples are open to anyone who observes the simple rules of removing his or her shoes and covering the head with a shawl (for women) or a round, Persian-style cap. Zoroastrians have a profound reverence for all of creation, especially for the basic elements of air, earth, water, and fire.

Death and the Tower of Silence

It is in Zoroastrian beliefs concerning death and the life to come that some striking features of this faith confront us. I knew about them, of course, from past study, but in order to see them afresh and to obtain them from a living source rather than written documents, I spent a morning at a Zoroastrian temple in Toronto. There are Zoroastrian communities today in India and Pakistan, as well as smaller ones in East Africa, London, Toronto, Montreal, Vancouver, Winnipeg, New York, Washington, San Francisco, and Los Angeles. The centre for the

Zoroastrian Society of Ontario (3,000 members) stands on a secluded, wooded corner, overlooking a branch of the Don River. It is only metres away from one of the busiest intersections in the north end of this sprawling metropolis, and yet it has about it the feeling of a rural sanctuary. The elected president of the society, Sam Vesuna, fifty-five, is an accountant with a multinational company. He met me, showed me the grounds and the temple, and then spent considerable time explaining what Zoroastrians believe about death and the hereafter.

Undoubtedly the most unusual aspect of the entire discussion was the description of what is known as "the Tower of Silence." Today there are only a few of them still in use, in Karachi, Pakistan, and in various parts of India. These circular structures are placed on the highest point of ground in the area and consist of high walls around three gratings, one for men, one for women, and another for children, where the corpses of the deceased are exposed. The sun beats down, the vultures and crows consume the flesh (one source said this takes an average time of about thirty minutes) and the rains wash the remains. The ground beneath the gratings slopes to a central drain where everything is filtered and rainwater is then filtered four more times before being allowed to dissipate into the earth. When the elements have bleached the bones clean, they are gathered and buried reverently. The idea behind all of this is to avoid any possible contamination of the earth with the corruption of decay.

Vesuna explained that Zoroastrians in Iran use normal burial for their dead and in Bangalore, India, where there is a Tower of Silence, the community is divided between those who use it and those who bury their deceased. Here in North America, some inter the body in a burial plot and many practise cremation, later scattering the ashes on a special plot of ground. Smiling, he said his mother tells him she is happy to be living in Canada and to know she will not be exposed in the ancient manner. But, speaking with obvious depth of feeling, he said he wished there was a Tower of Silence here. "Personally, I believe that from an environmental point of view it is the ideal and correct way to dispose of the material body. And besides, our sacred books, particularly the Gathas [seventeen songs of Zarathustra], ask us to preserve all the elements of creation."

Because death is regarded as a temporary victory of evil over good, it is a time when there is a risk of evil spirits being present, but a number of rituals limit or prevent their influence. The soul of the departed is believed to hover close to the physical body for three days after death. At dawn on the fourth day the soul begins to travel and goes to the bridge of judgement known as the Chinvat Bridge. The soul or consciousness, before crossing the bridge, meets face to face with the representation of his own conduct, a guide called his *daena*. If his good deeds in earthly life outweighed his bad, his guide appears in the form of a beautiful maiden who leads him across to "the best existence" or heaven. Where the bad has exceeded the good, the spirit guide takes the form of a "very ugly maiden" and leads the soul to "the worst existence" or hell. There is a third, neutral place called Hamista-gan, which is the temporary abode of those whose good and bad deeds balanced out. Here there is neither much happiness nor much pain.

Each of these "places" has several subdivisions depending upon the soul's "vibrations." The thinking here, Vesuna said, was that the holier a soul is the greater the frequency of its vibrations and consequently the better its place in the "astral world." However, and this is where Christianity might have done well to have followed more closely, according to Zoroaster, this is not the last of the story. For some to remain in hell would mean a kind of defeat for Light or Ahura Mazda. Consequently, one day there will come a collective, final resurrection in which all are redeemed to spend eternity with God. The good ultimately will prevail, and the earth and the heavens will be made new.

Vesuna told me that Zoroastrians believe in prayers for the dead as well as prayers asking the dead for their assistance. The Zoroastrians have a calendar with twelve months of thirty days each. The remaining five days are called the Days of the Gathas and constitute the major holy season. At this time, Vesuna explained, they thoroughly cleanse the sanctuary, recite the sacred Gathas, and remember all the departed. Among the things prayed for are the various attributes of Ahura Mazda himself such as "good mind," the power of self-control, perfection, and, ultimately, immortality.

"It's a very moving time for all of us," he said. "I like to dwell on the various good things about deceased relatives, friends, and others of my acquaintance. I have a deeply personal feeling that they are going to assist me as I try to live a better life."

The first time I ever met a Zoroastrian was in Rudyard Kipling's *Just So Stories*. In his story of how the rhinoceros got his wrinkly skin, Kipling has a character whom he calls The Parsee Man. When the Parsee teaches the rhinoceros a lesson for stealing his cakes by putting crumbs inside his skin while it hung out to dry in the sun, the Parsee chants: "Them as takes cakes that the Parsee Man bakes, makes dreadful mistakes!"[1]

19

◆

Hinduism

BECAUSE THE TWO CARDINAL TENETS OF HINDUISM – THE law of karma and the principle of the cycle of reincarnation – are by now so well-known in the West as to be almost commonplace, it is not necessary to set out a detailed description of this world religion here. Nevertheless, some background information is essential to our understanding of Hinduism's approach to an afterlife.

What has to be realized first of all is that Hinduism is a faith that is in many ways very different from most of those we examine here. Hinduism has no one founder or prophet, and there is really no such thing as a Hindu creed; it is more like a massive spiritual and cultural movement holding within itself many complex and diverse schools of thought and rituals. Its origins lie deeply obscured by the mists of thousands of years – just as the Himalayan peaks which inspire its loftier moments are so often hidden by clouds.

The very word "Hindu" is itself the creation of Islamic invaders who referred to those living beyond the Indus River as "Hindus" in about 1200 A.D. Radhakrishnan, a former president of India, is once said to have remarked that Hinduism is "more a culture than a creed." Certainly one cannot comprehend the "feel" and the essence of Hinduism without appreciating its deep-rooted relationship with the land of India itself – its mountains and life-giving rivers, its incredibly rich river valleys and broad plains, its demonstration of nature's nurturing kindness and of nature's fury, its cycles of teeming life and of unrelenting decay. For Hinduism, every rock and pebble, every aspect of the natural world, is filled with the energy of life and is part of the Divine. This is described by theologians as pantheism – everything is part of God – or as monism, all things are ultimately one.

The whole point of yoga, which means "yoke," is harmony with the one source of all being. Meditation has this same focus – inner attunement and union with ultimate reality or God. Brahman, the pure, absolute being or one God behind all and through all and in all, is defined (as in Christian mysticism) chiefly by negatives. In other words, Brahman is beyond any possible human descriptions. He is "the God beyond the word God." The many deities in the Hindu pantheon are all in varying degrees manifestations of aspects of Brahman. Another way of putting it is to say that they symbolize or express the broad range of energies active in nature and the cosmos.

Thus, while to westerners Hinduism seems like polytheism (and by inference, therefore, primitive and inferior), Hindus see themselves as truly monotheistic. There is but one Brahman, but there is a multiplicity of ways of approaching him. This accounts for the fact that the gods worshipped in one village in India may be quite different from those worshipped in the next, and also for the great tolerance shown by Hinduism for other faiths. Since there are many avatars or incarnations of the Divine in Hindu thought, the orthodox Christian view of Jesus or the saviours in other faiths make perfect sense to a Hindu.

What is important for our study is the belief that the *atman* or soul of each individual is a part or seed of Brahman. The divinity of the self must be perceived in order to see through the illusion of change and decay all around and ultimately achieve the peace of *moksha*, eternal release. This truth runs throughout the Hindu scriptures, but nowhere is it more eloquently described than in "the bible of Hinduism," the *Bhagavad Gita*. In this ancient, epic poem, "The Song of God" as it is often called, the core teaching is that our life on earth has one single end and purpose: to identify with our inner, eternal self and so attain the knowledge that we are one with the divine ground of the cosmos, God. For those familiar with John's Gospel, there are startling parallels. For example, Krishna, the incarnation of God, says to his friend, Arjuna:

> "For I am Brahman
> Within this body,
> Life Immortal
> That shall not perish:
> I am the Truth
> And the joy forever."[1]

Again, speaking of the life to come, Krishna tells Arjuna: "'At the hour of death, when a man leaves his body, he must depart with his consciousness absorbed in me. Then he will be united with me . . . Therefore you must remember me at all times, and do your duty. If your mind and heart are set upon me constantly, you will come to me. Never doubt this. Practise meditation and do not let your mind be distracted. In this way, you will finally come to the Lord, who is the light-giver, the highest of the high.'"

Krishna here is the form in which the impersonal, absolute God, Brahman, becomes the personal, tenderly loving friend of humankind. Though there are marked differences, anyone familiar with the cycle of stories in the Hindu scriptures about Krishna cannot help but see other features that echo Gospel themes. Krishna has a miraculous birth and later has a narrow escape from those who would do him harm. Just as Moses had to to be hidden from Pharaoh and Jesus from King Herod, so Krishna has to flee from his evil cousin Kamsa.

When it comes to reincarnation and the immortality of the soul, however, the Gospel parallels end. There are no words of Jesus to match Krishna's about the *atman*:

> "Know this *atman*
> Unborn, undying,
> Never ceasing,
> Never beginning,
> Deathless, birthless,
> Unchanging forever.
> How can it die
> The death of the body?"

And the same is true of Krishna's description of the rebirthing process:

> "Worn-out garments
> Are shed by the body:
> Worn-out bodies
> Are shed by the dweller
> Within the body.
> New bodies are donned
> By the dweller, like garments."[2]

Since Hinduism is as much a culture as it is a religion, to be born a Hindu and to be a practising believer are not necessarily the same thing. (A situation not unknown in "Christian" societies either!) Trying to set a figure for the number of Hindus worldwide is made even more difficult by the fact that there is no centralized form of ecclesial organization. No membership rolls are kept and so no precise figures are available. Various informed sources I have consulted put the total somewhere around 600 million globally.

The Afterlife: Rebirth or Liberation?

"The yogi's highest recompense is to become so firmly united with God after death that he need never again return to the status of migrating, mortal man. Several times in his life Mahatma Gandhi expressed the hope not to be born anew."[3]

Gokula Ranjana comes from New York City, and in 1969, having graduated from a Boston college in occupational therapy, was working as a therapist in a New England Baptist Hospital. At the same time, however, he was living a kind of bohemian, "hippyish" lifestyle and deeply aware that there was a spiritual vacuum in his life. He met with some Hare Krishna youth one day and, intrigued, decided like many other young people in the late 1960s to "give it a try." By 1971, he was ready to become a full member himself and today, at forty-one, he is an enthusiastic member of the Toronto Hare Krishna Temple.

Ranjana is an articulate spokesperson for a Krishna-centred form of Hinduism that has an ancestry going back centuries beyond the birth of Christ. In an interview, he explained the classical Hindu understanding of life after death:

"At the moment of death, the spirit-soul [*atman*] leaves the gross, natural body made up of the four elements of earth, air, fire, and water. There is also a subtle body made up of mind, intelligence, and the false ego. Depending upon the kind of life the person has led and what he or she is thinking of at the time of death, the spirit either takes this subtle body and enters another material body to be reborn or, discarding it, is liberated from the cycle of rebirth. This liberation is called *moksha*. The cycle of rebirth is *samsara*."

Ranjana was asked whether or not *moksha* or liberation was the result of one's own personal efforts (works) or a result of the gift of God (grace). The question, much debated in Christian circles, is solved, he said, by a combination of both. "Everything is of the grace of God or Brahman," he said. "But everything also depends upon how we as individuals use our free will to respond to this grace."

It is worth pointing out here that in Hindu thought this works-grace dilemma is illustrated by two theories. One, called the "kitten" approach, takes as its metaphor the way a mother cat carries her kitten in her mouth. The kitten is entirely passive, symbolizing the view that God's grace is the supreme element in salvation. The other theory, called the "monkey" approach, uses the way a mother monkey carries her young to make the point. The baby monkey is carried by the mother but plays his part by hanging on for dear life! The mother is ultimately responsible for the baby's life and safety, but not without some effort on his part as well. Most Hindu traditions take this latter view.

Ranjana went on to speak of the nature of *moksha*: "There are really two views of the liberation experience as well. The impersonalist view is that we are all God and there is no personal God. At the time of liberation from *samsara*, we are simply absorbed into the all and this itself is bliss. This union, however, is only for a time and then the process of rebirth will begin again. The predominant approach, though, is the personalist one. According to this, when one finally achieves liberation from *samsara*, the eternal person, with his or her spiritual body (a seed of which is always carried in the soul) goes into the spirit sky or 'heaven' to be with God forever. The individuality of the person always remains, but he or she is united in love with God and never returns to the cycle of rebirth again."

At this point, in spite of the differences, what he had to say was very close indeed to the Christian understanding of death and the life to come as I have defined it. Ranjana stressed that, in spite of the many gods and demi-gods of Hinduism, "there is but one God," but he can expand or make himself known in a thousand different ways. "After all, he is God!"

A Hindu Prayer
From the unreal lead me to the real!
From the darkness lead me to the light!
From death lead me to immortality!
(From the Briha-Aranyaka Upanishad)[4]

20

◆

Buddhism

IN CONTRAST TO WHAT WAS BELIEVED BY THE SCHOLARS OF the nineteenth century, we now have no doubt that there was in fact a historical person known as Siddhartha Gautama, later to become "the Buddha" or "enlightened one." However, because no "life" of the Buddha was written until several centuries after his death, the mixture of fact and legend is such that it is difficult to reconstruct his biography. Suffice it to say that he was born in or about the year 563 B.C. at Lumbini, on India's border with Nepal. Legend has it that his mother, Maya, gave birth to him miraculously. She had taken a vow of chastity but one day she dreamed that a white elephant had entered her womb. She died seven days after giving birth to Siddhartha Gautama and so, in a sense, like the Virgin Mary, can be said to have remained a perpetual virgin. The young man grew up as a prince in great wealth and splendour and was protected from all outside influences by his watchful father, a rajah, and by his sister.

Eventually, still inexperienced in the outside world, he married Yashodara and had a son by her, Rahula.

Even as a boy, he had shown an unusually keen intelligence with a remarkable thirst for knowledge. Anxious to know more about the world beyond the palace, he set out one day for a drive with his charioteer, Channa. The story tells how he took three journeys in all and each time saw something that caused him great questioning and disquiet. The first sight was that of a frail old man. The second was of an invalid, his body wracked with pain. The third was of a funeral cortège with its weeping mourners. When he asked Channa what these things meant, he was told that age, disease, and death are the common lot of all men. Pondering all of this and becoming increasingly dissatisfied with the luxury and unreality of his courtly existence, the young man came to the conclusion that the cycle of birth and rebirth was the source of all human misery. He determined to discover some way out of this morass of suffering and to teach it to others. On a fourth trip away from the palace grounds, he came across a holy man who was a beggar. The monk seemed the happiest man he had ever met, and he decided that that was somehow the way of life for him.

Thus, at the age of twenty-nine, Siddhartha Gautama bade farewell to his sleeping wife and child and set out on his personal journey alone. He travelled to famous gurus for a while and then, for a time, tried a life of even more extreme asceticism, almost ruining his health completely. Finally, he adopted a quieter, more meditative, trusting approach to his search.

One night, during the May full moon, having been deep in meditation for some hours under the Bo tree, enlightenment came. In a flash of illumination, he saw for the first time the origins of evil, the cause of all suffering, and the way by which it could be overcome. His first temptation was to enter into Nirvana, to be, as it were, a Buddha only unto himself. But he resisted this in the deep conviction that he was being called to preach the deliverance or way of salvation he had found to the rest of mankind.

The Buddha's first sermon was preached at Benares during the July full moon, and he won as his converts five ascetics who had previously spurned his company. Immediately, they were ordained by him and sent out to teach "the Dharma" (the Way) to their fellow Indians. Ignoring the Hindu caste system, Gautama Buddha took his disciples from every walk of life. As soon as there were sixty of them, he sent these out as missionaries as well. At first he didn't permit women to be disciples because they epitomized the cycle of rebirth and the craving for life; but before too long, he admitted them as well. He died at eighty years of age at a place called Kushinagara.

The Teaching

Although later developments moderated his teaching on this point, Buddha himself denied the existence of the gods of Hinduism and of other religions. Pure Buddhism can be described as a form of atheism. He took over the belief in karma and the cycle of rebirth from Hinduism, but with a significant difference. He did not accept the idea of an individual *atman*, or soul, which one day will be reunited with Brahman, or God. He believed that good deeds bring a good rebirth and evil deeds the reverse – that, he said, was the moral order of the cosmos and hence inescapable. But the basic components of the world are always coming together and dissolving to combine in new ways. It is an illusion, he believed, to hold that the individual is an independent or permanent unit. We are just a flowing together of constituent aspects which come to form a new person after death. There is no "self" to remain constant through these rebirths. Yet paradoxically, to us at any rate, though there is no immortal soul, karma links the consecutive lives together.

Buddha's need to deny the reality of the soul or self becomes apparent as soon as one examines his thought further. Here are the "Four Noble Truths," which were revealed to him at his enlightenment:

Suffering is universal, no human is free from it from birth to death;

The cause of suffering is desire or craving and these lead to rebirth and more suffering;

Deliverance from suffering is man's only salvation. This means escape from the enslavement of desire;

This can only be attained by following the eightfold path of right belief, right attitude or aspiration, right speech, right action, the right occupation or means of living, right effort, right memory or mindfulness, and right meditation or composure.

What this boils down to is an overwhelming concern with the moral principles of right living rather than with religious rites or ceremonies. The spread of Buddhism happened amazingly quickly. Its reverence for all life, its emphasis upon non-violence, and its high moral demands soon made it a way of life for most of Asia and beyond.

There are, as with other religions, two main branches in Buddhism today, the Theravadins, who are the stricter, more conservative group, and the much larger Mahasanghikas, the liberal movement. The Theravadins, more widely known as the Hinayana Buddhists, reject prayers to Buddha, images, rituals, and any form of divine help in the moral quest. The others, known today as Mahayana Buddhists, hold that salvation is not just for monks and sages but for all mankind. It's a broad, very humane religion with many concessions to the needs of popular piety. It comes close to Christianity with its belief in saviours and in its Paradise of the West, the land of Sukhavati, where the blessed live in ecstasy after death. Sukhavati was originally thought to be a stage on the way to Nirvana but it is now increasingly seen as an end in itself. In this form of Buddhism, worshipping a particular Buddha or enlightened one can be a way of holiness for those too weak to follow all the disciplines of stricter Buddhism.

Nobody knows how many Buddhists there are in China today or in the Soviet Union. That, together with the fact that

Buddhists are not organized in the way many other religions are, means that it is very difficult to say with precision how many there are worldwide. There are only some 5 million in India but, when you take into consideration Japan, Burma, Tibet, Sri Lanka, Korea, Campuchea, and other parts of southeast Asia, as well as emigration and the growing number of converts to Buddhism in the West, the total, according to some authorities, could be as high as 500 million.

"Life After Life" in Buddhism

Samu Su Nim is a Zen Buddhist master and spiritual head of a Zen Buddhist temple on Vaughan Road in Toronto. In an interview, he explained that Zen Buddhism, which originated in China and was further developed in Japan, doesn't make "a big thing" out of life after death. He said: "We prefer to speak of life after life, or of the emergence of a new birth rather than of death itself." He noted that classical Buddhism believes there are four stages or periods which are repeated continuously until the spirit escapes the wheel of rebirth and enters Nirvana. These are conception, one's earthly lifetime, death, and the intermediate stage known as "the Bardo."

Upon death, the spirit wanders to find its "proper place" for forty-nine days. In the cases of individuals who have had some very strong "attachment" to worldly ambitions, cravings and desires – even some strong emotional tie such as a deep resentment – this period can last up to one hundred days. But, at some point during this Bardo state, the decision is made and a new conception or rebirth takes place. Very holy people, sages, monks, and others, would normally be expected to escape rebirth at this point and go to Nirvana, Samu Su Nim said. But very often they are reborn because they have taken an oath to put off Nirvana for a specified series of cycles so that they can return to help others. The technical name for such a person is a Bodhisattva. He becomes more than just a teacher; he is a kind of saviour figure who assists others to attain enlightenment.

I asked the Zen master about what it is that survives from life to life. Since Buddhism asserts that the primary source of pain and suffering is illusion and that the chief illusion is the identity of the ego itself, it cannot be the self of the ego that carries on from life to life. He replied that this is precisely why Buddhists prefer to speak of rebirth rather than of reincarnation; the latter term suggests the ongoing experience of the same soul. Buddhists do not believe it is the same individual who survives but rather "the karmic forces" organized around him or her.

Nirvana, which means quite literally, extinction – as in the blowing out of a candle – is a difficult concept for westerners to comprehend. In fact, Samu Su Nim himself admits that Zen Buddhists, who like to work with paradoxical riddles known as koans, find the concept of Nirvana to have a koan-like or riddling nature. It is spoken of as extinction and as nothingness, and yet it is also described as ultimate peace and bliss. You can get the idea that it means total obliteration, but this would be to misunderstand. What is extinguished, he said, is all delusion, all defilement, all attachment to illusions of any kind. "Whatever is left is good and pure and enters into peace and happiness." When I asked him if this means some kind of absorption into the All or into the Source of all things, the master said he likes to think of it as entrance into a "universal identity" or into Buddhahood itself. As Hans Küng remarks, this is not as far from the Christian concept of heaven or paradise as a superficial glance might suggest. There is the promise of a kind of personal bliss which is entered into by trust in the teachings and power shown in and by the Buddha.[1]

The Tibetan Book of the Dead

Before leaving Buddhism, a few words must be said about this, one of the most remarkable treatises ever written. Its full title is The Tibetan Book of the Dead, The Great Liberation Through Hearing in the Bardo, the intermediate state before rebirth. The best modern translation of this singular work is by Chogyam

Trungpa, *Rinpoche*, with an introduction by Francesca Fremantle.[2] Chogyam Trungpa first received the tradition contained in
the book at the age of eight and was instructed in its teachings by
special tutors steeped in Tibetan Buddhist lore. He was given
intensive training in dealing with dying people and, while still a
child, began visiting the dead and dying. He tells us in the
preface:

"Such continual contact with the process of death, particularly watching one's close friends and relatives, is considered
extremely important for students of this tradition, so that the
notion of impermanence becomes a living experience rather
than a philosophical view."[3] The texts to be read in the presence
of the dying or recently dead are a means of guiding the
deceased through the various levels of post-death consciousness
so that, if possible, rebirth can be prevented. There are instructions on how to avoid the "mouth of the womb" and being
reborn in some animal, bird, or human form.

What is quite remarkable is that there are some extraordinary
parallels between the kind of experiences described here and
those attributed to the near-death experience by contemporary
researchers. Most notable of all is the sense of luminosity. The
text explains how at the moment after death the deceased will
see his loved ones gathered around and will not be certain
whether or not he is dead or what has happened. The sense of
being without one's ego brings a kind of "shakiness." But this is
quickly followed by a state of luminosity where one sees images
of light and then "dazzling light." To understand the book fully
would take a longer explanation of Buddhist psychology than
we have need of for our central theme. But it is important to be
aware that, whereas we in the West think of sin as always
associated with guilt and punishment, Buddhism looks beyond
sin and suffering to their root cause. This, as we have seen
above, consists of a false belief in the self and the illusory world
it projects. Instead of seeing the real world, the self creates a false
universe of its own. As Fremantle notes, the purpose of *The
Tibetan Book of the Dead* is to help the person to recognize his or

her projections and to be liberated from the ego in the light of reality. The various stages the book says the deceased spirit passes through are spoken of in terms of different deities. These are not really gods in the usual sense but a way of speaking symbolically about the energies and emotions that make up our conscious lives.

Thus, to quote Fremantle again, while the book was written ostensibly for the dead, "it is in fact about life . . . It is often emphasized that the purpose of reading the Bardo Thotrol [Book of the Dead] to a dead person is to remind him of what he has practised during his life. This Book of the Dead can show us how to live."[4]

Having been a parish priest myself and, as stated before, having been present with many dying persons at the end, I have been deeply impressed by the wisdom and depth of understanding shown by Chogyam Trungpa in his commentary on these texts, even though much of their content seems foreign to my own background. This is supremely true when he speaks about the need for honesty and for the communication of a deep sense of solidarity with the dying. "Fully being there is very important when a person dies," he instructs. "Just relating with nowness is extremely powerful, because at this point there is uncertainty between the body and the mind [of the dying]. The body and the brain are deteriorating but you are relating with that situation, providing some solid ground."[5] If those attending the dying person are very stable, he says, those entering the Bardo state will relate to that. "In other words, present a very sane and solid situation to the person who is going to die. Just relate with him, just open to each other simultaneously, and develop the meeting of two minds." Unfortunately, with so many of us dying in hospitals, heavily drugged and often full of tubes, this kind of "good death" is in the West today the exception rather than the norm.

21

♦

Judaism

THE JEWISH RELIGION, THE MOST ANCIENT OF THE WORLD'S three great monotheistic faiths, is parent to both Christianity and Islam. The current Jewish Year Book puts the number of Jews at just over 14 million, with 6.5 million of these living in North America and 3.5 million in Israel.

Unlike some other faiths, most notably Christianity, Judaism has no formal creeds to which one is required to give assent. The heart of the religion is found in the Shema (from the Hebrew word for "hear"), which is the name given to three passages of the Hebrew Bible that are recited twice daily by every deeply pious Jew. The Shema begins: "Hear, O Israel, the Lord our God, the Lord is one, and you shall love the Lord your God with all your heart, and with all your soul, and with all your might. And these words which I command you shall be upon your heart." Love of the one God is expressed by obedience to His law, the Torah, or first five books of the Bible.

The real distinctions to be made between the major branches of Judaism today are not primarily a matter of theology so much as of practice. The extent to which adherence to the rituals, dietary and other laws is maintained depends upon the attitude taken to the Torah, the "Books of Moses." Thus, while the Orthodox take the view that the words of Torah are divine and totally authoritative, and hence are very strict about adherence to all 613 commandments laid down there – on everything from personal hygiene to diet – more liberal Reform Jews take a much more relaxed position. Conservative Judaism stresses the importance of the tradition but tries to balance this with the kind of accommodations felt to be necessary in the modern world. Accordingly, although the Orthodox, who see themselves as the only "Torah-true" Jews, might deny it, it is very difficult to make the statement "Judaism believes or teaches this or that" about specific aspects of religious life. Among devout Jews of every major branch, Orthodox, Conservative, or Reform, there is widespread agreement or acceptance of the reality of an afterlife, but it ranges all the way from "a strong sense of hope" on the part of many Reform Jews to a literal belief in the physical resurrection of the body by most of the Orthodox. It would take several books to do justice to a theme as large as this where Judaism is concerned. Here I can just sketch the main outlines, and I have chosen once again to let representatives of Judaism do the talking rather than impose my interpretations on them.

We will begin with two Reform rabbis who are both internationally known and who have been friends of mine for some time. Rabbi Jordan Pearlson is the leader of the large congregation at Temple Sinai, in the north end of Toronto, and Rabbi Dow Marmur is the senior rabbi at Holy Blossom Temple, Toronto, one of the oldest and most prestigious centres of Jewish worship in Canada. Asked for his personal beliefs about the afterlife, Pearlson admitted to having been fairly sceptical when he first came out of college: "I felt then about theology the way (though I was still single) that I felt about doing marriage counselling. Since I was unencumbered by experience, I knew all the answers! But the longer I sit in the rabbi's chair and listen to my people, the more I become convinced that there are whole realms of life which can't be expressed mechanically or mathematically. I have found that the essence of spiritual maturity is the refusal to slam doors."

Noting that one distinguishing feature worth stressing about Judaism is that there never has been a concept of damnation or of eternal punishment, Pearlson said that in Reform Judaism there is a full range of options – all the way from a belief in reincarnation or the transmigration of souls to physical resurrection. He pointed out that there is unanimity among believing Jews (as testified to in prayers of memorial said for the deceased) about the concept that all souls rise to a higher level after a year in a kind of purgatorial state (She'ol). In other words, there is a period of spiritual cleansing which takes place. "An Orthodox boy will say prayers for his dead father for eleven months rather than the entire twelve to avoid the impression that he had not accumulated enough merit for at least one month."

Pearlson said that the idea of a physical resurrection has been unacceptable to the majority of liberal, western Jews, but that the belief that there is "something which does continue beyond physical death" is an important part of the Reform tradition: "In our memorial prayers we ask that God take notice of this particular soul." The rabbi noted that the idea of an afterlife is implicit rather than explicit in the Hebrew Bible. It became an important doctrine during the two centuries immediately preceding the beginning of the Common Era (the time since Christ's birth), when the old conviction that the righteous would be vindicated in this life was virtually impossible to hold in the face of repeated oppression of the Jews by foreign powers. It was the development of this teaching by the Pharisees (as opposed to the Sadducees) that ensured that life after death would remain a key tenet of Judaism for more than two thousand years.

Rabbi Dow Marmur told me he likes to express his personal approach to the matter of life beyond death in terms of hope rather than as a creedal proposition. "We don't know for certain what happens, but we have a lively hope. It is this hope that permeates our memorial prayers and our entire understanding of death." Marmur was critical of Reform Jews, particularly rabbis, who simply dismiss or skirt the issue of life after death and leave others to "fill in the gaps themselves." He said: "This is unacceptable to me. The rabbis and Rabbinic Judaism are heirs to the Pharisees and they were the party that believed in a future life."

Marmur agreed with Pearlson about the difficulties Liberal Jews have with a literal understanding of the resurrection of the body and made this interesting comment: "The ancients knew as well as we do what happens to the body when one dies. But because they believed in the unity of the body and soul – seeing man as a psychosomatic entity – they used the concept of a physical resurrection as a metaphor to express their belief that this unity continues after death." (I found, however, in talking to Orthodox and ultra-Orthodox or Hasidic rabbis, that most, though not all of them, take the language about physical resurrection literally.) In Marmur's view, the beliefs of both Orthodox and mystical forms of Judaism about the afterlife stem from the human "thirst for certainty, where hope is not enough."

Rabbi Barry Levy, Professor of Jewish Studies at McGill University, Montreal, belongs to the Orthodox tradition. He too stressed the broad spectrum of beliefs held by Jews about the afterlife, no matter which branch they belong to. He himself is "not sure" about the matter of a literal, physical resurrection. At the same time, he feels some sympathy with those Jews who quote a saying from an ancient rabbinical source in support of their literalist belief: "If God can put a soul into the body of a baby which doesn't yet exist, why can't he put a body which once did exist back together with its soul?" Levy also said he does not personally believe in repeated reincarnations, just the possibility that our soul or inner essence will be reunited with a body in the life to come. However, he pointed out that the Talmud and other Jewish sources do testify to an ancient belief in reincarnation among Jews and said that, while it is not preached as an article of faith, it is a position still widely held by traditional, Orthodox believers today.

Jewish Mysticism

Many ordinary Jews with whom I spoke in my research were totally unaware that there has also been a strong mystical tradition within Judaism from earliest times that holds quite firmly to a belief in reincarnation as part of its overall understanding of life after death. The Cabbala, (also spelled Kabbalah) a Jewish mystical tradition which developed in Spain in the thirteenth century but has roots going back at least to the second century A.D., used a kind of esoteric approach to the Hebrew Bible, including direct, mystical insights, allegory, various ciphers, and at times even astrology. The aim was to get at the "secret" meanings behind the surface texts. The most important Cabbalistic work is the Zohar, attributed to a second-century writer but actually written much later and edited into its final form by Rabbi Moses de Leon in Spain in the Middle Ages. It has been called the Talmud of Jewish mysticism and was a major influence upon Israel Baal Shem Tov (1700-60) who founded the Hasidic Movement. Hasidism began in Poland under Tov and has been from its inception a popular type of religious expression, combining passionate devotion to God – expressed in ecstatic prayer, singing, and dancing – and a strict commitment to the Law in every aspect of life. These ultra-Orthodox Jews are characterized by their old-world style of dress, with black coats and curled earlocks, and their enthusiastic approach to worship. They have many different sects around the world but the best-known in North America are the Lubavitch.

I spoke with Rabbi Dr. Ronnie Fine, who is at Chabad House, a synagogue in Montreal, and is a chaplain at the University of McGill. Fine is a Lubavitcher and totally convinced that reincarnation is an essential part of Judaism. He pointed out that the Talmud, which is "accepted by every observant Jew," has many stories and references to reincarnation. The purpose of reincarnation, Fine says, is to enable every soul to fulfill its purpose. "Every soul has a purpose and if it doesn't fulfill it in one life then it comes back again until it accomplishes it. A person could come back and live sixty or seventy years just to do a favour to one person – if that was their purpose and it hadn't yet been done." Cranston and Williams, in *Reincarnation, A New Horizon in Science, Religion, and Society*, devote a whole chapter to the Hasidim and include the following Hasidic prayer: "Master of the Universe! I hereby forgive anyone who has angered or vexed me, or sinned against me . . . in this incarnation or in any other." Those who wish to pursue the subject further should read *For the Sake of Heaven*, by Martin Buber, one of the greatest Jewish thinkers and literary figures of this century. The story concerns two Jewish mystics who were gifted with the ability to gauge from the lines in the foreheads and hands of those who came to them, as well as from their general auras, the paths their souls had taken in their previous incarnations and wanderings from life to life.

In our interview, Rabbi Fine went on to describe the position held by the Orthodox in general on the afterlife. After death, he explained, the soul goes through a period of cleansing and then goes to be with God. Once the Messiah comes, with the kindling of the "spark of God" in all who are alive at that time and the ensuing peace that will grow from that, the stage is set for the final resurrection. At that time, the soul will be reunited with the physical body and people will then be ready to live in a wholly renewed earth forever. The peace and wholeness of the original Eden will have been restored.

In summary, it can be said fairly that contemporary Judaism affords its members a very broad range of options regarding life after death and, since it is an area where absolute knowledge is not possible, most rabbis I interviewed are quite content with that. The uniting factor behind this spectrum of choices is, as already noted, the strong belief that the soul or whatever we choose to call the real person lives beyond the grave and ultimately returns to its Creator.[1]

22

♦

Islam

FEW NORTH AMERICANS ARE AWARE THAT THERE ARE NOW
more Muslims – 3.5 million – in the United States than there are
Episcopalians (Anglicans). This means that Islam is now a
major American religion. The same situation prevails in Canada, where some 300,000 Muslims exceed the number of Presby-
terians by more than 35 per cent. While Muslims do not need a
mosque in order to worship Allah, there are now well over 125
mosques in the United States and in at least one city in every
Canadian province, with several in Toronto and Vancouver.
Worldwide, there are about one billion Muslims – almost as
many as there are Christians. In spite of this, and in spite of the
fact that Islam is a religion of peace and conciliation, as its holy
book, the Qur'an, makes quite clear, there is a widespread
tendency in the West to equate "Muslim" with "terrorist." The
violent actions of a few fanatics in the Middle East, combined
with such events as the call for the death of author Salman

Rushdie on the publication of his novel *The Satanic Verses*, have tarnished the image of the entire religion. The view that all Muslims are extremists or terrorists has as much validity as the claim that all Catholics are thugs because of the bombings and shootings by the IRA, or that all Protestants are bigots and killers because of the outrages of a few Ulster Loyalists.

Space and the focus of our inquiry do not permit me even to skim the surface of the story of Islamic development or to begin to give details of the complexities of Muslim theology and laws. It would take a full volume just to describe the enormous contributions to art, architecture, and general learning that Islam has made down the centuries.[1] But, in order to set the teachings of Islam on the afterlife in their proper context, some introductory remarks must be made about the origin and leading tenets of the faith.

Since the cardinal affirmation of any true Muslim is: "There is no God but God [Allah] and Muhammad is his prophet," the place to begin is with the Prophet himself. But, it will help make things easier to look first at the etymology of the words, Islam and Muslim. In Arabic, the root *slm* means "to be in peace, to be an integral whole." From this comes Islam, "to surrender to God's laws and be an integrated whole." A Muslim, accordingly, is a person who surrenders to the rule and sway of God. Muslims believe that Islam is God's eternal religion. It was the religion of the Old Testament patriarchs and not just of Muhammad and his followers. Its central teachings about the one true God are those brought by every prophet of the past, including Jesus, or Issa ben Yussuf as he is called in Arabic. Muhammad, however, is regarded as the last and greatest of God's Messengers, "the Seal of the Prophets.'

Muhammad was born in Mecca, in what is now Saudi Arabia, in or about the year 570 A.D. Early in life he lost both parents and knew great poverty and hardship. At age twenty-five, however, having led several successful trade caravans for the wealthy widow Khadija, he married her and took his place among the privileged elite of the city. Mecca was already a prosperous and renowned centre both of commerce and of religious cults. Its strategic position made it a meeting place for the caravans trading between the Middle East and Asia, and its ancient shrine of the Ka'ba, which houses the sacred black stone, had been a focus of pilgrimages from earliest times. Polytheism and immorality were rampant. Muhammad, who was troubled by the religious and political divisions of the various competing tribes and disillusioned with the wealth and lifestyle of the privileged class, began to spend more and more of his time in solitude in the desert. About 610 A.D., while meditating in a cave on Hira Mountain, overlooking Mecca, he received the first of what were to be many revelations from the angel Gabriel. These messages, written down and collected together, eventually formed the Qur'an.

You have to read the Qur'an yourself (preferably in Arabic!) to get its full sweep and beauty, but its central theme can be briefly stated: That Allah is One God; his attributes are unbounded might and unlimited mercy. As creator and judge of every individual and nation, he will one day call all to account before his judgement throne. The greatest error is to assign divinity to any god or person other than Allah. Thus, while Jesus is highly respected as one of the greatest of the Messengers of God and his mother Mary is accorded the greatest of respect, the Qur'an explicitly condemns the view that Jesus is part of the Godhead.

In the Qur'an, there are provisions for every aspect of personal and community life. Thus, for the Muslim, there is no breach between religion and, say, politics. The faith is meant to be a total way of life. There are five basics of faith: belief in God, in angels, in revealed books, in God's Messengers, and in the judgement of the Last Day. Corresponding to these are the five rules of practice: bearing public witness at least once in a lifetime that there is no god but God and that Muhammad is his prophet; praying towards Mecca five times daily; paying *zakat* or charitable offerings; fasting during the month of Ramadan, the ninth month of the Islamic lunar year; and making the pilgrimage to Mecca at least once, provided one can afford to do so without harming close family members.

As with Buddhism and Christianity, there are two major denominations, the Sunni (90 per cent) and the Shi'a, who make up the rest. The split began as a dispute over who could properly succeed Muhammad as ruler over the Muslim community. The Sunnis believed that nobody could succeed the Prophet and so were content to choose a caliph or guardian of the prophetic legacy. He had to come from Muhammad's tribe but not necessarily from his clan or house. The Shi'as, on the other hand, insisted that after Muhammad, the rule had to pass to 'Ali, (his cousin, adopted son, and eventual son-in-law), and then from him to 'Ali's descendants. In the course of time, however, many theological and other differences emerged, none of which need detain us here.

The Afterlife

In regard to basic teachings about life after death, there are no major differences between the two main groupings. The key theme is that God has promised to reward those who do good and to punish those who do evil on the Last Day. In Islam, the moral significance of every earthly deed, thought, and word is taken to the highest intensity. The life to come, *Al-Aakhira*, is totally shaped by one's present life. The hereafter begins with the general resurrection of humanity and is followed immediately by "a moment when every human will be shaken as he is confronted with his intentions and his deeds, good and bad, and even by his failure to do good in this life."[2] By this means, the dilemma of why bad things happen to good people, while often the wicked seem to flourish, is ultimately resolved. Because of the nature of God's mercy and justice, the injustices of this present life will be compensated for.

The Qur'an more than once addresses the doubts and hesitations of those who find the idea of a physical resurrection impossible to believe: "O mankind! If you are in doubt concerning the Resurrection, [remember that] verily We have created you out of dust, then out of a drop of sperm, then out of a germ-cell, then out of an embryonic clump complete and yet incomplete, so that we might make your origin clear unto you . . . And [if you still doubt] you can see the earth dry and lifeless – and suddenly when we send down waters on it, it stirs and swells and puts forth every kind of lovely plant! All this happens because God alone is the Ultimate Truth, and because He alone brings the dead to life . . . and will indeed resurrect all who are in the graves."[3]

The judgement itself is expressed – as in many religions and myths – in terms of a weighing or balance of the good and evil to see which has predominated: "And We will set up a just balance on the Day of Resurrection, so no soul shall be dealt with unjustly in the least, and though there be the weight of a grain of mustard seed, We will bring it forth, and sufficient are We to take account."[4]

On reading through the Qur'an in its entirety, the non-Muslim will be struck by the vividly detailed descriptions both of heaven and of hell. They occur with almost startling frequency and there is no indication that they are meant to be taken as purely symbolic or metaphorical. For example, on hell: "Verily, We have prepared for the wrongdoers a fire whose flaming canopy shall enclose them. And if they cry for help, they will be helped with water like molten lead which will burn their faces. How dreadful the drink, and how evil is the Fire as a resting place!"[5] Heaven or Paradise, on the other hand, is described like this: "And He [Allah] will reward them for their steadfastness, with a Garden and a raiment of silk; reclining therein upon couches, they will find there neither excessive heat nor excessive cold. And its shades will be closed over them, and its clustered fruits will be brought within easy reach . . . And there will wait upon them youths who will not age."[6]

Interestingly, there will be different degrees or stations within both Paradise and Hell, and the Qur'an speaks as well of a kind of intermediary place between them where those who didn't incline either to good or to evil will go. "These are the indifferent ones. They will be placed in a station between Heaven and Hell, longing to go to Paradise and fearing to be put among the evil-doers."[7] In spite of the apparent starkness of this picture, there are some ameliorating factors. Those who are believers in God but whose balance of evil deeds outweigh their good deeds will only experience hell for a period of time. According to the Qur'an, God can and will forgive those who repent during this time – excepting the sin of *shirk*, which means the associating of others with his Godhead or glory. What is more, in one of the *hadith*, or traditions of the Prophet not in the Qur'an, he is reported to have said that even hell may not be a permanent place. "Surely a day will come over Hell when it will be like a field of corn that has dried up after flourishing for a while. Surely a day will come over Hell when there shall not be a single human being in it."[8] In the end, God's mercy triumphs over his justice and all shall be saved. As the Qur'an says, the divine invitation is always "to the Mighty, the Great Forgiver."

Reincarnation in Islam?

Under the heading "Religious Schools of Islam," the authors of *Reincarnation, A New Horizon in Science, Religion and Society* attempt to show that reincarnation has always been a signifi-cant part of Muslim teachings about life after death.[9] They cite a number of authorities and texts but this is certainly one of the weakest links in their overall argumentation. For example, they quote a couple of passages from the Qur'an which, in their view, support the case for Muslim belief in this doctrine. However, the meaning of the verses is quite plain and fits entirely within the framework we have already examined above. They are quite similar, and so it will be sufficient to quote one only: "Allah hath caused you to grow from the earth, and afterwards He maketh you return thereto, and He will bring you forth again."[10] This obviously means that Allah created us, is with us as we die, and will one day raise us up in the general Resurrection. To foist reincarnation upon such wording is to play fast and loose with the text.

It is true that there have been and are all kinds of different small sects and schools within Islam, as is true in the other great world religions. There is also little doubt that some of these tiny minorities have believed in a form of reincarnation. But it has never been a mainstream element in the way it has, for example, within Judaism. The overwhelming majority of Muslims and their leaders have always been stoutly opposed to reincarnational theories on the basis of "one lifetime, one chance to be responsible before God."

23

◆

Baha'i

"You shall, most certainly, return to God, and shall be called to account for your doings in the presence of Him Who shall gather together the entire creation."

– Baha'u'llah

THE BAHA'I FAITH IS A RELIGION THAT, ALTHOUGH IT draws heavily from all religions and honours all, nevertheless sees itself as a new revelation addressed by God to the entire world. Today, the Baha'is have national centres in over 145 countries and claim (though Muslims would dispute this) to be the second most widely distributed faith in the world after Christianity. There are an estimated 6.5 million Baha'is, with the majority of them concentrated in India (1.5 million) and other parts of Asia, Iran, where they have suffered constant and continuing persecution, and Africa. The figure for Canada is about 21,000 and for the United States some 110,000.

The religion of the Baha'is grew out of the teachings of two prophets or visionaries who lived in Persia (Iran) in the nineteenth century. The first was Mirza Ali Muhammed, who called himself "the Bab," which means "gateway." The Bab (1820-1850) saw himself as the latest in the long list of prophets going back all the way to Adam. Somewhat like John the Baptist, he predicted the coming of one who would be an earthly manifestation of God. He gathered a few followers but was executed in his thirtieth year for an alleged attempt to overthrow the Shah. His remains are entombed at the Baha'is' strikingly beautiful world administrative centre in Haifa, Israel. I have visited this shrine on several occasions and am always impressed by its panoramic view of the busy harbour below, and the sense of peace that emanates from its lofty interior and from the gorgeous gardens surrounded by soaring cypress trees.

The real founder and inspiration for this new religion, however, was Mirza Husain Ali (1817-1892) who took the name Baha'u'llah, meaning "the glory of God." In 1863 he declared himself to be the manifestation promised by the Bab, "Sent to redeem the world at the end of the age and to interpret God's will for a new era." He sent out notices to proclaim this fact to numerous kings and other heads of state in the Near East with the result that he was promptly persecuted, imprisoned, and finally exiled to a series of different cities from Constantinople to Acre in Palestine. Baha'u'llah wrote over one hundred volumes and, while his followers were few during his lifetime, this literary legacy, filled with spiritual truths of a very lofty calibre, became the foundation of a rapidly expanding movement.

Teachings

Baha'u'llah saw himself as the fulfilment of the predictions in all faiths of a coming Messiah or Holy One to renew the world. His mission was, he believed, to teach "the true religion of God," fill the world with justice, and save it from moral chaos and despair. He taught that truth is one, but traditions are many. All religions come from the same source and reflect the progressive revelation of divine wisdom to humankind. Religion and science are perfect partners and their resources must be brought into absolute harmony in building a better world. Sex discrimination must be abolished and all racial prejudice uprooted. Universal peace must be established. Universal and compulsory education must be provided for all. Extremes of poverty and wealth are to be eliminated through laws and the working of the individual's own conscience. There must be a universal language adopted and taught throughout the world, a single currency, and, eventually, one world government to regulate international affairs. The aim of the Baha'i religion is an inner transformation of man and society so that the world will move from the edge of ruin to harmony and lasting peace.

The whole of the Baha'i faith is marked by a moral seriousness and a commitment to the perfection of the social order that have made the Baha'is an effective and powerful presence wherever they have gone. The story of their persecution as a matter of public policy by various leaders in Iran, from the last Shah to the Ayatollah Khomeini and his successors, is one of the more tragic tales of this tragedy-torn century.

Life After Death

The best source for a concise account of Baha'i teachings on death and immortality is a paperback put out by the Baha'i Publishing Trust called *Unto Him Shall We Return*.[1] It contains selections from the writings of Baha'u'llah, the writings of the Bab, and from those of Baha'u'llah's eldest son, his official interpreter. Some of the meditations and insights are among the most comforting and inspirational I have read anywhere, particularly those dealing with the death of a child. The doctrine of reincarnation is regarded as an absurd "superstition," and there are warnings against mediums and trances as ways to commune with the dead. But, once again, rather than simply quoting from this or other books, I want to let a believing Baha'i explain her faith about ultimate reality.

Nancy Ackerman is the director of public affairs for the Canadian Baha'i National Centre, located in Thornhill, Ontario. In a lengthy interview, Ms. Ackerman said that as a Baha'i she believes deeply in the immortality of the soul, that "mysterious part of us which is the essential self, the capacity for conscious thought and moral striving." Baha'u'llah, she said, called the soul "a sign of God." It reflects God's light and then returns to him. Death "comes as a messenger of joy" to the believer. When a loved one dies, he or she is not lost but has stepped from one world to another. They live in everlasting companionship "immersed in an ocean of light." Quoting from the sacred writings, she said that it's as if a gardener were to uproot a flower or shrub not to destroy it but to transplant it from a narrow place into a wider room in which to grow.

From a human viewpoint death seems to be a rude end, but from the eternal aspect it is an enlargement of life and growth. She told me: "Our purpose here is to acquire the full spiritual capacities of which we are capable. We will strive and continue to make spiritual progress in the next life based upon the progress we've already made here. The qualities we attain to here are eternal, and we continue to mature and grow there until we attain the full presence of God." Heaven will be a purely spiritual existence but we will recognize and know one another, she believes. At death, the physical body disintegrates but nothing is annihilated. The various components live on in other forms. Death, then, is really a transformation or change of form. The body returns to the elements it was made up of; the soul returns to its Maker.

Ms. Ackerman said she and her fellow members see the life after death as "the world of vision where all concealed realities will be disclosed. We will know the truth. We will also discover those who influenced our lives unknown to us as well as those whom we knew." We will all one day be called to account for our lives; we will know we did right or wrong. But all of this will be seen in the light of the grace and mercy of God who alone knows the secrets of our hearts. There will be no physical hell, she said, but souls will be remote or close to God depending upon how they are judged. "That will be heaven or hell enough."

The Baha'is believe in praying for the dead and also that the dead can intercede on behalf of the living. She said: "When a person dies, loved ones here can assist the soul's progress [already helped by the grace of God] by special prayers and intercessions. Souls can also be assisted by good works or other acts of charity done here in their name." Finally, she noted that "everyone, believers and non-believers alike, enters the next realm in the spiritual condition they have attained to on Earth. The tests we failed to pass here will have to be passed in the world to come!" Interestingly, Baha'u'llah believed that dreams of dead loved ones and of another world to come are evidencce of a life beyond: "God, the exalted, hath placed these signs in men, to the end that philosophers may not deny the mysteries of the life beyond nor belittle that which hath been promised them."[2]

24

◆

Native Spirituality

"RELIGIOUS PERSONALITIES FROM THE EUROPEAN CULTURE have been especially limited in their ability to see the profoundly religious and spiritual qualities of the [North American] Indian traditions," according to cultural philosopher Father Thomas Berry.[1]

This is not the place to deal with the full implications of Thomas Berry's indictment of the failure of Christians and others to take the American Indian's spirituality seriously. This sad story is part of the worldwide crucifixion of aboriginal peoples over the past five hundred years. In many parts of the world, most notably in the Amazon River hinterland, this process of cultural, religious, and even physical elimination is still going on. Yet today, a remarkable resurrection of the religious traditions of indigenous peoples has taken place. What is more, it is coming precisely at a time when our devastation of the planet demands the insights into a new mode of relating to the Earth that Native spirituality has to offer. As Berry has said, "Awareness of a numinous presence throughout the entire cosmic order establishes among these peoples one of the most integral forms of spirituality known to us."[2] So far from being "primitive" in some pejorative sense, study of the original religion of the American Indian, for so long repressed and ignored by non-Indian society, shows that it contains some of the highest forms of spiritual teaching ever conceived. Indeed, its discernment of the importance of what is now called "the feminine principle" in nature, in human consciousness, and in the being of the Creator Spirit, coupled with its insistence on the sacredness of the natural world, reveals that it has possessed from time immemorial truths which are presently considered avante-garde in Christian theology!

Years ago, while at university, I spent three summers in one of the most remote Indian reserves in northern Canada working among the Swampy Cree. Since that time, and most recently as a journalist, I have had many close contacts with Native people, going with them on the caribou hunt on the eastern shores of James Bay, visiting them on the traplines, and researching numerous stories, from the impact of pollution on their ancient way of life to epidemics of teenage suicide in some Native communities, or the tragically high infant-mortality rate. This does not make me an expert on Native life, but it has given me a deep appreciation both for Indian suffering and for the enormous contribution these people have to bring to contemporary crises affecting us all. As Berry puts it, "The fate of the continent, the fate of the Indian, and our own fate are finally identical. None can be saved except in and through the others."[3]

Amerindian Religion

The most recent scholarly studies of so-called "primal religion" and the religious belief systems of native peoples around the world have revealed that the old view of a linear, evolutionary development of religion from simple superstition to the great, classical world religions is no longer valid. The myths, rituals, and beliefs of indigenous peoples are exceedingly complex and often show a theological sophistication – for example, in the insistence upon the concept of a Supreme Being – that surpasses that of supposedly "more developed" cultures. They uniformly witness to a rich view of the cosmos and of the relationship between humans, nature, and the supernatural dimension of existence.

Because of the extraordinary size and diversity of the North American continent and the cultural differences that have developed over the centuries, it would be foolhardy to suppose that the space available here is adequate to do justice to the full complexity of this subject. The religion of the Indians of the Great Plains is different from that of the Indians of the northwest coast or those of California and the intermountain region of the southwest. The Cree of the subarctic muskeg differ greatly from the Indians of the Maritimes or the southeast. Yet many traits or elements of Amerindian religion are shared not just by the Indians of North America but by aboriginal peoples the world over. Let me point to just two distinctive characteristics of the North American scene: the marked dependency of the North American Indian's religion on visions and dreams of the spirit world; and the extremely intricate and time-consuming ceremonialism of most tribes.

The traits held in common by all the Amerindians include:
◆ The belief in a spirit realm or dimension which permeates the whole of the creation. This world of spirits, gods, wonders, and numinous powers has a deep and abiding connection with the natural world. Certain natural features – rocky outcroppings, cliffs, waterfalls, lakes, forests, and islands – are regarded as sacred because at or around them the spirit presences can be felt in special intensity.
◆ There is a Supreme Being – sometimes, symbolized by a collectivity of divine beings – who most typically is a sky god, the ultimate maker of heaven and earth, the Gitchi Manitou. The

view of some scholars of a generation ago who argued that Amerindian belief in a Supreme Being postdated the arrival of the Christian missionaries has now been completely refuted. This belief, though not identical to Christian monotheism, was already there when the Christian Europeans first came ashore.

◆ The belief in the culture hero, the one who acts as a sort of intermediary between God and humanity in imparting the various aspects of the culture itself – language, the arts, hunting skills, and so on. At times, this figure is known as the trickster who acts as a quasi-opponent of the Creator and causes the divine intentions to go awry. At times, the trickster is there to explain the problem of evil, to help explain the quirkiness of fate. At others, his or her role (the trickster can take either male or female form) is to lampoon human frailties or to objectify human passions and longings. Often he or she is symbolized by a zoomorphic form: the hare, the raven, the coyote, depending on the tribe and its geographical range.

◆ The shaman or medicine man (in some tribes these could also be women) is the most powerful person in the community. By the aid of special spirit-helpers, he or she has a measure of influence or control over the power evidenced in the impact of the spirits upon the natural world. Shamans act as intermediaries between the tribe and the forces of the supernatural. Thus, the shaman is above all, a healer, a diviner of the future, an enabler who can change the weather, influence the crops, strengthen the hunter for the chase or the warrior for the fight. He or she can even communicate with other shamans across vast distances when special need arises. It is the shaman who wards off the evil spirits or the ghosts of enemies.

◆ The elaborate rituals are marked by a single overall aim – to maintain a balance or harmony between the individual, the tribe, nature, and the supernatural. The main tools of these rituals are prayers and the imitative acting out of supernatural events through dances, masks, chants, and drum music. The sun dance is undoubtedly the classic instance of this approach. At death, the traditional place of the departed is the southwest.

There the deceased live very much as they did on earth and so food and weapons – even a horse in some tribes – were left at the grave or cremation site for use on the journey.

◆ The vision quest marks the rite of passage at puberty for boys, and in some tribes for girls also. Through solitary fasting and meditation the initiate is given a dream or vision of the kind of future he or she is meant to follow. Sometimes this comes in the symbolism of a conversation with a particular animal or bird; sometimes the seekers are given the name of a specific spirit-helper or of a particular amulet to guide them into adult life. The practice of going on a vision quest is being widely revived among young Native people in the United States and Canada today. What's more, it is being emulated by many non-Natives who see in Native spirituality an openness to mystical experience that seems lacking in their own lives.

An Indian Elder Speaks

Rather than tell the story of Indian views on life beyond death myself, based upon the reading and research I have done, I spent several hours interviewing an elder of the Objibway Nation who is an internationally respected spokesperson for Native religion. I first met him in February of 1990 when he was a guest on "Harpur's Heaven and Hell," a weekly, hour-long interview program which I host on the Vision/TV network across Canada. His baptismal name is Art Solomon. His Ojibway name, which means "fast-moving cloud," is Kesheankwut. Solomon was born seventy-six years ago in the tiny, picturesque village of Killarney, on the northwest shore of Georgian Bay, Ontario. He was raised in a Jesuit-run Indian Residential School at Spanish, Ontario, but left it before reaching the ninth grade. Yet, while his formal education is meagre, his learning and leadership in Native spirituality have won him honorary degrees from Queen's University, Kingston, and Laurentian University in Sudbury. He lectures frequently on university campuses and, under the auspices of the World Council of Churches, has represented Native peoples at religious conferences in Nairobi, Melbourne, the Island of Mauritius, and at the Vancouver WCC Assembly in 1983.

Solomon is a quiet-spoken man, but when he is addressing issues such as the injustice of the penal system towards Native people – he worked for twelve years in one of Canada's best-known federal penitentiaries – or the way the missionaries and the government schools combined to suppress and destroy Indian language and culture, his words are powerful and disturbingly blunt. At the same time, he is a poet and storyteller. His creative work mixes a deep compassion with a righteous outrage. A new book about him, filled with his poems and prayers, is called *Songs for the People – Teachings on the Natural Way.*[4] Solomon renounced his Christian upbringing about twenty years ago and, while he has now come to appreciate the deep unities between the two faiths, he sees himself as totally committed to the traditional, Indian belief system. His wife, Edna, remains a practising Roman Catholic and two of his daughters (they have ten children) are nuns.

Solomon's description of Native beliefs concerning the afterlife has to be seen in the context of Indian spirituality as a whole. Briefly, he said that his people see the continuum of life and the universe as a sacred, delicately balanced harmony and whole. The idea of anyone owning any part of the natural environment, the land, the lakes and rivers, is anathema to him: "It all belongs to the Great Spirit; so it is like blasphemy to say that any individual or group owns any of it. It's a common heritage and we are here simply as caretakers." The aim of life is to live with deep appreciation of the natural world, struggling heroically against life's challenges and always seeking the help and guidance of the spirit world. All of the various rituals and ceremonies – burning offerings of sweetgrass or tobacco in prayer, passing the pipe of peace, the vision quest, enduring the rigours of the sweatlodge, or offering the cosmic renewal symbolism of the sun dance – emphasize this close communion between humankind, nature, and God. When Solomon talks about the way in which the Thunder People or spirit-helpers make themselves known, and when he describes the way in which the very elements are alive with God, you could well think this is a form of pantheism, the belief that everything is divine. Yet Native spirituality is monotheism of the highest kind. The Great Spirit, whom Solomon movingly calls "Grandfather-Grandmother of all creation," is one Lord over all.

Dr. Ed Newberry, who founded the Department of Native Studies at Laurentian University, Sudbury, Ontario, and who knows Solomon better than any other non-Indian, says that in many ways the kind of religion articulated by Solomon and other Native leaders resembles most the Process Theology of Christian thinkers like professor John Cobb at the University of California.[5] "There is the kind of witness to the relationship between the human and the natural world in Native religion that the rest of us so sorely need just now," Newberry says.

What struck me most in all Solomon had to say was the deep awareness he had of living in two worlds simultaneously. The spiritual sphere is so penetrated by the natural and the natural so imbued and surrounded by the spiritual that life and death, and life beyond death, all seemed to flow as part of a seamless unity. He described death as "just as completely natural as birth, part of the life process," and he went on to say he found it surprising and distasteful to hear anyone saying they feared or couldn't face death. "Only those who have no idea of how to live don't know how to die," he argues. "We are spiritual beings and our journey here on Earth is very short. It only makes sense that death is the gateway to our return to the spiritual world that gave us birth."

After death, he said, each one of us has to give an account of how we have used the gifts entrusted to us in the course of life. There is no concept of hell or enduring punishment, but he said his people believe there will be an experience of remorse or shame for misdeeds or failure to obey the spirit guides. Traditionally, it is believed that at death the spirit entity or soul travels southwest and goes down with the setting sun. He smiled when asked about the "Happy Hunting Ground" idea of heaven and said it was, in his view, simply a way of trying to put in human words a reality that is by nature indescribable. In conclusion, Solomon gave several examples of the dead returning as spirit-people to warn someone of impending trouble or to bring them a challenge to some heroic task or mission in life.[6]

I'd like to conclude here with a lovely Ojibway prayer which gives one an authentic "feel" for Indian spirituality:

> Grandfather,
> Look at our brokenness.
> We know that in all creation
> Only the human family
> Has strayed from the Sacred Way.
> We know that we are the ones
> Who are divided
> And we are the ones
> Who must come back together
> To walk in the Sacred Way.
> Grandfather,
> Sacred One,
> Teach us love, compassion, and honour
> That we may heal the earth
> And heal each other.[7]

◆

PART FIVE

PERSONAL REFLECTIONS AND CONCLUSIONS

◆

IT WAS A BRIGHT, SUNNY DAY IN SOUTH FLORIDA, JANUARY 28, 1990. The unprecedented hot, dry spell that had been going on since Christmas, causing a severe drought, persisted. The waters of the bay sparkled brightly and in the sky above several large buzzards wheeled in lazy circles above the royal palms. I was reminded of vultures in the desert and told my wife in jest that I hoped it wasn't an omen. The fact was, we were about to attend a lengthy seminar on death and dying at the Unity of the Palm Beaches Church in West Palm Beach. The birds were directly over the spot!

We were there to hear Dr. Raymond Moody, the pioneer explorer of the near-death experience, report on his twenty-five years of experience in the field. Moody, a round-faced, spectacled man in his late fifties, is a professor of psychology at West Georgia College, Carrollton, Georgia, and a psychiatrist with a large, active practice. His best-selling book, *Life After Life*, has

241

now gone through over forty printings. The title of his two-hour seminar was "The Light Beyond."

What struck me most about his presentation, apart from the fact that it was an opportunity to hear and talk with him firsthand, was the way he began it. Moody explained that in the past twenty-five years he has personally heard the NDE stories of some 2,500 patients. Describing himself as "a lapsed Presbyterian" whose father, a surgeon, was a hard-headed sceptic about matters of faith, he said he himself had always believed that being dead meant the end of all consciousness – finis, oblivion. His personal "conversion" came when he could no longer ignore or explain away the evidence his patients were bringing him. Moody made it plain that in the near-death experience we are not dealing with scientific proof of life after death but with "the relationship between different levels of reality." In other words, the evidence for life after death deals with a reality that science is not equipped to weigh, measure, or validate in a laboratory. He said: "The fact that it is not scientific proof doesn't worry me in the slightest. I want to tell you I have absolutely no doubt now that there is a transformation of consciousness at the point of death and we do go on." Describing the expanding research that has gone on intensely since the publication of *Life after Life*, and the fact that during his recent visit to nine European countries he discovered that doctors there are reporting exactly the same experiences he has documented, Moody summed up: "My own conviction today is that these patients have indeed had an experience of another life beyond."

I will return briefly to the Moody seminar shortly. For now, I simply want to point out that when this former sceptic was repeatedly faced by the unanimous testimony of those who had come close to death and returned, he found the evidence such that he was persuaded to change his mind. If this were the case with just one doctor, it would be interesting but hardly convincing. The truth is, however, that this is a phenomenon I have observed over and over again in my own research. It is remarkable how many atheists and agnostics have felt compelled to soften or change their stance on this issue when faced themselves with a near-death experience, or when they objectively examine those of others. What holds true of the NDE seems also to apply in regard to the wider picture. As Colin Wilson, the author of *Afterlife* and himself a case in point, concludes: "In every single case where a sceptic has persisted in studying the facts, he has ended up more or less convinced of the reality of life after death."[1]

My own conviction, following much thought and in light of what I consider to be the evidence and also the vast range of arguments for and against, can be put in far stronger terms. I am today fully persuaded and assured that death is very much like birth. It is the traumatic but essential passage into a new phase of life. It is not for some holy huddle or a select few, but for all. And it will so far surpass anything we have ever dreamed of as to make all present attempts to describe it, religious or otherwise, seem tawdry and utterly inept. What's more, it's my deep conviction that such a belief is completely congruent with the utmost respect for both intellect and science. Indeed, I am now convinced it would be flying in the face of intelligence and rationality to believe otherwise. I will give the grounds for what I call this "reasonable faith" in a life beyond and try to flesh out what I believe this life will be like in a moment.

First, though, I have to deal with an objection. There will be those who, knowing my background as an Anglican minister and a former professor of the New Testament, who will say that I came to this question not as a sceptic but as one within the tradition of faith – in other words, that I was already committed to my conclusion before beginning to study the matter. The point is, you have to begin from where you are and nobody is a *tabula rasa* completely without biases. But it is a serious error to suppose that where one comes from inevitably dictates where one will arrive.

When I began my study of the historic Jesus for my book *For Christ's Sake*, I had no idea the argument and evidence would lead me where it did. Those who knew my Low Church, evangelical upbringing were greatly surprised at my conclusions.

Indeed, the furore over the book, including organized attempts to have me dismissed both as religion editor at the *The Toronto Star* and from my lectureship in mass media at the Toronto School of Theology, would never have occurred had I not tackled Christology with an open mind. I have adopted the same approach in tackling the question of death and I have no doubt that some of my conclusions will not sit well with orthodox believers in many camps. No one can prove his or her attempt at objectivity, it has to be recognized as present or lacking from the work itself. I can only say that it would be a great mistake for anyone to think that because a person belongs to a particular religion or grouping that this is an unquestioned commitment or one arrived at easily and without intellectual effort.

I am extremely grateful to past teachers at Oxford who taught me the nature of evidence, especially my philosophy tutor, Richard Robinson, who constantly forced me to rethink all the faith presuppositions of my youth. He was, and still is at age ninety-two, an atheist and he has a mind like a steel trap. I owe him a lot. I am also indebted to the great philosopher, Gilbert Ryle, whose lectures on logical positivism – the view that only sense-data can give rise to true knowledge – were a must for every classics student during my Oxford days. His position denied the very possibility of knowledge about life after death. Ryle was wrong, but he forced me to confront one of the most formidable arguments I have ever encountered. I can only say that I came to this study with an open mind, fully prepared to follow wherever study, intelligence, and the evidence led. I simply ask that the reader do the same.

Why the sudden "Boom" of Interest?

One of the themes of my column for some time now has been that there is a vast spiritual hunger in western society just at a time when the influence and membership of traditional religious bodies are in decline. Organized religion has always addressed the existential issues of the meaning, value, purpose, and ultimate fate of human life, but today its answers are not being heard or no longer make sense to the greater part of the population. Partly, this problem arises from a communication gap of gargantuan proportions; partly, it seems to me, it stems from a certain embarrassment at a past, undue emphasis upon spiritual things to the neglect of the body and this world altogether. The present attempt to prove Karl Marx was wrong when he described religion as the "opium of the people," the search for justice and the "preferential option" for the poor as opposed to a religion of "pie in the sky when you die by and by" – all this is praiseworthy and long overdue. But instead of dealing with both sides of "what God hath joined together," the rush to social justice has left out the matter of personal, spiritual concerns virtually altogether.

I am not normally a great admirer of the pronouncements of Cardinal Josef Ratzinger, head of the Vatican's Congregation for the Doctrine of the Faith (the modern successor to the notorious Inquisition). Recently, however, I found myself in total agreement. Ratzinger was quoted in the *Catholic New Times* of Toronto saying that there is a great lack of teaching about "last things" in the Church of today. "Belief in eternal life has hardly any role to play in preaching . . . The Kingdom of God has been almost completely substituted by the utopia of a better future world . . . which becomes the true reference point of morality," he said. This lack, in my view, accounts in some measure for the growth of the more conservative and the fundamentalist groups, as well as that of various sects and cults.

But the real impact of this lack of teaching can be seen in the popularity and omnipresence in the media of New Age thinking and practices. There is the same abhorrence of a vacuum in the spiritual realm that there is in the world of physics. In the discussion of life after death, the spiritual gurus who fill the vacuum today are the Shirley MacLaines and the Dr. Raymond Moodys, not the Billy Grahams, the Pope, or the Archbishop of Canterbury. To be perfectly blunt, there is an incredible lack of intelligible teaching and thinking about ultimate matters in our churches and synagogues. The old formulae are either boring or nonsensical. What I believe we are seeing in the contemporary secular and in the non-traditional religious awakening regarding life after death is the voice of the collective unconscious. It is saying, If the traditional symbols, language, and thinking about so central an issue are so utterly inadequate, then new ones must emerge. Since there is such a thing as life after death, this is too essential a concern to be left to outdated concepts or worse, to total neglect.

Dr. Marie-Louise von Franz speaks of the "symbol impoverishment" of traditional Christian thinking about death and eternity.[2] It is this poverty that the modern NDE and other similar phenomena may be meant to enrich.

Wish fulfilment?

The most common criticism levelled against anyone who believes in a life beyond death is that it is simply wish-projection. It was the argument proposed by Lord Bertrand Russell, and you can hear it in almost every discussion of the subject. One of the respondents to a research questionnaire I sent out gave a typical version: "There is no life after death. Religious theories that maintain that the soul or spirit lives on or joins a universal spirit stem from fear of death. It is natural to have that fear but foolish to let it sustain illusion. What happens to the flame when the candle burns down? It is the same with consciousness . . . We humans have invented immortality because we do not want to die." But, as in the case of Sigmund Freud's thesis that belief in God is an illusion fostered by wish-projection, this argument cuts both ways. It is equally possible that an adamant refusal to believe either in God or in immortality is itself an instance of wish-fulfilment. Plenty of people with an absent or violently abusive father have abundant subconscious reasons for denying the existence of a deity characterized as a heavenly Father. Indeed, Freud's own atheism may well have had its roots in his acknowledged inner conflicts over his own father.

Similarly, those who cannot abide the thought of being answerable to any other being than themselves, those who wish to live completely self-centred, selfish lives, or those who know they have committed unspeakable crimes against their fellow humans all have cause to hope that death brings oblivion and that the grave is the end. There is more than one kind of fear where death is concerned. Historically, one can point to many bright people who sincerely wished that life after death were an illusion. Colin Wilson offers an interesting observation from the autobiography of the Cambridge philosopher C. D. Broad: "So far as I can tell, I have no desire to survive the death of my present body, and I should be considerably relieved if I could feel much surer than I do that no kind of survival is possible."[3] Broad told Wilson in an interview that he'd been so lucky and success-ful in this life that he wouldn't want to have to take a chance in another world. "I'd rather just come to an end."

I have tried to examine myself as honestly as possible, and I can truthfully say that I have not consciously allowed wishes of any kind to affect my own thinking. In fact, the more I contem-plate the matter the more I am convinced that just the very opposite of the wish-projection theory is true. I now believe that the near-universal, ancient human belief in personal survival after death is the result of the kind of experiences of contact with another world or reality we have already examined in this book. The so-called primitive belief of all aboriginal peoples in such survival, for example, flows not from wish-fulfilment but from the hard evidence of their own experience that death is not the final word.

Anthropologists and others have often noted the fact that native peoples, living much closer to nature and with their minds uncluttered by modern media babble, are in a much more intimate relationship with "other worlds." Their experi-ence of the phenomena described in the first two chapters of this book, plus other paranormal forms of awareness which we as sophisticated moderns may well have lost, have convinced these people down the ages. Not the other way around. This, I believe, is the true source also for the amazing congruence of thought about life after death in the world's great religions.

Escapism or Commitment to Life?

This leads directly to another key question. Why be concerned at all with this problem when there are so many burning issues to be faced right now in this world – poverty, global hunger, the AIDS crisis, the environmental deterioration of the planet, and much more? Isn't concern about ultimate survival a form of escapist narcissism? Obviously, I don't think so or I wouldn't have engaged in researching and writing this book in the first place. It is important, however, to answer this line of reasoning. Of course we must admit that undue concern about one's personal survival can indeed be a form of escape from tough realities close at hand. And it is all too true that at times in history religion has been exploited to keep the masses so preoccupied with rewards or punishments in the next world that they had little time or thought for the cause of their miseries in this one. But, as the old Latin proverb says, *abusus non tollit usum*, the wrong use of something in no way makes its proper use illegitimate.

Escapism goes in two directions. Individuals or groups can use undue preoccupation or busyness with this world's needs and problems as an escape from facing all spiritual questions completely. Many people refuse to think or talk about a hereafter because it reminds them very sharply of their own mortality. It may seem paradoxical, but they blot out the entire subject as part of their attempt to repress or deny the fact that in life we are all caught in what the iconoclastic British psychiatrist R.D. Laing once described as "a sexually transmitted disease with a 100 per cent mortality rate." In spite of a lot of progress in recent years, death is still a taboo subject in western society. At an international conference of more than five hundred people who deal daily with the dying and bereaved, in London, Ontario, in May 1989, Dr. Sandra Bertman, a professor of humanities at the University of Massachusetts School of Medicine, observed: "We're generally uncomfortable with death and dying because it brings us face-to-face with our own mortality." Bertman went on to say that people are most afraid, not so much of death itself, but of the dying process. "They especially fear a raw and agonizing death – the indignity of deterioration, dependence, and unlimited, hopeless pain," she said.[4]

Far from being escapist, the consideration of and commitment to a belief in a life beyond death lends an enhanced intensity to living in the here and now. It means that the whole of one's life is lived *sub specie aeternitatis* – in light of the eternal. Nobody in his or her right mind would want to argue that Jesus espoused any form of escapism. Indeed, the certainty that the whole of this life is lived under the shadow of and in preparation for a wider life to come is what fuelled and drove his involvement with the desperately needy folk to whom he directed his ministry. It eventually led him to lay down his life in the ultimate sacrifice of love for others. As the chairman of philosophy at Emory University in Atlanta, Thomas Flynn, told the conference: "We focus on death, not out of morbidity but to appreciate what life really is." What I have said about Jesus could, of course, be said of the leaders or founders of other world religions, and of saints and martyrs down the ages. I have seen and accompanied Mother Teresa in her mission of mercy to the poorest of the poor in Calcutta.[5] In my travels as a journalist, I have visited with many lesser-known but equally committed heroes of other denominations and faiths in remote corners of the world. All of these were eloquent witnesses to a faith that is firmly rooted in this world and its agony, and yet which draws its inspiration and hope from the conviction that there is a fuller life to come.

Recently, I did an hour-long interview with a Jesuit priest, Father Michael Czerney, for my television program. Czerney was about to leave Canada to replace one of the six Jesuits murdered by a right-wing death squad at the University of Central America in San Salvador in November 1989. He knew that he and the other Jesuits going to that strife-torn country to take up where the martyrs left off were marked men. There is extreme risk. Yet such is his passion for justice and his faith in unseen dimensions to life that he was eager to involve himself in the lives of struggling Salvadoran peasants. One could speak of the late Archbishop Oscar Romero in that same country, or of people such as Archbishop Desmond Tutu in South Africa. The point is clear. A firm understanding of and a belief in a destiny beyond the joys and griefs of this life infuse one's earthly life with a sense of depth and meaning and purpose that energizes the whole of one's being. Responsible, zestful engagement with practical, down-to-earth opportunities and problems results from the realization that what is done has lasting or ultimate consequence. It has a larger context or meaning than the surface one.

This is not a matter of seeking future rewards or of fearing future punishments, as some sceptics might argue. Rather, it's an awareness of being fully alive and in touch with a Source beyond oneself. Carl Jung, in *Memories, Dreams, Reflections*, talks about the great importance of everyone, especially as he or she grows older, having a faith or "myth" about death. He cites the way in which this can conjure up helpful, enriching pictures of life "in the land of the dead," and how these in turn lead to more intense living at the end of life: "The man who despairs marches towards nothingness, the one who has placed his faith in the archetype follows the tracks of life *and lives right into his death*. Both, to be sure, remain in uncertainty, but the one lives against his instincts, the other with them [my italics]."[6]

The Reality of Death

Some words of Chief Seattle are often quoted: "There is no death, only a change of worlds." This is an eloquent and epigrammatic way of affirming belief in a hereafter. We know what is meant. But, taken literally, it contradicts experience and harsh reality. I cannot accept the sometimes sentimental, sometimes overly ethereal explanations of those who sermonize at funerals or who erect elaborate philosophies on the theme that death is unreal or simply an illusion. Some, I know, having a strong commitment to the idea of human immortality or innate divinity, put these views forth with great sincerity and goodwill. But, after much thought and study, and in spite of the incredible persuasiveness of such writers as Plato and Plotinus, to name only two, I do not believe in the innate immortality of what is known as the soul or inner essence of the person, that is, in an eternal entity that inhabits the human body. I greatly respect the views of those who do so, and I cannot prove them wrong, but it is a late addition to Christian thinking, is nowhere to be found in the Bible, and the reasons for this belief do not seem to me convincing. Thus, when I see books with such titles as *You Cannot Die* (on reincarnation, by Ian Currie), or stories with similar headings in the press, I read them with more than a little suspicion.

I know that in our culture few people come into actual contact with death. It has been so sanitized and removed from daily life that its very naturalness as part of the human cycle is remote from all but a tiny minority. However, when you have been an active priest for seventeen years as I have, with more than eight years in a large parish setting, you come face-to-face with death and bereavement constantly. Someone who has never presided at the funeral and the graveside of a dead child, a beloved spouse, an esteemed friend, or a devoted parent cannot know fully what it is like. You know, as the casket is lowered into the grave and you turn to try and offer comfort to those closest to the deceased, that death is very real indeed. Yes, it can come as a friend when one has suffered long, or when one is old and "full of years." But even then it has a finality and marks a separation which is tragic and real for those who remain.

Death, no matter how firmly committed one may be to the conviction that it is the gateway to a new stage of being, is an end of something very important. We have a deep, inner sense that it is an intruder or, as the New Testament firmly declares, an enemy. It is not the last word, but it is a word that has to be heard by each of us. It is the gateway to life beyond but it is a narrow one – with all the pain as well as all the joy of birth. It is the one supreme act which no one else can undertake for us. To minimize it or to attempt to gloss it over with pretentious terms is to trivialize and mask its significance in the total drama of what it means to be a human being.

Weighing the Evidence

I have said that I am compelled by the evidence to believe that death is ultimately transcended by new life. This evidence does not provide by itself total, irrefutable proof. There is an act of faith or trust involved here, just as there always is with belief in God as well. But it cannot be stated too strongly that this is supremely not an act of what is commonly called "blind faith." It is faith firmly supported by and based upon a process of sound, rational thought.

The great philosopher of religion, William James, said that the evidence for life after death is "abundant" but it always leaves room for doubt.[7] This principle, of course, holds true for most of the areas of life that really matter. We do not have hard-and-fast scientific proof for our ultimate values of goodness, beauty, justice, love, fidelity, or the sanctity of life either. As I have written elsewhere, "All of us, scientists, agnostics, believers, or unbelievers alike hold values and truths which no scientific experiment could ever verify."[8] What matters most to me in reaching the decision I have regarding life after death is the amount and the quality of the evidence on its side. If one is to have a "reasonable faith," as opposed to "blind trust," one ought to have some very sound reasons. It is time to state mine as succinctly as possible. None by itself would be sufficient. Cumulatively, though, they make a body of argument which I, at any rate, find thoroughly convincing.

The Principle of Catholicity

By catholicity, of course, I mean universality. It has always been a criterion for orthodox Catholic doctrine that it be what has always and in all places been believed by everyone. Belief in life after death extends far beyond any Church dogma in meeting this test. It is one of the most fundamental, most universal of all human convictions, whether we consider the earliest cultures of our primitive ancestors or take public opinion polls of North Americans in the late twentieth century. It is expressed and understood in a myriad of different ways, but the essential intuition is identical. Critics will say, of course, that truth is not a matter of opinion polls or weight of numbers. If the majority of people, for example, were convinced that the earth is flat, that wouldn't make it so. But that's too facile. There is overwhelming evidence on the other side that this quaint belief, however popular we hypothetically agree it could be, is dead wrong. Such is not the case with life after death.

I doubt if one could find one scientist, philosopher, intellectual, or even high school student for that matter who would come forward to espouse the flat earth view. But with life after death we're not just talking about billions of people down the ages from every race and continent, we're talking about some of the most brilliant minds of all time, many of them scientists or doctors, as well as the great mystics or the founders of various religions. For example, Sir Bernard Lovell, one of Great Britain's most distinguished astronomers, is a committed believer and can be found on Sundays serving as a lay reader in his parish church. In summary, then, when a belief is as ancient and as widespread as this, it would be unscientific to take it as proof of anything, but it would be even more unscientific to disregard it or to try to slough it off with clever but hollow quips.

Science

I do not believe that science will ever "prove" life after death because, by definition, it concerns a dimension or level of reality with which science can never deal. The idea that only science can give us true knowledge stems not from science but from its bastard offspring, scientism, and is itself incapable of scientific proof. What weighs heavily with me, however, is not just the number of scientists today who themselves believe in an afterlife but the way the new physics and the findings of neurosurgeons in regard to brain/mind functioning have opened a path for belief through difficulties once thought insurmountable.

We have seen how the majority of modern physicists have moved to the view that the whole of the material universe is a cosmic dance of energy. Indeed, physicists such as David Bohm and others speculate that the universe is essentially an indivisible whole. The material, visible world is but the unfolded or "explicate order," which is the surface or outer layer, so to speak, of an invisible, implicate order of being.[9] Consciousness or mind would belong to this underlying, psychic order of being and would be the cause of matter rather than emerging from it as was previously thought.

It is significant to me that so great an authority on the human psyche as Marie-Louise von Franz has concluded from her study of the dreams of the dying that the symbolic statements there about another realm beyond this natural world have "relevance to the fact that modern physics has also begun to speak about universes 'with which we cannot communicate.' We stand at a great turning point in modern science, which points towards the healing discovery that we are everywhere surrounded by rationally impenetrable mysteries."[10]

At the same time, brain specialists such as Sir John Eccles have now postulated that the human psyche exists independent from the physical brain.[11] This was the belief of William James, of Wilder Penfield, Sir James Jeans, and even of the man who was a scientist, sceptic, and materialist for most of his life, Thomas Huxley. In his *Essays on Some Controverted Subjects*, published in 1892, Huxley said that there is more to the universe than just matter and energy: "There is a third thing . . . consciousness, which I cannot see to be matter or force, or any conceivable modification of either." He went on to say that a student who admits the existence of immaterial phenomena in the form of consciousness must also admit the possibility of "an eternal series of such phenomena."

An article in *Science Digest* (July 1982) refers to Sir James Jeans's book *The Mysterious Universe*. Even in the early thirties Jeans foresaw that scientific knowledge was headed towards belief in "a non-mechanical reality; the universe begins to look more like a great thought than a great machine. Mind no longer appears as an accidental intruder into the realm of matter; we are beginning to suspect that we ought to hail it as the creator and or governor of . . . matter."[12] Then, from Albert Einstein himself: "Everyone who is seriously involved in the pursuit of science becomes convinced that a Spirit is manifest in the Laws of the Universe – a Spirit vastly superior to that of man, and one in the face of which we, with our modest powers, must feel humble."[13]

Should anyone still doubt the significance of the kind of thrust I'm describing here towards a belief in life after death, I suggest he or she read Guy Murchie's latest book, *The Seven Mysteries of Life*.[14] Murchie, who is now eighty-three, with a science degree from Harvard and a lifetime of observation and philosophizing about the universe, argues strongly for transcendence as we engage in "the inexorable drift from our present earthly finitude toward some sort of an infinitude far beyond." In his preface, Murchie says "the seventh mystery of life, the greatest of all," is divinity or whatever one chooses to call "the unknowable essence that leading thinkers have long believed somehow exists behind the creation and maintenance of all body, mind and spirit." This kind of growing consensus from those who take science seriously can no longer be ignored.

The NDE Revisited

I do not agree with Hans Küng's view in his book *Eternal Life?* that one cannot be a believing Christian and a believer in reincarnation. Some notable Christians of the past, as we have already seen, have believed in it. However, I respectfully must say I do not find the evidence produced to be either firm or persuasive. Reincarnation does not solve the problem it first came into being to deal with, that of suffering and injustice, and the more I read and hear of alleged past lives the more convinced I am that these are the induced products of the imagination, repressed memories, and what Jung calls the collective unconscious of the participants in these hypnotic regressions.

The case with the near-death experience seems to me to be quite different. I have no doubt that the roughly 8 million North Americans who have experienced an NDE have experienced the threshold of another mode of being. At the seminar in Florida with which I introduced these reflections and conclusions, one had to be impressed with the vividness of the details described and with the results in the lives of those who had these experiences. Dr. Bruce Greyson, a psychiatrist at the University of Connecticut where much of the leading research on NDEs is being done today, said on a "Man Alive" program on CBC TV (April 3, 1990) that he has been amazed at the way in which personalities have been changed by the NDE. Whereas psychiatrists might work for months or even years to effect very small modifications in someone's behaviour and outlook, "the NDE seems to achieve so much more almost overnight."

Moody says that his patients reported that, so far from being a kind of dreamlike reality, what they experienced had such a compelling clarity and power that it made this life seem like a dream in comparison. "They became quite convinced that our consciousness here is quite limited," he said. "In the realm where they went, to think something was to communicate it. To see something was to feel you had it under a microscope and could vision its very being." Moody's patients, corroborated by thousands of others, said they had no sense of space or time during the NDE. "They are aware of having a body," he said. "But it's like a cloud of light." The biggest difficulty of all, Moody reports, is that the NDE is so ineffable, so unlike anything previously experienced, that the experiencer can scarcely find words to come close to it. "They do the best they can but they keep telling you that they can't really describe it."

It is my considered opinion that while these people have not been dead, they have obviously been very close to death, and so what they have to say must be listened to. Their experience, tying in as it does with similar experiences down the ages and in every culture, must be taken seriously. It is evidence that something quite extraordinary begins to happen at death. It also suggests very strongly that the glimpses and hints of an afterlife in the great religious literature of the world may well be based not upon flights of fancy but upon a kind of knowledge we are only now beginning to understand.

The uniform witness of those who have NDEs, whether they are atheists, agnostics, lapsed religionists, or devoted believers, is that to enter the dying process is to be led towards an incredible light. This is why Moody has entitled his latest book *The Light Beyond*. But the near universal testimony of mystics and prophets from the beginning has also been that the ultimate source of all being, God, is Light. Well over two thousand years ago, the prophet wrote: "Arise, shine: for thy light is come . . . The sun shall be no more thy light by day; neither for brightness shall the moon give light unto thee: but the Lord shall be unto thee an everlasting light, and thy God thy glory."[15]

There are those who claim too much for the NDE and feel they now have the elusive proof that many have sought for immortality. They don't have any such proof. But, again, I would argue that it is foolish and unscientific to go to the other extreme and pretend that all of this has no relevance. No natural explanation has been found that can sweep this phenomenon away. In its absence, there is little alternative but to accept some kind of transcendental explanation in its stead. The NDE is only a plank in the platform of evidence, but it's an important one, in my view.

Religion

We have already looked at the testimony of Christianity, Judaism, Islam, and other religions regarding death and a life to come. There is no need to repeat that here. I resist as well the temptation to cite the relevant passages from the scriptures of the world's great faiths to illustrate my point. The majority of dedicated believers in these various folds may feel it is grounds enough for certainty that their sacred books affirm life after death. But as a critic of fundamentalism of any kind, whether it be religious, political, or economic, I cannot follow that route myself. It is not enough to say "It's in the book" and demand assent. As I have said elsewhere, one of the most serious mistakes of ultra-conservative Protestantism is that it has rejected the idea of an infallible Pope only to create the idol of an infallible "paper Pope" – the Bible. Other religionists too are guilty of this type of bibliolatry concerning the Qur'an, the *Bhagavad Gita*, or whatever. On the other hand, it does not follow from this that one loftily dismisses the wisdom and insights of the world's inspired scriptures. Quite the opposite. Standing as I do within the Christian tradition, I take the witness of the Old and New Testaments with total seriousness. I have studied them for years and find new spiritual light and truth breaks out from them continuously. I believe God speaks powerfully through them to our human condition.

Thus, when the Bible and other sacred books describe unseen realities beyond this present order, I find it the intelligent thing to do to listen carefully. If I wanted to learn about any other area of life, from fly-fishing to gourmet cooking, I would listen to the experts. I would read the most experienced writers in the field. I would pay particular attention to the "superstars." It makes sense, then, to do no less when it comes to the most central issue anyone can face: Is there a life to come and what is it like?

Those who know my work, particularly my newspaper columns, know that I am only too aware of the shadow side of religion and that I am far from blind to its failures and shortcomings.

But still, for me, as for countless millions of others, the really great, inspired geniuses of history are those who pioneered and taught in the spiritual arena, who addressed the ultimate questions of God, origins, meaning, ethics or conduct, and the final purpose and destiny of all things. Their voices, their willingness to die for their vision of an eternal truth, and its resonance within my own innermost being, the sense that their testimony confirms what I have already unconsciously known to be so – all these constitute essential evidence indeed.

The Resurrection of Jesus, of course, is of utmost importance for me. I find the evidence for it even more convincing today than in 1985, when *For Christ's Sake* was written. It plays a large part in my thinking about an afterlife. I believe the evidence shows that God raised up Jesus from the dead. We can differ widely over what kind of "event" we think this was; the bottom line, as they say, is that something quite extraordinary took place that first Easter. It was not the resuscitation of a corpse. It was a total transformation into an entirely new mode of being, a sign and seal of the New Age to come. I believe the New Testament witness that, as he was raised, so too shall we all – and all humanity.

The reader must form his or her own conclusions. I can only say this: there are very few areas of life where absolute certainty is possible. One of the more tragic seductions of religion, as well as other spheres of thought, is the promise of total certainty. What we have to do in most cases – indeed as they do in any court of law – is weigh up the available evidence and make our decision. When it comes to life after death, I can say with humility that I am now convinced the overwhelming weight of evidence falls on its side.

God, Faith, and Life After Death

In the course of my research, I received a very thoughtful letter from a sceptic in which he chastised me for giving any thought to "evidence" whatever. His point was that, since belief in God and belief in a life to come are really matters of faith, it is a sign of weakness or of unbelief to look for concrete signs or reasons. I believe he has a restricted view of faith, and that any "leap" of faith must be based upon a right-brain as well as a left-brain approach. Theology, for example, is *fides rationem quaerens*, faith seeking a rational basis and mode of expression. Our belief in God is certainly not an irrational act; its final step of trust is better described, perhaps, as non-rational instead. It is an act of commitment like marriage or friendship. But, at the same time, my critic had a point. When all is said and done, my belief in life after death is ultimately rooted in the nature and grace of God.

Though I have radically revised many of my understandings of my own faith, Christianity, over the years, I am more convinced and sure of the reality Whom we call God today than ever before. It is because of the kind of God revealed by the teachings of Judaism, Christianity, and Islam in particular – "the People of the Book" – that I am persuaded of the truth of spiritual planes beneath, through, and beyond this world of space, sense, and time. It is for this reason that I believe God has a destiny for each of us that transcends the grave. We will live in a dimension of being where all of life's promises will be fulfilled, not because of our inner merit or innate immortality, but because of God's faithfulness and love. Because God is God, the forces of evil, disease, decay, and death do not have the last word. When one stands by the grave of anyone, be they dearly beloved or total stranger, it is this faith that is the source of all comfort and hope. You believe it with your intellect; in your heart you know it to be true.

What Will It Be Like?

In "The Love Song of J. Alfred Prufrock," T. S. Eliot depicts Prufrock at a tea party in a room where women "come and go Talking of Michelangelo."[16] Upset by the idle chatter and tormented by existential doubts about the meaning of life, he wonders what would happen if he were to try to squeeze the universe into a ball, "to roll it toward some overwhelming question." To say, in fact, "'I am Lazarus come from the dead,/Come back to tell you all.'" He imagines what he would feel like, if, having done this, someone "settling a pillow by her head," should say: "'That is not what I meant at all. That is not it, at all.'"

This is more than a mere indictment of the triviality of much of what passes for social conversation; it recognizes the overwhelming importance for humanity of the issues we have been discussing. If there is a God, and if there is a destiny beyond the grave, the questions of what kind of God and what kind of destiny become absolutely crucial. Unfortunately, there is no Lazarus, come back from the grave, to tell us all.

I know that throughout the centuries there have been individuals who have claimed to have gone farther than our modern NDErs and to have actually been given the privilege of touring heavenly realms. Those who are familiar with the voluminous writings of Emanuel Swedenborg (1688-1772) will know that this brilliant scientist-turned-theologian claimed to have had direct contact with angels and the spiritual world. In his longest, eight-volume treatise, the *Arcana Coelestia* (*Heavenly Mysteries*) from 1756, Swedenborg gives detailed descriptions of the world to come. Without wishing to offend his current followers, however, I have to say that I have found his and other, similar visionary expositions interesting but unconvincing. They are a testimony more to the inner, imaginative life of those concerned than to an objective reality.

Leaving the visionary approach on one side, then, what can be said with any degree of certitude? One thing is for sure, life after death will be utterly different from what we, from our limited stance, have supposed. As T. S. Eliot has reminded us, words sometimes crack and strain under the burden we impose on them. If there is one thing all those who have ever tried to describe otherwordly realities agree upon it is that ordinary language cannot express the glory. We see as yet, to quote Paul, "through a glass darkly; but then, one day, face to face."

Judgement

After leaving a tunnel of light, those who have had a near-death experience say that they are drawn to a Being of Light and that in this Presence they have a review of everything they have ever said or done. Some patients of Dr. Moody described this as a kind of "memory theatre." They saw their lives from a third-party perspective and were able to feel how their actions had been injurious or helpful to others. "There is some regret," he said, "but it is not a harsh experience." Reading both modern and ancient accounts of the NDE, you have to be impressed by the constancy of this theme of an evaluation or judgement process of some kind. In religions and mythologies of every type the symbolism of weighing scales, of judgement thrones, of difficult bridges to cross, or of narrow gates witness to the near-universality of this belief. It lies behind the use of such antithetical images as heaven and hell, damnation and bliss.

Several things combine to convince me there will be a reality corresponding to these descriptions or metaphors – my own inner, moral sense, my belief in justice, and my understanding of God's nature. In the words of the Anglican prayer, we have all done and said things "we ought not to have done" and we have left undone the "things we ought to have done" during a lifetime. There is both justice and wisdom in seeing the real meaning and implications for ourselves and others of all we have been. Part of our being human consists of our awareness of responsibility to our Creator, the ground of our being. The judgement or evaluation process is a necessary corollary of that. I think it would be a serious mistake to downplay or attempt to gloss over this aspect of a future life. While I have already made it abundantly clear that I cannot find any rational grounds for a belief in a literal hell, Purgatory, or any other form of temporal or eternal punishment, we will realize just what we have been and done, and this could bring more than mere regret. It could be a terrible experience indeed, and will surely be so for the murderous tyrants and torturers of this age. But it will be in the presence of the Light which not only reveals and brings judgement but brings love, mercy, and forgiveness as well. That, I believe, is why the researches of Moody and the others have shown that the millions who have had an NDE testify to the incredible sense of love and of healing that surrounds them, even at the moment of deepest remorse.

Healing and Growth

The word "salvation" is an old-fashioned one and greatly misunderstood as well. It comes from the Latin words *salvus* and *salvatio*, meaning wholeness. In fact, it comes close to the essential meaning of our word "holy," which also refers to a wholeness of mind, body, and spirit. In any case, all the sacred literature of the major religions and mythologies speak of the life after death as a restoration to wholeness. It is salvation. It is tempting here, because of their great emotional power and haunting beauty, to quote an entire anthology of such passages, but space does not permit it. These words speak of the crooked being made straight, the blind to see, and the deaf to hear. All imperfections of mind or body will be done away forever. Let me just cite one such vision: "And God shall wipe away all tears from their eyes; and there shall be no more death, neither sorrow, nor crying, neither shall there be any more pain . . ."[17]

What is fascinating in this respect is that when you examine the experiences of the millions who have now had an NDE you find these people – many of them agnostics, atheists, or lapsed believers – saying that when they are greeted by deceased loved ones they appear whole and in the very prime of life. According to Moody, the "dead" are said to seem to be as they were (or would have been) at about age thirty rather than the age at which they died. But it will not be solely a matter of physical and mental healing. As St. Augustine said, "We shall know, and we shall grow." Life after death, as we have hinted already, will not be a static, boring contemplation of eternity. Our spiritual journey has only just begun in this life.

There is much to discover ahead, much maturing to do, many new challenges to understand and overcome. In *Harpur's Heaven and Hell*, I suggested that it may well be that God will allow us to become co-creators of entirely new, unimaginable worlds and universes yet to come. Consider the possibility of having one's deepest questions answered – how this world was made, why God thought our free will worth the risk of all the terrible suffering we have inflicted upon each other and the planet, what the inner meaning of our own lives really was. As a writer, I know how often the vision in my mind and what I can actually find words to express differ when the work is done. Imagine the joy of a Mozart, a Beethoven, or a Glenn Gould on hearing and being able to express for the first time the music behind the music they were able to write or play! Think of the scientists or the philosophers who once wandered along the shore of the ocean of knowledge now able to plunge right in. As Paul says, "I shall know even as also I am known."

To know like this is to grow beyond the shadow to the reality of what we are meant to become. We will not all start at the same place, and no doubt we shall assist one another as the grace of God assists us all. There is a lovely passage in a book by Jungian analyst Marion Woodman called *The Pregnant Virgin* in which she is talking about the way in which the various stages in our earthly lives can resemble the caterpillar's metamorphosis into a butterfly. She notes that we can look back at our own lives and see this process at work. Then she adds: "As we mature, we are astonished at the accuracy with which fate uses one situation to develop the attributes necessary for another. From the soul's standpoint, it is possible that life as we know it now is a uterus in which the subtle body is preparing itself for the world in which it will be born when our physical body dies. Many of us, at one time or another, have felt a propensity for wings."[18]

Space and Time

We have already had reason to comment on the way in which language, designed to deal with this world and its experiences, fails us badly when we try to express feelings and thoughts about other dimensions and levels of reality. This becomes very evident when you examine the semantics involved when we talk specifically about death and a transcendent life to come. We realize that such a life will be one that is somehow freed from the shackles of time and space. Yet, because these are the spectacles through which we look at things, we repeatedly use time and space metaphors or imagery. Thus, for example, we speak of life *after* death, a time-based formula, or of life *beyond* death, which reveals a spatial bias. Indeed, much of what seems like crudity or incredulity in our language about heaven – "above the bright, blue sky" as the children's hymn puts it – stems from this kind of linguistic inadequacy. It is not easy to escape from this trap, but we must at least be aware of the problem and make some attempt to surmount it. Not to do so is to put an unnecessary obstacle in the way of those who are struggling for understanding in this area yet are put off by most descriptions of it.

When I was an undergraduate at Oriel College, Oxford, I belonged to a group called The Socratic Club. The president at the time was the well-known writer and Christian apologist, C. S. Lewis. Lewis, an articulate agnostic who then found faith, was then a don at Magdalene College and later became professor of English Literature at Cambridge. I well remember one evening when he was talking about coming to grips with the notion of an existence or state of being free of space or time. He used the example of a novel and its author. Within the pages of the book, the story unfolds and the characters develop in an orderly fashion. They live inside a certain pattern of both time and space. But to the author (or the reader) standing outside the confines of the drama, these limitations need not apply. We accept them tentatively as we read, but there is a sense in which everything in the book is here and now for us. We can open it at any part of the story we wish to. We can see it all happening in a flash. Neither the late Professor Lewis nor I would have argued that there are not faults with this illustration, but it does help a little. At death, it is as though we have stepped out of the book. The old restrictions will be replaced by a new kind of freedom.

Significantly, one of the points Dr. Moody says has impressed him in the NDE accounts of his own patients and those of other researchers is the way in which those who have the experience testify to this phenomenon. He told us at the Florida seminar: "While our language is either temporal or spatial when talking about this subject, the NDErs uniformly report that there is no awareness of space or time in the experience they have had. Nevertheless, they are aware of having a body which they describe as being 'like a cloud of light.'" All of this brings us back to what was said earlier about eternal life. This, we saw, describes not an endless or infinite time stretching menacingly and forever before us but rather a totally different quality of life lived in an everlasting *now*.

If this interpretation is correct, as I am convinced it is, it is of enormous help because it surmounts what I consider to be one of the greatest difficulties in the Christian teaching about what happens at and after death. Unable to escape from the snare of time-space thinking, the Christian view (as well as that of other religions) is that there is a considerable waiting period between the decay of the physical body and the general resurrection for the life to come. While the soul or spirit struggles in Purgatory or waits, disembodied, in some other place, the body is not resurrected or somehow reproduced until the end of the world. We are never told how this is supposed to occur.

Dr. Marie-Louise von Franz rightly calls this a "gap" in Christian thinking that is both striking and serious in its consequences for belief. But if to die is to escape immediately from the whole time-space web of being, then the entire concept of waiting periods or intervals between death and final resurrection falls to the ground. The resurrection is at the moment of death. As Paul rightly says, "To be absent from the body, is to be present with the Lord." The miracle of the resurrection of the body – be it the emergence of an astral or subtle body or some other form – occurs immediately.

This is not the place to elaborate upon the ramifications of this approach for some of the more bizarre timetables for the afterlife erected by religions both ancient and modern. But it is the chief reason why I find such predictions so totally wanting. In conclusion, I find it encouraging that several important contemporary theolgians, Karl Rahner and Ladislaus Boros in particular, have also espoused this approach. They, too, argue that the resurrection and final judgement take place immediately after death. Linear or historical time stops at death and the new life in its fullness begins. They see the resurrection no longer as "a recreation of the old body" but rather as a prolonged existence of the person in a spiritual body.[19]

Who Goes to Heaven?

Asking the question, Who will go to heaven? is not my preferred way of posing this concern. Nevertheless, I have phrased it so because it is a quickly recognizable formula. The traditional teaching of most religions, particularly Judaism, Christianity, and Islam, has been that some will and many will not "inherit eternal life." Indeed, talking with some groups or watching the television preachers, one gets the impression that the next life will be a very restricted one indeed. They and their followers will be in and the rest of us will be out! I'm reminded of the familiar but not terribly sound (theologically speaking) hymn that declares: "When we all get to heaven, what a day of rejoicing that will be." Of course, when it says "all" it doesn't really mean all. It means all those who think as we do, all those who belong to our particular little group.

I recently wrote a column in which I described an experience my wife and I shared at an Anglican church where we live. The preacher said quite bluntly that only those who have been "washed in the blood of Jesus" will go to heaven. When I told him at the door of the church that it seemed he had a very narrow view of heaven he simply nodded and agreed that he had indeed. It was evident he liked it that way. In this view, only a small minority of fundamentalist Christians will end up in heaven, never mind the vast majority of other Christians, the Muslims, the Jews, the Hindus, and all the others of different faiths or of none.

But it's not just extreme Protestants who take this route. The other day, *The New York Times* carried a front-page story on the threat by the assistant Roman Catholic Bishop of New York, Austin Vaughan, that the state's Governor, Mario Cuomo, "is in danger of going to hell" for being pro-choice on abortion. Vaughan said: "I think for a believing, educated Catholic to take the position he's taken, he takes a very serious risk of going straight to hell."[20] Frankly, I find such a rigid, short-sighted pronouncement almost incredible. I would have thought the days of preachers spending the first half of their sermon making people feel guilty and afraid, dangling them over a fiery hell, and then the second half telling them the Church just happens to have a remedy for their remorse and terror, were over and long past. Unfortunately, that's not so, and a great deal of unnecessary grief and harm results.

You can, it is true, read the Bible in such a way as to make it appear that life in a world to come is only for the chosen few. But you can interpret the Bible to make it teach almost anything you want. The truth is that, while I do not belong to the "It's in the Book" school, there are many passages that make it clear that it is God's will and intention to reconcile the entire cosmos, including every human who has ever lived, to Himself / Herself. There will ultimately be "one fold, one shepherd." My own deep conviction is that none of us deserves or earns eternal life no matter who we are or what we have done or not done. It is not a reward for good works; it is a sheer gift of love. Therefore it makes both sense and justice to recognize that the grace of God by which we are given it is there for all humanity. If we truly believe in an all-loving, gracious Source of all things, the kind of accepting presence imaged by the father in the parable of the prodigal son, then it seems to me to be utterly incongruous to hold that anyone will be ultimately "lost." We are all God's offspring or children, as New Testament Christianity – and most other religions – makes clear.

If none of us would ever want to see our own children separated from us forever, how much more will this be the case with "Our Father in Heaven"? God wills to bring all his children home. All will be "saved," to use an oldtime Gospel expression, not by compulsion or abrogation of their free will but by the attraction and transforming power of the Divine Love. Personally, I fail to see how heaven or eternal life would be bliss of any kind unless one were assured that all will be sharers in it. At this ultimate family occasion there will finally be no empty chairs, no missing faces.

Will There Be Animals In Heaven?

While some may regard the question of whether or not there will be animals in a life beyond death as quite frivolous, there are many for whom it is of very great importance. I once wrote a feature on this issue and it provoked an astonishing amount of mail, much more than on many other topics one might have thought to have been of greater urgency.

It seems to me there are two reasons why there are those who believe in some form of life after death yet treat this matter as irrelevant or foolish. One is what is now called "speciesism" – the arrogant supposition that human beings are all that matter in the sight of God or the universe. We are only now beginning to realize that the ecological crisis is in no small measure attributable to precisely this kind of misguided hubris. On the other hand, if we see ourselves not as lords and exploiters of creation but as very much an integrated part of the whole fabric of life, it is natural to wonder whether the future will contain all of those creatures who shared this mortal coil with us and, in so many cases, brought us such great joy.

The second reason is the way many religious people, particularly Christians, think about the soul. Animals, they argue, don't have souls, therefore they don't figure into God's ultimate salvation. This reasoning is based upon a serious error. It assumes that humans "have" something called a soul. But this is not what the Bible teaches. In the Genesis myth, it says: "And the Lord God formed man of the dust of the ground, and breathed into his nostrils the breath of life; and man became a living soul." Notice it doesn't say that God *gave* mankind a soul. It says plainly that Adam (which means simply human beings) *became* a living soul. People don't have souls in the same way they have arms or noses. We *are* souls. We are living centres of energy, thought, and personality. We bear the *imago Dei* in our freedom to choose and in our power of self-reflection. Animals, birds, and fish may not be "made in the image of God" but they are God's creatures whom He/She saw to be "very good" at the Creation. In my view, to the extent that they have consciousness at all, they are souls too.

I just want to say I have very great sympathy with those animal-lovers who feel instinctively that "heaven wouldn't be heaven without them." A friend of mine who is an avid bird-watcher looks forward, she says, to one day seeing those birds she has never seen before – especially those species that have already vanished from the Earth!

Rigidly orthodox religious people who bridle at any of this need to be reminded of some aspects of scripture that have been much neglected. Nearly all the passages in Jewish and Christian scriptures, particularly those that deal with "the age to come," speak of the restoration or re-creation of nature itself. There will be a "new heaven and a new earth," the scriptures say. The lion will lie down with the lamb and there will be no more killing – but he will remain a "liony" lion all the same, not an emasculated cat.

Epilogue

Hans Küng has written: "Eternal life is seen at its deepest level as a matter of trust." He quickly goes on to add, however, that such a trust must be rooted in reality. It must be "an absolutely reasonable trust."[21] That is precisely what we have been concerned with throughout this book: a rational foundation for such a trust. But it would be wrong to leave the reader feeling that this has been a merely academic discussion calling simply for assent or dissent. Something much more profound is at stake. It is, I believe, significant that those in our time who report that they have come back from the brink of death with an experience of a transcendent "beyond" do not just say they have lost their fear of death. With virtually total unanimity, they say they have come back with an intensified commitment to life. Their new certainty that death is a gateway or entrance into glorious, unseen dimensions of being has filled them with a greatly enhanced sense of purpose and meaning here and now. Old anxieties and problems that once seemed intractable, even overwhelming, are seen in a new perspective. There is an inner assurance that God or the Cosmic Spirit is in ultimate control.

Thankfully, we don't all have to have a close brush with death to come to this kind of spiritual experience. To conclude that there is life after death is to recognize that there is an Author or Creator of that life. The act of trust by which we commit ourselves to the one involves a commitment of ourselves to the other. In the end, it is because of that numinous Presence that brought us into being and that sustains the cosmos that we believe in a life after death. To trust that there is a life after death is to trust God. It is to trust that the ultimate energy at the foundations of the universe is love. With that kind of commitment, we can face both life and death with fearlessness and hope. Trust, hope, and love are the most powerful, most revolutionary forces the world has ever known. They are needed today more than at any previous moment in history.

Finally, to those of you who have read this book in grief seeking solace and understanding in the face of the death of someone dearly loved, let me just say this. All sorts of questions and mysteries surround you right now. Nobody can answer them all. But I assure you that I am as convinced of this as I am of anything in this world: A day is coming when all separations will be over. We will one day be reunited (in the words of the old hymn) with those "whom we have loved long since and lost a while." We will return to the source of our being, not as rivers return to the ocean and are swallowed by it, but as recognizable individuals. As Eliot says, we will find that our end is our beginning. We will "arrive where we started/And know the place for the first time."[22] The deepest longings of all our hearts will be satisfied. Meanwhile, we can safely entrust ourselves, our loved ones, and all the human community to the grace and mercy of God. In one of the most magnificent, most comforting pieces of writing ever penned, Paul says: "For I am persuaded that neither death, nor life, nor angels, nor principalities, nor powers, nor things present, nor things to come, nor height, nor depth, nor any other thing in all creation, shall ever be able to separate us from God's love."[23] That's not a narrow, one-faith vision. It is an insight into the heart of reality for the whole human race.

NOTES

Introduction
1. *The Toronto Star*, 11 May 1987, p. C3.
2. *The Toronto Star*, 21 Oct 1987, p. A27.
3. A. E. Wallis Budge, *The Book of the Dead – The Papyrus of Ani* (New York: Dover Publications, 1967), pp. xlviii-lv.

PART ONE: THE SECULAR WITNESS

Chapter 1: Strange Encounters
1. Andrew Greeley, "Mysticism Goes Mainstream," *American Health Magazine*, (January/February 1987), 47ff.
2. Reported by Tom Harpur, *The Toronto Star*, 2 April 1983.
3. Terry Clifford, "Shirley MacLaine's Spiritual Dance," *American Health Magazine*, (January/February 1987), p. 50.
4. Cited by Colin Wilson, *Afterlife* (London: Grafton Books, 1987).
5. Tom Harpur, *The Toronto Star*, 5 July 1987.
6. For further information on the mystical "boom" in North America, I recommend all the relevant articles in the 1987 issue of *American Health Magazine* already referred to above. For further polling regarding American attitudes to life after death, see George Gallup, Jr., *Adventures in Immortality*, (New York: McGraw-Hill, 1982).

Chapter 2: The Near-Death Experience
1. Raymond Moody, *Life After Life* (Georgia: Mockingbird Books, 1975).
2. *Philadelphia Enquirer*, December 1988, and the IANDS *Newsletter*, passim. (See bibliography for IANDS address.)

3. Carol Zaleski, *Otherworld Journeys: Accounts of Near-Death Experience in Medieval and Modern Times*, (New York: Oxford University Press, 1987.)
4. Raymond Moody, *The Light Beyond* (New York: Bantam Books, 1988), p. 2.
5. Canadian Medical Association *Journal*, 104 (May 1971), p. 889-90.
6. Aniela Jaffe, ed., *Memories, Dreams, Reflections* (New York, 1965).
7. For further documentation of the NDE and related experiences, I recommend Dr. Michael Sabom, *Recollections of Death: A Medical Investigation* (New York: Harper & Row, 1982) also Dr. Kenneth Ring, *Life at Death, A Scientific Investigation of the Near-Death Experience*, and *Heading Towards Omega, In Search of the Meaning of the NDE*. (See bibliography for details.)
8. Maurice Rawlings, *Beyond Death's Door* (Nashville: Thomas Nelson, 1978).
9. Margot Grey, *Return From Death: An Exploration of the Near-Death Experience* (London: Arkana, 1985).
10. *Ibid.* p. 41.
11. Karlis Osis, review of *Return From Death*, by Margot Grey, *Journal of Near-Death Studies*, 7, no. 3, (Spring 1989), pp. 183ff.
12. Grey, *Return From Death*, p. 72.
13. Carol Zaleski, *Otherworld Journeys*, p. 7.
14. *Ibid.* p. 161.
15. *Ibid.* p. 167.
16. Moody, *The Light Beyond*, pp. 181ff.
17. Zaleski, *Otherworld Journeys*, p. 175.
18. Carl Jung, quoted by Moody, *The Light Beyond*, p. 198.
19. Judith Miller, review of *The Light Beyond*, by Raymond Moody, IANDS *Journal of Near-Death Studies*, Spring 1989, pp. 191ff.

Chapter 3: Channelers: The New Spirit Mediums

1. A full account of the actual conversation between Pike, Fletcher, and Spraggett can be found in Martin Ebon, ed., *True Experiences in Communicating With the Dead* (New York: Signet Books, 1968).
2. *Ibid.* p. 18.
3. Colin Wilson, *Afterlife*, (London: Grafton Books, 1987), pp. 100-102.
4. *Ibid.* pp. 92-96.

5. Henry Gordon, *Channeling into the New Age* (Buffalo: Prometheus Books, 1988), p. 100.
6. Shirley MacLaine, *Out on a Limb* (New York: Bantam, 1984).
7. Gordon, *Channeling into the New Age*, p. 128.
8. *Ibid.* p. 95.

Chapter 4: Reincarnation

1. Hans Küng, *Eternal Life?* (New York: Image Books, 1985).
2. Sylvia Cranston and Carey Williams, *Reincarnation, A New Horizon in Science, Religion, and Society* (New York: Julian Press, 1984).
3. *Ibid.* pp. 106-7.
4. Geddes MacGregor, *Reincarnation in Christianity* (Wheaton, Illinois: Quest Books, 1978), p. 118.
5. Mark Albrecht, *Reincarnation, A Christian Critique of a New Age Doctrine* (Downers Grove, Illinois: InterVarsity Press, 1982), p. 65.
6. Ernest Hilgard, *San Francisco Examiner*, 17 March 1977, p. 24.
7. Albrecht, *Reincarnation, A Christian Critique*, p. 69.
8. Colin Wilson, *Afterlife* (London: Grafton Books, 1987), pp. 21ff.
9. Dr. Ian Stevenson, *Xenoglossy* (Charlottesville, Va: University Press of Virginia, 1974), and *Unlearned Language* (Charlottesville, Va: University Press of Virginia, 1984).
10. Sri Sri Somasundara, quoted in Albrecht, *Reincarnation, A Christian Critique*, p. 129.
11. Joel L. Whitton and Joe Fisher, *Life Between Life* (New York: Doubleday, 1986).

Chapter 5: Dreams of Death and Dying

1. Fraser Boa, *The Way of the Dream* (Caledon East, Ont.: Windrose Films Ltd., 1988), p. xii.
2. Dr. Marie-Louise von Franz, *On Dreams and Death, a Jungian Interpretation* (Boston: Shambhala Press, 1986).
3. Von Franz, *On Dreams and Death*, p. viii.
4. *Ibid.* p. ix.
5. *Ibid.* p. ix.
6. *Ibid.* p. xvi.
7. John 12:24.
8. Von Franz, *On Dreams and Death*, p. 64.
9. *Ibid.* p. 64.
10. *Ibid.* p. 89.

11. *Ibid.* p. 156.

Chapter 6: New Light From Science

1. Dr. Wilder Penfield, *Second Thoughts* (Toronto: McClelland & Stewart, 1970).
2. Bertrand Russell, *Why I Am Not a Christian* (London: Unwin Paperbacks, 1957), p. 45.
3. Thomas Henry Huxley, quoted in *The New Story of Science*, Robert M. Augros and George N. Stanciu, eds. (Chicago: Gateway Editions, 1984), p. 9-10.
4. Russell, *Why I Am Not a Christian*, p. 107.
5. Augros and Stanciu, *The New Story of Science*, p. 6.
6. Dr. Marie-Louise von Franz, *On Dreams and Death* (Boston: Shambhala Press, 1986), p. 152.
7. Augros and Stanciu, *The New Story of Science*, p. 6.
8. Sir Charles Sherrington, quoted in *The New Story of Science*, p. 11-12.
9. Sir John Eccles, *Facing Reality* (Berlin and New York: Springer-Verlag, 1970), p. 162.
10. Adolf Portmann, *New Pathways in Biology* (New York: Harper & Row, 1964). Quoted by Augros and Stanciu, *The New Story of Science*, p. 27.
11. Dr. Wilder Penfield, *The Mystery of the Mind, A Critical Study of Consciousness and the Human Brain* (Princeton: Princeton University Press, 1975).
12. Augros and Stanciu, *The New Story of Science*, p. 34.
13. Penfield, *The Mystery of the Mind*, p. 80.
14. *Ibid.* p. 12.
15. Sir John Eccles, *Facing Reality*, p. 174. See also Augros and Stanciu, *The New Story of Science*, p. 35.
16. Carl Jung, *Letters* vol. 2, p. 45, quoted in von Franz, *On Dreams and Death*, p. 144.
17. Von Franz, *On Dreams and Death*, p. 144-5.

PART TWO: THE RELIGIOUS WITNESS: CHRISTIANITY

Chapter 7: The Witness of St. Paul

1. Gal. 1:15-16.
2. II Cor. 12:2-4.

3. I Cor. 2:9.

4. I Cor. 13:12.

5. II Cor. 4:16ff.

6. II Cor. 5:1-10.

7. Phil. 3:20-21.

8. II Cor. 5:8.

Chapter 8: The Teachings of Jesus

1. Carl Jung, *Memories, Dreams, Reflections* (New York: Pantheon Books, 1961), p. 325.

Chapter 9: The Gospels and the Resurrection of Jesus

1. For a fuller treatment, see Tom Harpur, *For Christ's Sake* (Toronto: Oxford University Press, 1986).

2. Matt. 28:16ff; John 21:15ff.

3. Matt. 28:9.

Chapter 10: Hell

1. I Sam. 28:8-15.

2. W. O. E. Oesterly and Theodore H. Robinson, *The Hebrew Religion – Its Origin and Development* (London: Society for the Propagation of Christian Knowledge, 1930), p. 322.

3. Gen. 37:35.

4. *The Oxford Dictionary of the Christian Church*, F. L. Cross, ed. (London: Oxford University Press, 1958) p. 1250-1.

5. Psalm 16:10.

6. Psalm 38:18.

7. Psalm 6:5.

8. Psalm 88:5.

9. F. W. Beare, *The Gospel According to Matthew* (San Francisco: Harper & Row, 1981), p. 148, and see the other references there.

10. Job 19:25-6.

11. Oesterley and Robinson, *The Hebrew Religion*, p. 314.

12. *Ibid.* p. 348.

13. Rev. 21:1.

14. Beare, *The Gospel According to Matthew*, pp. 148-50.

15. Tom Harpur, *For Christ's Sake* (Toronto: Oxford University Press, 1986), pp. 26ff.

16. Beare, *The Gospel According to Matthew*, pp. 148-50.

17. Mark 9:42ff.

18. Jer. 32:35; II Kings 23:10.

19. Luke 12:5.

20. James 3:6.

21. Beare, *The Gospel According to Matthew*, p. 149.

22. Oesterley and Robinson, *The Hebrew Religion*, pp. 333ff.

23. J. N. D. Kelly, *Early Christian Doctrines* (San Francisco: Harper & Row, 1960), p. 482.

24. Kelly, *Early Christian Doctrines*, p. 484.

25. Luke 11:11-13, and other Gospel parallels.

26. De Principiis, 2, II, 2. Quoted in Kelly, *Early Christian Doctrines*, p. 473-4.

Chapter 11: What About Purgatory?

1. Matt. 12:31.

2. I Cor. 3:11-15.

3. *The Oxford Dictionary of the Christian Church*, F. L. Cross, ed. (London: Oxford University Press, 1958), p. 1125.

4. Hans Küng, *Eternal Life?* (New York: Image Books, 1985) p. 139.

5. *Oxford Dictionary of the Christian Church*, p. 810.

Chapter 12: Muddying the Waters

1. *The Oxford Dictionary of the Christian Church*, F. L. Cross, ed. (London: Oxford University Press, 1958), p. 901.

2. Rev. 21:1ff.

Chapter 13: Reincarnation and the Bible

1. Shirley MacLaine, *Out on a Limb* (New York: Bantam, 1983), pp. 234-5.

2. For more on this see pp. 211ff.

3. Job 14:14.

4. Geddes MacGregor, *Reincarnation in Christianity* (Wheaton, Illinois: Quest Books, 1978).

5. Sylvia Cranston and Carey Williams, *Reincarnation, A New Horizon in Science, Religion, and Society* (New York: Julian Press, 1984), p. 201.

6. John 10:15.

7. John 8:12ff.

8. John 9:1ff.

9. Cranston and Williams, *Reincarnation, A New Horizon*, p. 209.

10. Matt. 16:13-14.

11. Northrop Frye, *The Great Code* (Toronto: Harcourt Brace Jovanovich, 1983).
12. Geddes MacGregor, quoted in Cranston and Williams, *Reincarnation, A New Horizon*, p. 210.
13. *Ibid.* p. 209.

Chapter 14: The Christ Myth as the Ultimate Myth of the Self

1. Joseph Campbell with Fraser Boa, *This Business of the Gods* (Caledon East, Ontario: Windrose Films Ltd., 1989), p. 39.
2. John P. Dourley, *The Illness That We Are* (Toronto: Inner City Books, 1984), pp. 80-81.
3. Tom Harpur, *For Christ's Sake* (Toronto: Oxford University Press, 1986), p. 100.
4. Joseph Campbell, *This Business of the Gods*, p. 34.
5. *Ibid.* p. 134.
6. *Ibid.* p. 38.
7. *Ibid.* p. 40.
8. *Ibid.* p. 106.
9. *Ibid.* p. 83.
10. *Ibid.* p. 137.
11. Dourley, *The Illness That We Are*, p. 80.
12. *Ibid.*

PART THREE: THE RELIGIOUS WITNESS: THREE CHRISTIAN SECTS

Chapter 15: The Seventh-Day Adventists

1. For further reading, see any good encyclopedia of religion. Also, The Ministerial Association, General Conference of Seventh-Day Adventists, *Seventh-Day Adventists Believe. . . .* (Hagerstown, Maryland: Review & Herald Publishing Assoc., 1988).

Chapter 16: Jehovah's Witnesses

1. For further reading, see: *United in Worship of the Only True God*, (New York: Watchtower Bible and Tract Society, 1983). Also, Alan Rogerson, *Millions Now Living Will Never Die* (New York: Constable Publishing, 1969).

Chapter 17: Christian Science

1. For further reading, see: *Science and Health, with Key to the Scriptures* (Boston: First Church of Christ, Scientist, 1971).

PART FOUR: THE RELIGIOUS WITNESS: OTHER WORLD FAITHS

Chapter 18: Zoroastrianism

1. For further reading, see: "The Cosmic Battle: Zoroastrianism" in Eerdman's *Handbook to the World's Religions* (Grand Rapids, Michigan: William B. Eerdman's Publishing, 1982) pp. 80 ff.

Chapter 19: Hinduism

1. *Bhagavad Gita*, Swami Prabhavanands and Christopher Isherwood, translators (New York and Scarborough, Ontario: New American Library, Mentor Books, 1944), p. 29.
2. *Ibid.* p. 37.
3. Louis Fischer, *Ghandi: His Life and Message for the World* (New York: New American Library, Mentor Books, 1954), p. 19.
4. For further reading, see: Eerdman's *Handbook to the World's Religions* (Grand Rapids, Michigan: William B. Eerdman's Publishing, 1982).

Chapter 20: Buddhism

1. Hans Küng, *Eternal Life?* (New York: Image Books, 1985), pp. 57-8.
2. *The Tibetan Book of the Dead*, Francisca Fremantle and Chogyam Trungpa, Rinpoche, translators (Boston: Shambhala, 1975).
3. *Ibid.* p. xii.
4. *Ibid.* p. xx.
5. *Ibid.* p. 29.

Chapter 21: Judaism

1. For further reading, see "Afterlife" in *The Encyclopedia Judaica*, vol. 2 (Jerusalem and New York: Macmillan, 1971), pp. 335-39.

Chapter 22: Islam

1. For further reading, see the articles on "Islam" in *The Encyclopedia of Religion*, vol. 7, Mircea Eliade, ed. (New York: Macmillan, 1987).
2. Abdul Wahid, *Islam, The Natural Way* (London: Mels Publishing, 1989), p. 164.
3. The Qur'an, 22:5-7.
4. *Ibid.* 21:47.
5. *Ibid.* 18:30.

6. *Ibid*. 29:13-20.
7. Wahid, *Islam, The Natural Way*, p. 170.
8. *Ibid*. p. 169.
9. Sylvia Cranston and Carey Williams, *Reincarnation, A New Horizon in Science, Religion, and Society* (New York: Julian Press, 1984), pp. 175-7.
10. The Qur'an 71:17-18.

Chapter 23: Baha'i
1. Hushidar Motlagh, *Unto Him Shall We Return* (Wilmette, Illinois: The Baha'i Publishing Trust, 1985).
2. *Ibid*. p. 17.

Chapter 24: Native Spirituality
1. Father Thomas Berry, *The Dream of the Earth* (San Francisco: Sierra Club Books, 1988), p. 182.
2. Berry, *The Dream of the Earth*, p. 184.
3. *Ibid*. p. 193.
4. Michael Posluns, ed. *Songs for the People – Teachings on the Natural Way* (Toronto: NC Press, 1989), p. 287.
5. John Cobb and Charles Birch, *The Liberation of Life* (New York: Cambridge University Press, 1985).
6. For further reading, see Jordan Paper, *Offering Smoke* (Vancouver: Rain Coast Books, 1989). Also, *Handbook on the North American Indian*, in 20 volumes, William C. Sturtevant, (Washington: The Smithsonian Institute, 1978–). And Jamake Highwater, *The Primal Mind* (New York: Harper & Row, 1981).
7. George Appleton, ed., *The Oxford Book of Prayer* (London: Oxford University Press, 1985), p. 351.

PART FIVE: PERSONAL REFLECTIONS AND CONCLUSIONS
1. Colin Wilson, *Afterlife* (London: Grafton Books, 1987), p. 144.
2. Dr. Marie-Louise von Franz, *On Dreams and Death, A Jungian Interpretation* (Boston: Shambhala Press, 1986), p. xi.
3. C. D. Broad from *The Philosophy of C. D. Broad*, quoted in Wilson, *Afterlife*, p. 266.
4. Dr. Sandra Bertman, *The Toronto Star*, 25 May 1989.

5. See my account in *Harpur's Heaven and Hell* (Toronto: Oxford University Press, 1984), pp. 175ff.

6. Carl Jung, quoted in von Franz, *On Dreams and Death*, p. x.

7. William James, quoted in Wilson, *Afterlife*, p. 183.

8. Tom Harpur, "Reasonable Faith," *The Toronto Star*, 11 Feb. 1990.

9. Von Franz, *On Dreams and Death*, pp. 152ff.

10. *Ibid.* p. 157.

11. Sir John Eccles, *The Human Psyche* (Berlin and New York: Springer-Verlag, 1980).

12. *Science Digest*, July 1982; Sir James Jeans, *The Mysterious Universe* (New York: Macmillan, 1931).

13. Albert Einstein, *The Human Side*. H. Dukas and B. Hoffman eds. (Princeton: Princeton University Press, 1979).

14. Guy Murchie, *The Seven Mysteries of Life* (Boston: Houghton Mifflin Co., 1989).

15. Isa. 60:1, 19.

16. T. S. Eliot, "The Love Song of J. Alfred Prufrock," in *T. S. Eliot, Selected Poems* (London: Faber & Faber, paperback ed., 1961), pp. 11ff.

17. Rev. 21:4.

18. Marion Woodman, *The Pregnant Virgin* (Toronto: Inner City Books, 1985), p. 73.

19. Von Franz, *On Dreams and Death*, p. xi.

20. *The New York Times*, 22 Jan. 1990.

21. Hans Küng, *Eternal Life?* (New York: Image Books, 1985), p. 78.

22. T. S. Eliot, "Little Gidding," from *The Four Quartets* (London: Faber & Faber, paperback ed., 1959), pp. 49ff.

23. Rom. 8:38-9.

SELECTED BIBLIOGRAPHY

Albrecht, Mark. *Reincarnation, A Christian Critique of a New Age Doctrine*. Downers Grove, Illinois: Inter Varsity Press, 1982.

Aries, Phillippe. *The Hour of Our Death*. Trans. by Helen Weaver. New York: Random House, 1981.

Augros, Robert M. and Stanciu, George N. *The New Story of Science*. Lake Bluff, Illinois: Gateway Editions, 1984.

Boris, Ladislaus. *The Mystery of Death*. New York: Crossroad, 1973.

Budge, Wallis, A.E. *The Book of the Dead – The Papyrus of Ani*. New York: Dover Publications, 1967.

Campbell, Joseph. *The Power of Myth*. New York: Doubleday, 1988.

Campbell, Joseph, with Boa, Fraser. *This Business of the Gods*. Caledon East, Ontario: Windrose Films Ltd., 1989.

Capra, Fritjof. *The Tao of Physics*. Boulder, Colorado: Shambhala, 1976.

Cranston, Sylvia, and Williams, Carey. *Reincarnation, A New Horizon in Science, Religion, and Society*. New York: Julian Press, 1984.

Dumont, R.G., and Foss, D.C. *The American Way of Death: Acceptance or Denial*. Cambridge, Mass.: Schenkman, 1972.

Eccles, John C. *Facing Reality: Philosophical Adventures by a Brain Scientist*. Berlin and New York: Springer-Verlag, 1970.

_____ *The Human Mystery*. New York: Springer-Verlag, 1979.

_____ *The Human Psyche*. Berlin and New York: Springer-Verlag, 1980.

Eerdmans' *Handbook to the World's Religions*. Grand Rapids, Michigan: William B. Eerdmans Publishing, 1982.

Einstein, Albert. *The Human Side*. H. Dukas and B. Hoffman, eds. Princeton: Princeton University Press, 1979.

Encyclopedia Judaica, vol. 2, "Afterlife," pp. 335-39. Jerusalem and New York: Macmillan, 1971.

Encyclopedia of Religion, Mircea Eliade, ed. New York: Macmillan, 1987.

Gallup, George, Jr., with Proctor, William. *Adventures in Immortality*. New York: McGraw-Hill, 1982.

Gordon, Henry. *Channeling Into the New Age*. Buffalo: Prometheus Books, 1988.

Grey, Margot. *Return From Death*. London: Arkana, 1985.

Greyson, Bruce. "Near-Death Experiences and Attempted Suicide." IANDS, *Anabiosis*, 11 (1981) pp. 10-16.

Greyson, Bruce, and Flynn, C.P., eds. *The Near-Death Experience: Problems, Prospect, Perspectives*. Springfield, Illinois: Charles C. Thomas, 1984.

Hanson, Paul. *The Dawn of Apocalyptic*. New York: Fortress Press, 1979.

Harpur, Tom. *Harpur's Heaven and Hell*. Toronto: Oxford University Press, 1984.

_____ *For Christ's Sake*. Toronto: Oxford University Press, 1984.

_____ *Always On Sunday*. Toronto: Oxford University Press, 1988.

Heinberg, Richard. *Memories and Visions of Paradise*. Los Angeles: Jeremy P. Tarcher, Inc., 1989.

Huxley, Thomas. *Essays on Some Controverted Subjects*. New York: 1892.

Ingber, D. "Visions of an Afterlife." *Science Digest*, Jan./Feb. 1981.

James, William. *The Will to Believe and Human Immortality*. New York: Dover Press, 1956.

Jeans, Sir James. *The Mysterious Universe*. New York: Macmillan, 1931.

Journal of Near-Death Studies (formerly *Anabiosis*). The International Association for Near-Death Studies (IANDS), P.O. Box 7767, Philadelphia, PA 19101.

Jung, Carl G. *Memories, Dreams, Reflections*. New York: Random House, 1961.

Kelly, J.N.D. *Early Christian Doctrines*. San Francisco: Harper & Row, 1960.

Kubler-Ross, Elizabeth. *On Death and Dying*. New York: Macmillan, 1969.

———— *Living with Death and Dying*. New York: Macmillan, 1981.

Küng, Hans. *Eternal Life?* New York: Image Books, 1985.

MacGregor, Geddes. *Reincarnation as a Christian Hope*. London: Macmillan, 1982.

Mead, G.R.S. *The Doctrine of the Subtle Body in Western Tradition*. London: Stuart and Watkins, 1967.

Moody, Raymond A., Jr. *Life After Life*. Georgia: Mockingbird Books, 1975. New York: Bantam, 1976.

———— *Reflections on Life After Life*. London: Corgi Books, 1977.

———— *The Light Beyond*, New York: Bantam, 1988.

Motlagh, Hushidar. *Unto Him Shall We Return*. Wilmette, Illinois: Baha'i Publishing Trust, 1931.

Osis, Karlis, and Erlendur, Haraldsson. *At the Hour of Death*. New York: Avon, 1980.

Oxford Dictionary of the Christian Church. F. L. Cross, ed. London: Oxford University Press, 1958.

Penfield, Wilder. *Second Thoughts*. Toronto: McClelland & Stewart, 1970.

———— *The Mystery of the Mind*. Princeton: Princeton University Press, 1975.

Rawlings, M. *Beyond Death's Door*. Nashville: Thomas Nelson, 1978.

Ring, Kenneth. *Life at Death: A Scientific Investigation of the Near-Death Experience*. New York: Coward, McMann & Geoghegan, 1980.

———— *Heading Toward Omega: In Search of the Meaning of the N.D.E.* New York: William Morrow, 1984.

Russell, Bertrand. *Why I Am Not a Christian*. New York: Simon & Schuster, 1957.

Sabom, Michael B. *Recollections of Death: A Medical Investigation*. New York: Harper & Row, 1982.

Short, Robert. *Something to Believe In*. San Francisco: Harper & Row, 1980.

Siegel, Ronald K. "Hallucinations." *Scientific American* 237 (October 1977), pp. 132-40.

———— "The Psychology of Life After Death." *American Psychologist* 35 (1980), pp. 911-931.

Stevenson, Ian. *Cases of the Reincarnation Type*. 3 vols. Charlottesville, Va.: University Press of Virginia, 1975.

The Tibetan Book of the Dead. Francesca Fremantle and Chogyam Trungpa, Rinpoche, trans. Boston: Shambhala, 1975.

Von Franz, Marie-Louise. *On Dreams and Death*. Boston: Shambhala, 1986.

Wilson, Colin. *Afterlife*. London: Grafton Books, 1987.

Zaleski, Carol. *Otherworld Journeys*. New York: Oxford University Press, 1987.

INDEX